Moving Your University Course Online

This book equips higher education professionals with a roadmap for the design, development and delivery of a successful online degree.

Responding to the evolving landscape of higher education, the text offers reflections and practical insights from staff who transformed a campus-based Humanities and Social Sciences degree into a ground-breaking online learning experience at an Australian university, contributing to a dynamic culture of interdisciplinary collaboration and continuing professional development. The chapters follow the development process of an online degree from inception to delivery. Taking an applied focus, they guide readers to anticipate and navigate challenges encountered in implementing curriculum change. The authors explore how to embed student-centred digital pedagogies, approaches taken to develop skills for staff and students and thoughtful ways to integrate technology into learning and teaching whilst preserving the spirit and integrity of multiple academic disciplines. Alongside relational and strategic aspects of curriculum enhancement, the book offers practical case studies on implementing dynamic online learning to enhance the student experience.

This is an indispensable guide for educators, learning designers, higher education leaders and higher education professionals who support and enhance online higher education programs.

Michael Kilmister is an academic developer at the University of Reading, UK. He was awarded his PhD in History from the University of Newcastle, Australia, where he worked in several teaching and learning roles for over a decade. He has published widely on academic development and education.

Annika Herb is the education development lead at the University of Newcastle, Australia. Her research explores academic development, teaching and learning and young adult literature. She is an associate editor of *IJYAL* and a co-editor of *Storying Plants in Australian Children's and Young Adult Literature* (Springer, 2023).

Clare Lloyd is the senior manager of Education Development at the University of Newcastle, Australia. Her research focuses on online education, academic development and technology-enhanced learning. She is on the editorial board of *Advances in Online Education: A Peer-Reviewed Journal*.

Moving Your University Course Online

Case Studies on Design, Development and Delivery

Edited by Michael Kilmister, Annika Herb and Clare Lloyd

LONDON AND NEW YORK

Designed cover image: Getty Images

First published 2026
by Routledge
4 Park Square, Milton Park, Abingdon, Oxon OX14 4RN

and by Routledge
605 Third Avenue, New York, NY 10158

Routledge is an imprint of the Taylor & Francis Group, an informa business

© 2026 selection and editorial matter, Michael Kilmister, Annika Herb and Clare Lloyd; individual chapters, the contributors

The right of Michael Kilmister, Annika Herb and Clare Lloyd to be identified as the authors of the editorial material, and of the authors for their individual chapters, has been asserted in accordance with sections 77 and 78 of the Copyright, Designs and Patents Act 1988.

All rights reserved. No part of this book may be reprinted or reproduced or utilised in any form or by any electronic, mechanical, or other means, now known or hereafter invented, including photocopying and recording, or in any information storage or retrieval system, without permission in writing from the publishers.

Trademark notice: Product or corporate names may be trademarks or registered trademarks, and are used only for identification and explanation without intent to infringe.

British Library Cataloguing-in-Publication Data
A catalogue record for this book is available from the British Library

Library of Congress Cataloging-in-Publication Data
Names: Kilmister, Michael editor | Herb, Annika editor | Lloyd, Clare A. editor
Title: Moving your university course online : case studies on design, development and delivery / edited by Michael Kilmister, Annika Herb and Clare Lloyd.
Description: Abingdon, Oxon ; New York, NY : Routledge, 2026. | Includes bibliographical references and index.
Identifiers: LCCN 2025024775 (print) | LCCN 2025024776 (ebook) | ISBN 9781032827087 hardback | ISBN 9781032817644 paperback | ISBN 9781003505785 ebook
Subjects: LCSH: Web-based instruction | Internet in higher education | Distance education
Classification: LCC LB1028.57 .M68 2026 (print) | LCC LB1028.57 (ebook)
LC record available at https://lccn.loc.gov/2025024775
LC ebook record available at https://lccn.loc.gov/2025024776

ISBN: 978-1-032-82708-7 (hbk)
ISBN: 978-1-032-81764-4 (pbk)
ISBN: 978-1-003-50578-5 (ebk)

DOI: 10.4324/9781003505785

Typeset in Optima
by Apex CoVantage, LLC

Contents

List of contributors viii
Foreword xi
Acknowledgements xiv

PART 1
Creating an online degree 1

1 **Moving your course online: it's translation, not conversion** 3
  ANNIKA HERB, MICHAEL KILMISTER AND CLARE LLOYD

2 **Creating the BA Online: reinventing the degree through pedagogical innovation** 13
  CATHARINE COLEBORNE

3 **Reflections on the partnership between FutureLearn and a regional Australian university: an ecological perspective** 28
  MONTY KING

PART 2
Case studies in online teaching and assessment 43

4 **FutureLearn as a learning environment: striving for a community of inquiry** 45
  MITCHELL J. TAYLOR AND JULIA COOK

5 **Creating engaging videos for online teaching** 59
  SACHA E. DAVIS AND ADAM KHAMIS

6 **Teaching screen and cultural studies online** 78
  HAMISH FORD AND REBECCA BEIRNE

PART 3
Challenges and opportunities in adaptation   95

7 **Designing a history course for online and face-to-face
   delivery: 'the Australian experience'**   97
   MICHAEL KILMISTER, KATE ARIOTTI AND JAMES BENNETT

8 **Teaching challenging material: technological affordances of
   staggered asynchronous online learning**   110
   JESSICA FORD

9 **Funking it up: teaching poetry as creative writing in
   the digital age**   122
   DAVID MUSGRAVE

10 **Fantasy cricket: from ethnographic film to virtual
   anthropology fieldwork**   134
   HEDDA HAUGEN ASKLAND, MICHAEL KILMISTER, KATE SENIOR, ADRIAN
       MERELES, CHRIS LAWRENCE AND TIM GARSIDE

11 **Easing eco-anxiety in an online environmental sociology course**   150
   JAI COOPER AND CHRIS LAWRENCE

PART 4
Impacts and evaluation   167

12 **Academic development for effective online learning design**   169
   CLARE LLOYD, ANNIKA HERB AND MICHAEL KILMISTER

13 **Student evaluation of online teaching and learning: notes on
   theory and practice**   187
   PAUL SIJPKES AND ELIZABETH ROBERTS-PEDERSEN

14 **Being an online educator: reflections on iterative design
   of a transdisciplinary humanities course**   199
   JULIE MCINTYRE

15 **Australian underworlds: online teaching as a pathway to
   building scholarly networks**   213
   NANCY CUSHING, ALANA PIPER AND VICKY NAGY

16 Conclusion: reflecting on the BA Online project 225
CATHARINE COLEBORNE AND CLARE LLOYD

Afterword 231
MICHAEL KILMISTER, CLARE LLOYD AND ANNIKA HERB

Index *232*

Contributors

Kate Ariotti is an Australian Research Council (ARC) DECRA senior research fellow in the School of Historical and Philosophical Inquiry at the University of Queensland, Australia. She specialises in the study and teaching of Australian war history.

Hedda Haugen Askland is an associate professor of Anthropology at the University of Newcastle, Australia. She has been teaching Anthropology for over a decade, developing courses for face-to-face and online delivery. Her publications on decolonial teaching in Anthropology represent her drive to advance a justice- and student-centred curriculum.

Rebecca Beirne is a senior lecturer in Screen and Cultural Studies at the University of Newcastle, Australia. She has written extensively on queer representation in popular culture, as well as about representations of mental ill health on television and online film distribution.

James Bennett is an honorary academic at the University of Auckland in Aotearoa New Zealand. He has published widely on aspects of Australian and New Zealand history. Most recently, he co-edited the anthology *Gay Conversion Practices in Memoir, Film & Fiction* (Bloomsbury, 2024).

Catharine Coleborne is a professor of History at the University of Newcastle with interests in digital histories and interdisciplinary learning. Coleborne was the head of school/dean of Arts (2015–2022) and led the project to both reinvent the Bachelor of Arts degree and create the BA Online (launched in 2019).

Julia Cook is a senior lecturer in Sociology at the University of Newcastle. Her research addresses the sociology of youth, housing and credit-debt. She is an ARC DECRA fellow (2022–2025), a chief investigator on the Life Patterns research program (2021–2026) and a co-editor-in-chief of the *Journal of Applied Youth Studies*.

Jai Cooper is an environmental sociologist and currently a consultant with the Institute for Regional Futures at the University of Newcastle. Jai has an extensive background in both the university and vocational sectors, including working in outdoor adventure, community natural resource management and Aboriginal and youth environmental training programs.

Nancy Cushing is an associate professor in History at the University of Newcastle on Awabakal and Worimi Country. Her research focus is Australian animal history while teaching has drawn her into the field of crime history. Her most recent book is *A History of Crime in Australia* (Routledge, 2023).

Sacha E. Davis lectures in History at the University of Newcastle, Australia. He completed his doctorate at the University of New South Wales. His research interests examine minority nationalism and the nation-state in the east of Europe. He has also written on German diaspora communities in Australia and North America.

Hamish Ford is a senior lecturer in Screen and Cultural Studies at the University of Newcastle, Australia. A film studies researcher of 25 years in the areas of 1960s European modernist cinema and the relationship between film and philosophy, he is the co-editor of *A Companion to Ingmar Bergman* (Wiley-Blackwell, 2025).

Jessica Ford is a senior lecturer in Media at the University of Adelaide, Australia. Her research examines women and feminisms on screen, and she teaches in media and cultural studies. She is a contributing editor of *MAI: Journal of Feminism and Visual Culture* and a Fellow of the Adelaide Education Academy and AdvanceHE.

Tim Garside is a learning designer at the University of Newcastle, Australia. He holds a Bachelor of Engineering (Honours) in Mechatronics and a Graduate Certificate in Education. His work focuses on designing interactive and engaging online learning experiences, underpinned by principles of accessibility and constructive alignment.

Adam Khamis is a learning media producer at the University of Newcastle, Australia. He has over 20 years of experience in film, television and advertising. His portfolio includes special effects on feature films for Disney and Fox Studios, directing and editing commercials, comedy sketches, interviews and branded content for leading clients.

Monty King is an educational researcher and a learning designer based in London. Between 2018 and 2021 he worked at FutureLearn, where he was the partnership manager working with the University of Newcastle during the development of the Bachelor of Arts degree. He is currently the Learning Design Manager at University of the Arts London Online.

Chris Lawrence is a senior instructional designer with the Australian Education Research Organisation. He has an extensive background in tertiary education and digital learning design, with expertise in developing engaging, learner-focused solutions. Chris is passionate about evidence-based pedagogy and takes delight in convincing subject matter experts to try wild ideas.

Julie McIntyre is an associate professor of History at the University of Newcastle, Australia, and an award-winning author. Her research into commodities such as wine and coal in environments, society and the economy informs her interdisciplinary teaching. Her next book is a global history of Australia for Princeton University Press.

Adrian Mereles has a background in software development, design and operations, with a strong focus on full-stack web technologies. Having developed a variety of bespoke web applications primarily within the teaching and learning space, Adrian enjoys weaving creativity into his work, leveraging a diverse range of experience and influence.

David Musgrave is one of Australia's leading poets. In 2005 he founded Puncher & Wattmann, the foremost publisher of poetry in Australia. Since 2010 he has also taught creative writing at the University of Newcastle.

Vicky Nagy is a senior lecturer in Criminology at the University of Tasmania with a particular interest in historical and contemporary socio-legal responses to women's offending and incarceration in Australia. Vicky is the co-editor of *Women's Criminalisation and Offending in Australia and New Zealand* (Routledge 2023).

Alana Piper is an interdisciplinary researcher whose work draws together the social and cultural history of crime in Australia with criminological, legal and digital humanities approaches. Piper has authored over 40 academic works and co-edited (with Ana Stevenson) *Gender Violence in Australia: Historical Perspectives* (Monash University Publishing, 2019).

Elizabeth Roberts-Pedersen is a historian and former convenor of the Bachelor of Arts program at the University of Newcastle. She has designed and taught both general Humanities and specialist History courses and has published on the history of warfare, psychiatry and medicine.

Kate Senior is a professor of Anthropology at the University of Newcastle and is currently the Acting Director of the Institute of Regional Futures and the Purai Indigenous Global History Centre. She has 25 years of experience working in collaboration with Indigenous communities in Northern Australia.

Paul Sijpkes is a learning designer at the University of Newcastle. He has project managed, designed, taught and developed learning experiences across general Humanities and Science, Technology, Engineering and Medicine (STEM). Paul is undertaking a PhD at the University of Technology, Sydney, in designing learning tasks that support epistemic cognition.

Mitchell J. Taylor is a lecturer in Sociology at the University of Newcastle. His research focuses on sociological theory, philosophy of social science and the history of social thought.

Foreword

Worldwide, universities have been challenged by the rapidly changing needs of learners, digital innovation and new and adapting pedagogies. It has therefore been an exciting time to be involved in learning and teaching transformation, redefining the way we design, develop and deliver education. *Moving Your University Course Online* charts the journey of reinventing the Bachelor of Arts (BA) degree at the University of Newcastle in Australia as an online learning experience. We are introduced to the opportunities offered by partnership with an innovative social learning platform provider, the ability to challenge the way we teach and assess, and the importance of evaluating the output and impact of any educational transformation.

As the book demonstrates, the journey to reinvent the BA degree at the University of Newcastle began in late 2016 and was, in part, a response to a sector-wide decline in BA degree enrolments. However, the timing of the BA reinvention project and the resulting exploration of pedagogical shifts, innovative approaches and new technologies coincided with a wider institutional transformation of education. In 2017 I joined the University of Newcastle as Deputy Vice Chancellor (Academic) and was tasked with redesigning the approach to learning and teaching, especially in the area of digital delivery. It was clear to me that disruptions through technology, global connectivity, and the democratisation of access to knowledge meant students had different and varied expectations of what a university experience should be and what they wanted to achieve from it. Universities are creators of knowledge and a crucible for the development and application of new ideas. In spite of this, universities are typically seen as responding to, rather than guiding and leading, global trends. Given the pace and scale of change, there is a real risk that traditional higher education will become characterised by a value proposition that does not add up for students, industry or government. Therefore, as part of a new plan for learning and teaching I was focused on providing students with more control over their learning, particularly through greater flexibility and opportunities to tailor their experience, and building on the University of Newcastle's history of, and commitment to, equity and inclusion in education.

The resulting New Education Framework in 2018 was the culmination of collaborative discussion and development. The framework was a holistic and multifaceted approach to learning and teaching with learner-centred design at its heart. It was delivered within the context of an overarching education redesign strategy that was not only focused on learning and teaching transformation but also on a reimagining of the portfolio of programs and courses the university offered, a more flexible program and course architecture, and the development of an agile and streamlined approach to program design and approval. The framework consisted of eight interconnected frames covering aspects such as educator enablement, innovative curriculum design and delivery, transformative technologies and dynamic student support for learning. The composition of the framework was such that initiatives could be planned within each of the individual frames whilst relating and interconnecting to the main vision. In many cases, and by design, initiatives spanned, fed into or impacted a number of frames. To jump-start the implementation of the framework I chose to invest university funds into prototype projects focused on the redesign of four-degree programs across the institution as identified through an expression-of-interest process. The ever-growing prevalence of online learning in the educational landscape meant that the university needed to prioritise the expansion of its online delivery and ensure that it provided relevant, engaging and quality experiences for learners. It was therefore important that at least one of the prototype initiatives was directed at developing a fully online degree, and so the proposal to reinvent the BA by designing a BA Online degree was selected.

The University of Newcastle was in no way at a standing start when it came to online delivery, having had a long history in flexible delivery learning. The university had also embarked on the delivery of a small set of massive open online courses (MOOCs) with the edX platform, with one of the courses (Natural History Illustration) receiving the edX prize in 2017 for exceptional contributions in online learning and teaching. However, we recognised that we needed to shift our approach to focus more on student engagement and collaboration, and this strongly influenced our decision to design the BA Online in partnership with the UK educational provider FutureLearn, whose platform was based on a social learning pedagogy. I had been fortunate to work with FutureLearn previously when I was Pro Vice Chancellor (Learning and Teaching) at Monash University, when we became their first international partner in developing MOOCs, and I had been really impressed by their philosophy, innovative approach and design and delivery processes. In partnering with FutureLearn for the BA Online, the University of Newcastle became the first partner offering online undergraduate degrees on the platform. The announcement of the partnership emphasised the proposed flexible nature of the degree as well as the access to an international online classroom of learners.

From there colleagues in the School of Humanities and Social Sciences, under the enthusiastic leadership of Professor Catharine Coleborne, along with Dr Clare Lloyd, Academic Director of Online Learning Initiatives team and staff from the central teaching and learning support unit, embraced the opportunity and set to work on the design and development process. Educators recognised that in an online social learning model they needed to shift to become facilitators of the learning process to activate and promote conversation, collaboration and interaction, as well as produce different learning materials and resources that would focus on improved engagement and accessibility for learners. The great thing about this book is that it documents the experience of educational leaders, educators and learning designers in the creative process and, crucially, also includes analysis and reflection, providing an informative and fascinating narrative. Whether you are embarking on a similar design journey, a pedagogical researcher analysing the expansion and impact of online learning, someone interested in pedagogy and the changing nature of learning and teaching, or someone who simply enjoys learning from others' experiences, I think this book has a lot to offer.

Education has the power to transform lives, but we need to be able to transform how we deliver education in a changing world to ensure we provide learners with the relevant, accessible and engaging experiences they require. We must therefore continue to create opportunities for those involved in education to think outside the box, try new things and keep being learner centred.

Darrell J. R. Evans, BSc, PhD, FAS, FAAA, FRSB, FRMS, FHEA
Honorary Professor (formerly Deputy Vice Chancellor [Academic]),
University of Newcastle, Australia

Acknowledgements

We are grateful to all the authors who have contributed to this book for their commitment to this work. We were heartened by their enthusiasm in contributing to the book, seeing it as a testament to the lasting influence of the BA Online on teaching and learning at the university.

There are many colleagues who played an important role in bringing the BA Online to life and whose stories we were unable to include in the book, including the numerous teaching staff who contributed to the project. We want to particularly thank colleagues in Learning Design and Teaching Innovation (LDTI) Unit, who worked tirelessly to support academic staff in their transition to online learning. Our thanks also go to the sessional teaching staff who weathered mode of delivery changes, along with learning management system changes and COVID-19 lockdowns.

Thank you to our generous reviewers, whose practical and critical insights have indelibly shaped the chapters in this collection. We are indebted to Liz Burns for her support with the images and figures.

And finally, thank you to our loved ones for giving us the time and space to attend to this work.

Part 1
Creating an online degree

1 Moving your course online

It's translation, not conversion

Annika Herb, Michael Kilmister and Clare Lloyd

Introduction

Over the last decade, the higher education sector has witnessed a burgeoning demand for flexible and accessible learning pathways from increasingly diverse student demographics, prompting a need for innovative approaches to degree design and delivery. The Bachelor of Arts degree has faced particular challenges, from declining student enrolments in traditional degrees to media and governmental criticism and pressure to adapt teaching models. In response to this, in 2018, the University of Newcastle (UON) designed a fully online BA degree in partnership with the online learning platform FutureLearn. This book seeks to aid leadership and stakeholders in teaching and learning at higher education institutions (HEIs) to understand the process of translating traditional campus-delivered degrees online. Drawing on a diverse pool of academics, learning designers, and other professional staff, it interrogates the evolving roles of staff and institutions in the context of online learning, and how digital transformation influences institutional cultures of academic development, curriculum design, and ways of learning. Drawing on their extensive experience in designing, developing, and delivering online education at the tertiary level, the contributors have adopted a strategic and scholarly approach as they detail their experience of effective course development, offering models and strategies for success.

Recognising a convergence of factors shaping higher education, including an increasing need to effectively integrate digitally enabled learning (Kelly & Zakrajsek, 2020), dwindling enrolment and support for Humanities courses (Ikpe, 2015), and new disruptions in the form of generative AI (genAI) (Gruenhagen et al., 2024), we suggest online learning can help Humanities and Social Sciences programs navigate this challenging landscape. We do so through exploring an Australian university's experience of designing a Bachelor of Arts degree for online delivery (the 'BA Online'), from conception to delivery and beyond. This collection, drawing from staff involved in all aspects of course design, articulates the challenges and affordances of designing and

DOI: 10.4324/9781003505785-2

delivering courses for online education platforms. We note there are few applied case studies of successful online learning design initiatives in the Humanities – especially from the perspective of professional staff – and fewer still that bridge the periods before, during and after the COVID-19 pandemic. The BA Online's integration of open courses (also known as massive open online courses [MOOCs]) into its program structure is pathbreaking in the Australian context (see Chapter 2) and possibly unique globally in Humanities education. As such, we hope documenting the process and the impacts on students, staff, and the institution broadens the discussion of what is possible in Humanities and Social Science education.

The UON's strategic initiative to introduce the BA Online was a pioneering effort in Australian higher education. By incorporating MOOCs and prioritising accessibility and inclusivity, this endeavour not only increased student engagement and recruitment but also amplified the institution's global presence. The lessons learned and experiences gained from this ambitious project form the crux of this edited collection, providing a roadmap for other institutions aiming to initiate or navigate similar transformations. The book therefore responds to an observed demand for practical guidance in redesigning higher education curricula, especially in the Humanities.

We focus on the 'meso' level of program change, a facet frequently overlooked in the existing literature. While most online education scholarship primarily concentrates on theory ('macro') or instructional design and learning environment dynamics ('micro'), this collection delves into the intricacies of strategic educational projects and how practitioners working across various areas and at varying levels of seniority can affect change. It illuminates the crucial interplay between pedagogy, academic and professional staff, technological integration, and institutional culture necessary for the successful execution of quality online learning at the program level. The interdisciplinary case studies within this collection hope to appeal to any staff involved in teaching and learning: educational leaders, faculty members, learning designers, learning media producers, digital developers, educational technologists, and academic developers.

While this is an Australian case study, the principles and challenges it focuses on are experienced globally in HE. The project was an international project – it was delivered on a UK-based platform from an Australian university, with learners joining the open courses from all over the world. Additionally, discussion of approaches and concepts common to online learning globally, such as Universal Design for Learning, ensures this collection will appeal internationally, particularly in the United States and the United Kingdom due to similarities in the higher education (HE) context.

In framing our exploration and reflection of the process of translating a BA degree to an online learning experience, we acknowledge that contextual factors may likely mean different institutions are unable to directly replicate our experience. As such, we aim to provide an exploration of personal experiences, offering insights into the challenges to expect and how they may be overcome; the process of collaborative design and delivery; and the affordances of online teaching and learning. Readers are invited to consider the following collection as a reflective guide on the process of translation.

The origins of this collection

This book serves as a guide and testament to successful collaboration in whole-program curriculum redesign undertaken by academic and professional staff, who were at the coalface of reshaping a traditional BA degree into a fully online learning experience.

In recent years, the emergence and fast evolution of third-party online program management (OPM) providers and forces that encourage or oppose their partnership with HEIs have highlighted a sector conversation around the value of nurturing online learning capacity 'in house.' This edited collection demystifies the course and program development from face-to-face to a fully online and asynchronous learning experience from end-to-end process.

A note on terminology

Given the international nature of curriculum design and development and HE, it is important to define our use of language and note the differences in terminology between UON and FutureLearn. We use UON's terminology, explaining FutureLearn's use where necessary for clarification (see Figure 1.1 for more information). In the context of this book, a 'course' is a semester-long unit of study for credit that sits within a degree program. Courses were further modularised, that is, split into chunks. All courses comprise four 3-week modules, but the content focus of a module is principally determined in consultation between the educator(s) and the learning designers. Students need to satisfactorily complete all assessments across all modules in a course to be awarded credit for that 12-week course. Chapters 2 and 3 will further explain the rationale behind this structure.

University of Newcastle	FutureLearn	Using
Degree	Degree	Degree
Course	Program	Course
Module	Course	Module

Figure 1.1 Terminology differences between UON and FutureLearn.

Pedagogical approach and learning design methodology

The pedagogical approach to the project was multifaceted, reflecting research on curriculum design, engagement, active collaborative learning, and institutional pedagogic frameworks. A central tenet to this approach ensured that the process was always pedagogy-led, where technological affordances were carefully integrated into the pedagogical approach but did not dictate the curriculum design. As an undergraduate degree was a first for the FutureLearn platform, they were happy to collaborate and learn from UON as we led the structure and build of how the degree would take shape on the platform.

Groundwork for the pedagogical approach had been laid by the Bachelor of Arts Working Group in the BA Reinvention Project in 2016–2018 within the School of Humanities and Social Science (see Chapter 2). One of the priorities of the BA Online project was moving digitally enabled learning away from traditional, teacher-centred approaches – in other words, the prioritisation of knowledge transfer and the centring of the educator – and towards more active, collaborative, and student-centred learning. At the same time, this reinvention of the Bachelor of Arts was occurring, an institution-wide curriculum framework project was initiated, the New Education Framework (NEF). Embedded within the NEF were curriculum design principles that all new and redesigned courses needed to follow, including ensuring the learning journey included opportunities to 'prepare and discover,' 'explore and reinforce,' and 'consolidate and apply' (see Figure 1.2). They encompassed broad design principles that enabled constructive alignment, while the framework approach provided room for appropriate discipline, cohort, and faculty flavouring. All online courses designed by the University were expected to enable a constructive alignment approach and include experiences that the UON online learning environment could support.

Furthermore, the NEF encouraged courses to be 'Indigenous enlightened,' which is an acknowledgement not only of the University's campuses being built on the land of the Awabakal, Worimi, Biripai, Wonnarua, Eora Nations, and Darkinjung peoples but also of the institution's commitment to Indigenous studies and education collaboration with Aboriginal peoples and ways of knowing.

Local pedagogic priorities were aligned with the pedagogical underpinnings of the FutureLearn platform and good practice in designing learning for online. This meant enacting Young and Perović's (2018) ABC (Arena Blended Connected) learning design methodology, adapted from Laurillard's (2012) Conversational Framework which is at the core of FutureLearn's pedagogy (FutureLearn, 2024; Sharples, 2017). As its name implies, the focus of the Framework is on bi-directional dialogue between educator and student. This approach aligns closely with other learner-centred learning theories like constructionism and social constructivism (Mnasri & Papakonstantinidis, 2023). The ABC methodology underpins FutureLearn through its emphasis on thoughtfully integrating technology into learning through the concept of

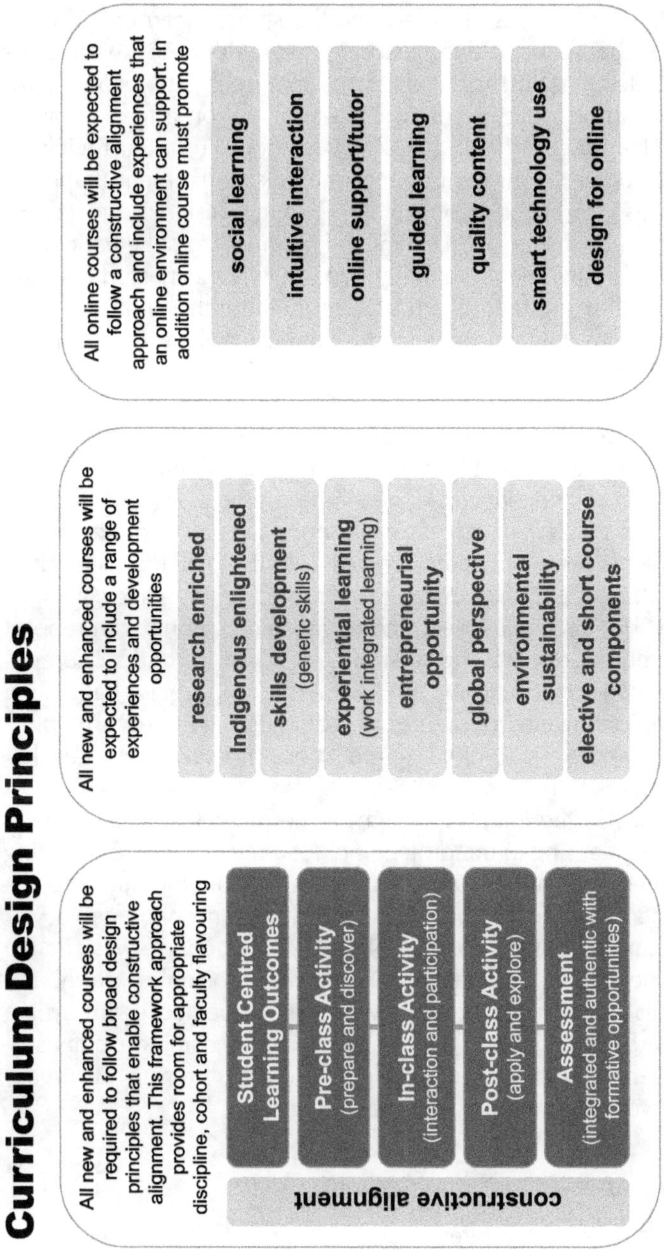

Curriculum Design Principles

All new and enhanced courses will be required to follow broad design principles that enable constructive alignment. This framework approach provides room for appropriate discipline, cohort and faculty flavouring

- **Student Centred Learning Outcomes**
- **Pre-class Activity** (prepare and discover)
- **In-class Activity** (interaction and participation)
- **Post-class Activity** (apply and explore)
- **Assessment** (integrated and authentic with formative opportunities)

constructive alignment

All new and enhanced courses will be expected to include a range of experiences and development opportunities

- research enriched
- Indigenous enlightened
- skills development (generic skills)
- experiential learning (work integrated learning)
- entrepreneurial opportunity
- global perspective
- environmental sustainability
- elective and short course components

All online courses will be expected to follow a constructive alignment approach and include experiences that an online environment can support. In addition online course must promote

- social learning
- intuitive interaction
- online support/tutor
- guided learning
- quality content
- smart technology use
- design for online

Figure 1.2 Curriculum design principles of the New Education Framework.

'learning types,' of which there are six: acquisition (i.e., reading/watching/listening), collaboration, discussion, investigation, practise, and production (Laurillard, 2012; Young & Perović, 2018). The types are an effective language for staff and students to discuss and describe the student learning process. Learning designers operationalised the learning types within ABC workshops facilitated with academic staff. These workshops entailed creative storyboarding to ensure that innovative curriculum design is built on a foundation of active and social learning. Prior to an ABC workshop, an initial review of content, syllabus, course learning outcomes including alignment mapping, and assessment was conducted between the learning designer and course coordinator. This was to ensure consistency and quality across the entire program and constructive alignment (i.e., alignment between expected learning outcomes and how they are taught and assessed) within the online offering and across the different delivery modes and campuses where the course is offered.

Engaging and adhering to the agreed pedagogical principles within the NEF and the FutureLearn principles of "storytelling, discussion, visible learning, and using community support to celebrate progress" (FutureLearn, 2024) enabled one of the core concepts used: 'teacher presence.' Establishing and maintaining a strong teacher or educator presence is vital in online learning to ensure students feel connected, engaged, and motivated (Alharbi & Dimitriadi, 2018; Zhang, 2025). Zhang notes, "Instructor immediacy, encompassing behaviors that foster closeness and engagement, along with rapport characterized by mutual respect and trust, are identified as critical components in creating a conducive learning environment" (n.p.), yet is challenging to incorporate in an online environment (Cui et al., 2012); FutureLearn's principles enabled our approach to create connection through student-teacher and student-student relationships.

Another key focus in the learning design of the project was assessment. The design of online learning in the project included reviewing and rewriting assessment and integrating authentic assessment with more formative opportunities for students. This included the creation of a short online course for UON students, 'Learning Online with UON.' The 2-week course was created to support first-time online learners, debunking myths of online study and supporting students to learn the skills they needed to be successful online learners. It outlined the benefits and how to overcome common pitfalls. It also provided students with study tools, including resources for staying organised, taking effective notes, and assessment writing skills.

Structure and content

The chapters in this collection address elements crucial to the holistic development of online learning and degree change, providing insights into the process from the perspectives of academics and professional staff. They explore topics including pedagogical reform, educational technology integration, collaboration with stakeholders, and embedding inclusivity to support a diverse cohort of students. Some of the chapters here are personal narratives of how humanities scholars transitioned to online teaching. Other chapters address challenges and affordances of online teaching from the micro to the macro in project management, such as convincing stakeholders to engage in pedagogic change, adopting alternate opportunities for engagement and assessment, and sustaining shifts in teaching and learning practices beyond project timelines.

Chapters and case studies are aligned to four themes: Part 1: Creating an online degree; Part 2: Case studies in online teaching and assessment; Part 3: Challenges and opportunities in adaptation; and Part 4: Impacts and evaluation. Chapters in Part 1 range across pedagogy, partnerships, and affordances of learning technology. Signature pedagogical approaches and assessment situated in a variety of Humanities disciplines are the focus of Part 2. Part 3 addresses particular obstacles and affordances for traditional face-to-face delivery in adapting to online learning. Finally, Part 4 explores the project's outcomes and aspects of evaluation for iterative course design.

In Part 1, Catharine Coleborne explores the transformation of the Bachelor of Arts degree at the UON from her perspective as the Head of School for Bachelor of Arts. She provides an overview of the institutional and sector context for the changes to the degree between 2019 and 2022 to ensure future success, and she discusses how the model for the BA Online radically challenged both form and content delivery in the disciplines, and created new collaborative relationships and capability within the institution that aided staff during a global pandemic and enhanced tertiary education design and delivery. Monty King provides insight into the FutureLearn partnership from his role as partnerships manager external to the institution, detailing how the university leveraged the platform to host an online undergraduate degree, and the benefits and challenges of this collaboration. He argues UON's clear vision for its degree offering, its established foothold in the online learning space and the resources required to design and produce online courses, as well as the incorporation of the physical campus space into the learning experience, were key factors in the BA's success. He reflects on the opportunities this partnership provides for universities looking to move their online course design and production in-house.

In Part 2, Mitchell J. Taylor and Julia Cook reflect on the ability of online learning platforms to create and sustain effective learning communities through constructivist pedagogies. They evaluate the benefits and drawbacks of the FutureLearn platform with respect to a Community of Inquiry model approach. Sacha E. Davis and Adam Khamis share their experiences from producing over 200 educational videos for three online courses across all levels of undergraduate learning. Drawing on Khamis' 15 years of experience working in film, television, and advertising, along with Davis's 16 years of educator expertise and passion for the subject matter, they emphasise the importance of engaging multimedia content and performance for fostering engagement, student satisfaction, and learning in online teaching, through a mutually collaborative, creative process. Hamish Ford and Rebecca Beirne analyse the redesign of a Screen and Cultural Studies major for online delivery, highlighting the benefits and potential of asynchronous learning and addressing challenges such as content availability and copyright issues. They detail the strategies involved in this redesign, as well as broader questions regarding the creation of content in the online environment to maintain core objectives and outcomes to best foster active student participation in learning and the acquisition of core skills that enable successful completion of their degree and diverse employment futures. Finally, Michael Kilmister, James Bennett, and Kate Ariotti reflect on the redesign of a flagship first-year History course that challenges traditional approaches to teaching History. They argue that adapting the course to online delivery was vital to respond to the needs of its multiple cohorts and create a student-centred learning environment. Their discussion addresses the importance of collegial conversations and the creation of interactive learning materials to develop key concepts and skills.

In Part 3, Jessica Ford explores how online learning can facilitate the teaching of sensitive topics by allowing students to self-pace and approach challenging content with caution. She unpacks how teaching certain topics, namely, online pornography, sexting, and mediated violence, can utilise the specific opportunities of online learning, including flexibility, asynchronicity, physical anonymity, and self-directed learning, for student comfort and success. David Musgrave outlines his adoption of innovative digital technologies and methods for teaching creative writing, highlighting their positive impact on student engagement and learning. He discusses digital methods of composition, such as the compositional method of Deer Head Nation, Meaning Eater, speech (mis)recognition, and ChatGPT, and how these techniques can be deployed digitally to aid the central task of teaching creative writing through workshopping in an online environment. He examines the strengths and weaknesses of these approaches and the challenges for employing such methods in the tertiary pedagogical context. Next, Hedda Haugen Askland, Michael Kilmister, Kate Senior, Adrian Mereles, Chris Lawrence, and Tim Garside discuss the distinct challenges of teaching ethnography in anthropology courses, and the affordances of the virtual learning environment to navigate these challenges. They reflect on how the pandemic prompted a shift to virtual anthropology fieldwork, using gamified learning and authentic assessment to teach ethnography. Finally, Jai Cooper and Chris Lawrence consider key challenges to education for the environment that are heightened by the online learning space. Focusing on 'bringing the outside in,' they detail strategies for addressing eco-anxiety in online environmental sociology courses, including interactive engagement with outdoor adventure, sequential and progressive conceptual framing of course content, and comedic interventions as a unique pedagogical tool.

Part 4 opens with Clare Lloyd, Annika Herb, and Michael Kilmister exploring the role and importance of collaborative and continuous academic development in designing and implementing a fully online degree. Drawing on a range of data to assess the success of the academic development, they advocate for the implementation of collaborative and distributed learning design frameworks, continuous and bespoke professional development opportunities, and robust institutional support structures that take account of the voices of all involved in the learning experience. Paul Sijpkes and Elizabeth Roberts-Pedersen reflect on the value of student feedback data to inform pedagogical design and teaching strategies for online Humanities courses. Drawing on existing literature and program-level data, they evaluate the effectiveness of student feedback processes for the BA Online to effectively support learning needs and aid in determining trends in student satisfaction and their usefulness for informing pedagogical design and teaching strategies. Julie McIntyre discusses the importance of iterative design principles in online course management, highlighting the need for adaptability in digital education. Employing an autoethnographic case study as an educator new to online teaching, she posits iterative design principles for asynchronous online course management are skills in being readily adaptive to the continual manifold change of educating in the digital age. Nancy Cushing, Alana Piper and Vicky Nagy demonstrate how online teaching can extend to enhance academic profiles and foster collaborative networks, leading to significant scholarly opportunities, including an invitation to publish a textbook on a History course designed for the BA Online. The final chapter is a conclusion from Catharine Coleborne and Clare Lloyd reflecting on the achievements and impacts of the BA Online. They emphasise the project and book's contributions to accessibility, innovation, and pedagogical renewal, showcasing the program's success in expanding the degree's identity and creating spaces for global learners. This reflection ties together these various threads discussed throughout the book. The book concludes with an afterword from the editors, which shares a brief personal history to the story of this book.

Conclusion

It is hoped that this edited collection will empower higher education providers to translate traditional learning – or to design a degree from the 'ground-up' – for the fully online mode. The investment in people and the learning infrastructure required, not to mention the risks involved in 'getting it wrong,' can be daunting for university leaders and their staff. This book will therefore address strategic and practical challenges involved in designing and delivering online learning, including driving and sustaining meaningful change in teaching and learning practice. The implementable approaches, solutions, and recommendations at the heart of the book, learned through lived experience, will be in conversation with established research literature in the fields of online learning design and digitally enabled learning pedagogies, developing academic practice, and leading program change.

References

Alharbi, S., & Dimitriadi, Y. (2018). Instructional immediacy practices in online learning environments. *Journal of Education and Practice, 9*(6), 1–7. https://centaur.reading.ac.uk/102105/

Cui, G., Lockee, B., & Meng, C. (2012). Building modern online social presence: A review of social presence theory and its instructional design implications for future trends. *Education and Information Technologies, 18*, 661–685. https://doi.org/10.1007/s10639-012-9192-1

FutureLearn. (2024). *Learning on FutureLearn: The power of social learning: An effective way to learn.* https://www.futurelearn.com/using-futurelearn/why-it-works

Gruenhagen, J. H., Sinclair, P. M., Carroll, J., Baker, P. R. A., Wilson, A., & Demant, D. (2024). The rapid rise of generative AI and its implications for academic integrity: Students' perceptions and use of chatbots for assistance with assessments. *Computers and Education: Artificial Intelligence, 7*. https://doi.org/10.1016/j.caeai.2024.100273

Ikpe, I. B. (2015). The decline of the humanities and the decline of society. *Theoria: A Journal of Social and Political Theory, 62*(142), 50–66. https://doi.org/10.3167/th.2015.6214203

Kelly, K., & Zakrajsek, T. D. (2020). *Advancing online teaching: Creating equity-based digital learning environments.* Taylor & Francis.

Laurillard, D. (2012). *Teaching as a design science: Building pedagogical patterns for learning and technology.* Routledge.

Mnasri, S., & Papakonstantinidis, S. (2023). The teaching-learning dynamic from behaviourism to social constructionism: A communication-centred narrative. *International Journal of Learning and Change, 15*(3), 312–327. https://doi.org/10.1504/IJLC.2023.130629

Sharples, M. (2017). Pedagogy of FutureLearn. *Slideshare.* https://www.slideshare.net/slideshow/pedagogy-of-futurelearn/80057298

Young, C., & Perović, N. (2018). *Introduction to the ABC learning design workshop.* University College London. https://abc-ld.org/wp-content/uploads/2020/05/01-ABC_LD-Toolkit-Intro-Erasmus-v02.pdf

Zhang, Q. (2025). The role of EFL teacher immediacy and teacher-student rapport in boosting motivation to learn and academic mindsets in online education. *Learning and Motivation, 89*. https://doi.org/10.1016/j.lmot.2024.102092

2 Creating the BA Online
Reinventing the degree through pedagogical innovation

Catharine Coleborne

Introduction

Creating the Bachelor of Arts as an online degree at the University of Newcastle signalled new possibilities for learning and teaching. In the context of a wider debate about the direction of higher education, degree reinvention was becoming more urgent and responsive to student enrolment trends. These trends promoted new conversations about the need to revitalise learning engagement for tertiary students. Our ambition was to transform both student and educator experiences by building on changes to the degree structure and its relaunch to the student audience, a challenge that was largely successful over time. This chapter provides a contextual overview of the BA reinvention between late 2016 and 2018 and the progression to the creation of the BA Online, which launched in 2019. It establishes the scene for other chapters in this book by setting out the underpinning concepts of the degree program and what we hoped to achieve over time as we considered the pressing need for change in pedagogies, delivery modes, and the student experience of learning.

By 2018, the BA degree taught in face-to-face mode had been through a lengthy reinvention process designed to tackle a decline in enrolments, counter student attrition and improve retention, and address enduring negative perceptions of the degree. Perceptions of the Bachelor of Arts degree in Australia, and elsewhere, tend to revolve around notions that the degree is less useful than the many vocational degree programs on offer to undergraduate students.[1] However, in 2018, the reinvention of the structure of the 3-year degree program (which comprised 240-units, an 80-unit major, and the opportunity for discipline minors), as well as emerging approaches to student retention, remained to be tested by the student cohort.[2] It therefore made sense to extend the potential of the redesign by tackling the problem of how to offer an arts degree to learners online. The catalyst for these changes was market insight data that demonstrated the risk to our enrolments, as well as to the sustainability of the degree, but more importantly, we identified the need to modernise our pedagogical approaches to ensure degree relevance and currency for students. Market insight also helped us determine the focus

DOI: 10.4324/9781003505785-3

areas and disciplines for our chosen online majors. The opportunity to continue the refashioning of the degree and its delivery modes was made possible by institutional leadership and investment in a relationship with the higher education online learning platform FutureLearn.

In 2016, I was a new Head of School/Dean of Arts and was tasked by the university with curriculum uplift and redevelopment. The BA degree was not the only area of the curriculum that was perceived to be lacking in innovation or which presented a challenge in terms of student retention, but it was the focus of the most attention. This was due to the serious decline in student enrolments over the preceding 5 years, with previous attempts to address the issues of student interest and outcomes mostly unsuccessful following a review of the degree in 2012. Although discipline and major 'capstone' courses (or courses that allow students to demonstrate their expertise and deep knowledge by the third year) had been developed and introduced after the 2012 review, the external visibility and marketing of the degree had no new 'story' to offer. It was this external and internal institutional identity for the BA that became the focus of our work over 2 years.

The surrounding context in the higher education sector was (and remains) unhelpful. With students and their parents choosing to seek vocational outcomes from expensive tertiary degree education, the reputation of the arts degree in Australia has suffered, evidenced by numerous radio talkback discussions and newspaper pieces.[3] Repeated slurs on the degree that date back to my own days as an undergraduate student in the mid-1980s tend to emphasise the negative perception of the arts graduate as a 'jack of all trades and master of none,' to use a gendered epithet. More problematically, this view has most recently been embedded in government policy and a university funding model. In 2019, the conservative Coalition government in Australia led by former Prime Minister Scott Morrison proposed the 'Job-Ready Graduates' policy funding package which was later endorsed by legislation making the cost of an arts degree far more expensive for students while many vocational degrees became less expensive (Coleborne, 2023).[4]

The changes to the Bachelor of Arts degree at Newcastle were also precipitated by a steady sector-wide decline in BA degree enrolments. The BA degree in Australia has showed a pattern of decline over time with an increasing emphasis on the marketing of vocational degrees and their perceived relevance and value, and evidence of shifting student interest favouring new degrees which are seen to offer distinctive outcomes, such as a Bachelor of Criminology paired with Psychology. The University of Newcastle's proud reputation for accessible education in the form of enabling pathways including Open Foundation has played a part in keeping the appetite for the BA degree strong as an entry degree for higher education (see Bennett et al., 2018). Yet this was also a factor in attrition from the degree, with students using their entry to gain access to other qualifications after improving their educational outcomes. Student retention in the degree is historically related to both academic and non-academic factors such as student poverty, life crisis, and mental health (Harvey & Luckman, 2014; see also Mestan, 2016). The degree also suffers from an unfair stigma, given decades of erosion of higher education as a mechanism for young people to grow their intellectual interest through post-secondary education.

Given all these factors and challenges, the intrinsic value of the humanities to life-long education was failing to capture the imaginations of future students. This was a shared problem, with higher education experts, peak bodies such as Learned Academies and the Australasian Council of Deans of Arts, Humanities and Social Sciences (DASSH), and educational researchers all focused on analysing how to renew and revive the generalist BA degree. In particular, DASSH collated decades of data about the degree and its changing fortunes over time.[5]

A collaborative approach to degree reinvention

Educational researcher Deanne Gannaway, who collaborated with the past Board of DASSH, worked with several universities to encourage academic staff to devise new forms of education in the degree through curriculum renewal (Gannaway, 2015). Approaches that Gannaway explored with colleagues in a range of institutions included rethinking authentic assessment, relevant core learning outcomes, and Work Integrated Learning (WIL) experiences as embedded in degrees, with several universities between 2016 and 2018 experimenting with models for reinvention. Gannaway worked with our academic staff to steer vibrant discussions about the BA at Newcastle. We also invited Aotearoa New Zealand colleagues from the Massey University to engage with the group as we developed our approach. Massey's BA degree had been a successful model in the New Zealand context and included a strong Māori and Pasifika identity from the first year of study. This was an appealing idea because, like Massey, we also aimed to engage First Nations Australian students and educators in our revised degree as we developed new module content. 'Place-based' approaches which offer students exposure to understanding knowledge relevant to their own experience of places including the University's own regional location were also the focus of discussions with other invited experts.

During the BA Reinvention Project, our academic team explored many exciting concepts. However, the ideas also tended to clash and compete for attention as degree reinvention became a flashpoint for staff concerns about changes to their teaching foci and expertise, as well as workload demands. The consistent message to the academic educators in the School was that we needed to adapt as educators, and to become able to respond to shifts in student demand for non-vocational 'generalist' degrees. From the start, I wanted to embed the core learning outcomes for the degree, as mapped against the Australian Quality Framework (AQF) Level 7, to a set of core courses in the degree. This had the added benefit of creating a student learner cohort and would allow us to shape the traditionally large, sprawling generalist degree in Australia into a more focused semi-directed degree, but at the same time maintaining choice in majors, minors, and electives.

The actions we took in the BA Reinvention were designed to support colleagues teaching in the BA degree disciplines to embrace change and to consider thinking differently about interdisciplinary learning and course content. The formation and constitution of the BA Working Group (BAWG) was important. It was designed to include emerging researchers and educators at the start of their careers as well as staff with reputations for excellent teaching and innovative examples of pedagogy. These were staff who had used the University of Newcastle's formative Blended and Online Learning Design (BOLD) Lab facilities for blended and online learning development, which was transformed to be the new Learning Design and Teaching Innovation (LDTI) Unit, and includes support such as the Lightboard (educators could film themselves writing or drawing on a transparent board), the One-Button Studio (individual educator recording booth), and the Film Studio (green screens, space and scope for seated interview or standing recordings; see Chapter 5). The BAWG team functioned as a large 'ideas tank' and also challenged hierarchies and distinctions, building in the involvement across units: academic and professional staff worked in a layered process, which created useful conditions for further collaboration between academic educators and learning designers (see Gormley, 2014). It was also possible for me, as Head of School, to support staff through training, work allocation, recognition, and several points of celebration.

In addition, we used relevant data to share an understanding of the need for change. This data included enrolment patterns and was benchmarked with other higher education sector (HES) institutions. A formal partnership between the University of Newcastle and the University of Wollongong allowed us to track student satisfaction scores and learner behaviours for a period of time as agreed by the institutions. This sharing of sensitive data also gave us insight into the differences between our learner cohorts and equity groups such as low socio-economic status (SES), 'First in Family' to attend university, Aboriginal and Torres Strait Islander (ATSI), gender and age, and school leavers or mature student groups.[6] The theme of equity, diversity, and inclusion was a particular focus for us, given that traditionally, many learners commencing their degree studies at the University of Newcastle were adult learners and not school leavers; many also joined the university via entry programs such as Open Foundation. Whatever we did with this degree, we wanted it to *enable* students in our cohort. The emerging focus of WIL was also a powerful theme for discussion; the university had not yet embarked on the project to transform WIL into 'career-ready placements' for all, but we envisaged WIL as a more adventurous step in our initial planning and effort to transform the 'Newcastle BA' into one that could be more distinctive in the sector, with tentative plans for an applied WIL course as part of the core course suite of offerings. We took inspiration from our colleagues in Social Work and other applied degree programs. Interestingly, online education emerged in these reflections as a positive learning delivery mode for parents, people living with disability, and other social groupings sometimes identified as equity cohorts (Stone, 2022).

The BAWG worked together from 2016 to 2018 and involved a sizeable group of up to 25, and the group also partnered with external stakeholders, such as past, present, and future students, and future employers of graduates from the BA program. All this work occurred during an organisational change process in the School which impacted the humanities and social science disciplines, with some areas disestablished, some reduced to minors, and some combined. The BAWG facilitated the need in the School to work together in collaborative approaches (Gormley, 2014). Academic educators could learn about curriculum design together; later, they were able to leverage this peer learning in relation to technology and overcome any fears of using the online tools we needed them to incorporate in their online courses. The process also led to academic recruitment to teach the core courses in the new degree program; ultimately, the process provided the School with a sense of new ownership of the BA program.

Reinventing the BA degree for future students rested on the need to reconfigure the degree through the introduction of an interdisciplinary core curriculum via three courses: BA Futures (HASS1000), BA Practice (HASS2000), and the newly envisaged degree capstone course, BA Project (HASS3000). Each of these was a 10-unit course in the 240-unit degree program with an 80-unit major. This means 2–3 hr of instruction per week per 10-unit course, with full-time enrolled students at Level 1000 required to study 8 courses over 1 year. These evolved over time and were originally floated as courses on language and culture, narrative and power; global encounters with culture; and applied humanities. The core was imagined as the 'spine' of the degree and allowed us to incorporate common skill strands for all students in the BA. The BA attracted students from combined law-arts programs, as well as from psychology; it was vital that we could reach all students in the creation of the core and provide transferable skills to all learners. In part, this mission was to uplift the reputation of the BA degree. A document was circulated in 2018 to explain the rationale for the proposed changes:

- To provide a *group study experience* and *peer-to-peer* support.
- To *showcase* and *embed our strong disciplines*.
- To offer new *interdisciplinary pathways* into majors.
- To impart a set of important *transferable skills*.
- To create an innovative focus for *our UON identity* through the BA.[7]

We also envisaged the potential use of learning streams to help better define the role of the core courses and the majors in the degree. In addition to choosing majors, minors and structured program pathways, students were given the opportunity to focus their studies through optional learning pathways such as an entrepreneurial stream with WIL components; a global stream focused on language acquisition and international mobility opportunities; an innovator stream focused on creativity and innovation; and an online stream for students pursuing work and study and blended learning in their degree. These learning streams or pathways proved to be difficult to fully enact over time, in part due to perceptions of degree structures, rules, and marketing approaches. It is important to note here that one of the streams was dedicated to existing online offerings that were delivered via the Learning Management System (LMS) at that time (Blackboard; the university has since moved to work with Canvas). This helped to model the future offerings for the BA Online.

The new core courses in the degree were created using a modular structure (four modules within each core course; our semester of 12 weeks would accommodate 4 modules). This was in part devised to aid collaborative team teaching because it brought academic staff into new conversations about course content and delivery. In terms of our focus on students, we looked to prioritise the learner experience and student retention. In particular, our team wanted to see a peer-to-peer approach through student learning circles in tutorial workshops in the first year of the degree. Theoretically, we wanted to place emphasis on peer-to-peer learning and the importance of feedback. Peer-to-peer learning is, as Boud et al. (2014) argue, a valuable tool in the hands of the adviser. Their pedagogical research indicates that students learn not just from teaching staff but also in more informal ways in the classroom and that this is a valid and important form of academic instruction (Boud et al., 2014, pp. 3–5).

Identifying changes to humanities pedagogy

The BAWG also worked hard to identify the kinds of pedagogical challenges facing academic educators. University educators were concerned about academic and disciplinary integrity and depth across the degree. There was mistrust of the interdisciplinary courses and whether these could provide the deep knowledge students might reasonably require for positive outcomes from the traditional BA degree especially due to the controversy that some disciplines, notably Philosophy, were being removed from the degree. This often manifested as a discussion about the volume of learning. Presenting humanities topics in new modes, as well as discussions about the function of learning scaffolds for students, often surfaced in our planning. Finding ways to ensure that new content would continue to develop the thinking skills central to humanities degrees prompted careful and deliberate discussion of the design of the core courses. These critical thinking skills would need to be developed further in the online environment (Tathahira, 2020).

It was important that we did not work in isolation but that we engaged with a variety of stakeholders. The consultation process widened the participation from the BAWG membership to other staff, students and other stakeholders, and our focus was on the potential for the core to attract and retain students in the BA, as well as to convey learning outcomes. At different stages of the process we held focus groups and surveyed employers. Once we had a draft design for the BA core, we did some market testing with all of our stakeholders through both a large survey and individual phone calls. Interestingly, many students – secondary, tertiary, and higher degree research – were captivated by the traditional values of arts and humanities knowledge-based acquisition. Meanwhile, in our survey of 400 employers from the Hunter region and Sydney, we found that they were interested in skills and currency for the BA degree and were hungry to learn more about the value of the degree for future workforces. Students cited stigma around their degrees as a concern when they participated in our stakeholder engagement, a valuable reminder of the need to provide educational uplift and meaningful outcomes as part of the reinvention. Comments included "it is about everything and nothing," "unwanted debt," and as having a quality "that is not listed in any job description."[8]

The challenge, therefore, related to modes of delivering humanities content in new ways, not abandoning deep inquiry and knowledge expertise, but understanding how to reach newer generations of students with their future approach to learning, especially using digital tools and interactive learning modes. At the time of writing this chapter, we are grappling with the impact of generative artificial intelligence (GenAI) on students and learning, especially assessment and academic integrity. The particular moment of designing the new BA between 2016 and 2017 may well have been a signal about the future; it proved to be a tipping point in terms of upskilling academic staff in the use of educational technology, especially GenAI and new concerns about academic integrity.

The major change in the pedagogy was underpinned by a focus on active or inquiry-based learning. The first-year core course HASS1000 deliberately starts with questions such as "What does it mean to be human?" To examine the theme of epistemology, students are asked "How do we know what we know?' This is an important departure from the idea of introducing a more traditional canon of 'great thinkers' or 'big ideas' for students to know about, which may have encouraged passive learning in the past. The shift to 'big concepts and big questions' signaled an inquiry-based approach which requires students to actively participate in the acquisition of new knowledge as learners. In addition, we asked students to engage with the concept of humanities learning for the future. For instance, in the first year of the new degree, students wrote short opinion pieces as an authentic assessment that required them to comment on the utility of the BA to public audiences and to make the case for the degree.[9]

Designing with FutureLearn: a model for online pedagogy

These pedagogical shifts in the degree led to the creation of the BA Online in partnership with the UK educational provider FutureLearn, which went live in 2019. This undergraduate degree was a first for FutureLearn and it offered new opportunities to present our Australian humanities educators and content to international learners via open massive open online courses (MOOCs).[10] We were able to advance this project through a 'prototype' investment from the Office of the Deputy Vice Chancellor (DVC) Academic under the 'New Education Framework' which outlined a program of work to revitalise educational models at the institution. The announcement of the partnership emphasised the flexible nature of the degree as well as the promise of an international online classroom.[11] We wanted to work with FutureLearn because they offered a social learning model which has been the focus of some academic scholarship (Tubman et al., 2016). Research indicates that designing for online participation and interaction is critical to the success of a large online course. Informed by theories of constructivism, which highlight the centrality of social interaction to learning outcomes, the model reinforces the value of people learning from and with each other, as well as from their educators and instructors. The role of the educator changes in this model: teaching becomes a facilitation of dialogue and conversation, the creation of safe and well-bounded spaces for discussion of topics and the expression of views (Bell, 2009; Huang, 2002, p. 29; p. 33).

This was an important shift and distinction because the student experience of other models of online learning – such as placing lecture materials online via the LMS and creating 'discussion boards' – tended to be both uninspired (with learning content quickly dated) and also disengaging, belonging to an older format for distance education, but mostly without intensive learning blocks as part of the program. FutureLearn offered a visually appealing and digitally sophisticated platform for learners and educators, including linking visual materials and short articles to podcast audio pieces, dynamic and interactive maps, and video interviews with experts, all of which form an engaging set of learning moments that students could interact with, as well as sharing their comments with peers. In addition, FutureLearn elevated the learning experience through mobile-friendly design, contextualised discussions, and a clear and simple layout to navigate content.

As the chapter has highlighted at various points, reinventing the Bachelor of Arts as an online degree has involved pushing out from the degree reinvention itself to thinking about new ways to present disciplinary content, core curriculum, and inquiry-based learning in the online environment and with teams of educators. This is a challenge faced by educators working in blended teaching modes in other contexts (Crawford & Jenkins, 2017). In devising the online degree, we added the impetus for a more radical vision of the BA degree by adding to the modularised set of core courses with a set of majors and around 30 more individual courses to be developed in a similar mode for the degree to move into a fully online environment. The choice of four majors was based on internal institutional benchmarking data across 12 other Australian universities offering online arts degree qualifications including several in New South Wales and institutions in other states. The University of New England, for instance, had a reputation for offering most of its humanities online. Our objective was to be distinctive in this market and also to compete with universities encroaching on our student catchment area of New South Wales. We chose to focus on History, English and Writing, Sociology, and the field of Film, Media, and Cultural Studies to both differentiate ourselves and help develop those disciplinary colleagues to innovate their curricula and pedagogies. Sociology also offered us the potential to reach out to learners enrolled in the Bachelor of Social Sciences who were able to experience the online offerings. These majors were also popular with teacher education students. The open MOOC 'What is poetry?' taught by Associate Professor Caroline Webb, proved to be one of the most successful MOOCs on the FutureLearn platform at the time.

Overall, we were aiming to play to our strengths; to provide opportunities to educators to innovate; and to capitalise on student interests and exposure to online courses. Some courses on the LMS also gave us some additional areas to fold into the narrative about online learning, such as languages Japanese and French, where some development of online classes and options had existed for a period of time. The main reason these language disciplines were not further developed in FutureLearn related to the crowded marketplace for language learning provision online but also to the nature of the learning experience.

This was a highly ambitious development for a fully online Bachelor of Arts degree at UON (Lloyd & Devine, 2019), as later chapters in this book demonstrate. Over time, it involved more than 25 academics in hands-on practical work. Educators worked with a team of skilled learning designers using curriculum design principles to ensure the purpose-built courses were optimal for online learning (Gormley, 2014). There were two specific challenges: first, breaking down the content of educational experiences for online learners with a focus on the learner experience; and second, experimenting with the online teacher presence in the humanities classroom for globally engaged students.

In planning the delivery of content on the FutureLearn platform, educators were asked to create large storyboards, collaboratively designed with a learning designer, breaking down their course content into 'steps,' and encouraged to aim for around 15 steps for each week of content on the platform. These steps could comprise short videos, articles, interactive exercises such as Padlet posts, polls, links to readings and discussion points, and real-world exercises. The educators were creating content for students who would actively learn together online by accessing the program's courses in 4 modules of 3 weeks. Their task would be to keep up with the narrative of the course, all of which is acknowledged through weekly completion achievements. As described earlier, the value here is that students engage as social learners: they participate through an inquiry-based pedagogy rather than as passive learners in a lecture/tutorial format (Lloyd et al., 2021). Formal course assessment would still take place in the LMS to allow for the interface with institutional systems for grading and moderation.

Making the move to FutureLearn involved thinking about social learning and student cohorts in a different way. We also had to think hard about creating the online teacher presence. Academic educators gained new skills in creating short introductory videos, learning to personalise their teaching personas for online, and also learning to interact with students online in ways that were contained in the FutureLearn platform. (Some academics added online drop-in sessions via Blackboard 'Collaborate' and later Zoom; this practice was encouraged by the learning designers but was not adopted widely.) This was to be asynchronous learning, developed as clearly as possible to help stage learning elements in each week linked to formal assessments and feedback via the LMS. Critically – and appealing as a way to engage – the platform had inbuilt learning milestones, achievements, and completions. As an educator, I have continued to use this idea in my face-to-face teaching to help show students their own progress from module to module in the core course HASS1000. Online teacher presence was also important in our mission to improve student retention.

Online teacher presence was critical in the open courses (some of our course offerings included an open MOOC in the first module), where our own university students mixed with global learners. There was much excitement about how these online classrooms would provide our own students with a global learning experience. International students living all over the world interacted with Newcastle-based students in open courses, and also attracted attention to our degree identity and content, and our educators. We wanted to be able to showcase the Australian identity in the BA degree for all of our learners online.

There are many examples of where this happened in the different program offerings, including in the core courses. The HASS1000 core, BA Futures, focuses on the concept of place and placemaking in the second module. For this module, we engaged experienced Indigenous Australian academics in the creation of audio-visual materials to evoke a sense of the place where our campus is located on the lands of the Pambalong clan of the Awabakal peoples. These educators created 'hero videos,' showing Week 4's educators: linguist and Dhanggati and Gumbayngirr man Raymond Kelly, and literary studies senior lecturer and Murri woman, Brooke Collins Gearing. Kelly and Gearing are shown walking students through the Birabahn Trail, a scenic bush walk through Newcastle's primary campus that reveals the University as a site of culture, rich in Indigenous history and meaning. Following their viewing of this piece, online students were encouraged to use Google Maps to locate and share the story of how or why a publicly accessible place is personally significant to them. This active learning prompt was designed to help students meet one of the learning outcomes of the course, showing that humanities disciplines give heightened attention to local places and different social/cultural distinctions and facilitate an empathetic connection to places framed through Indigenous ways of knowing. This element allowed our online students access to the campus identity and understandings of the physical 'place' shaping our virtual learning experience.

Other courses in the BA Online offer similar examples of learning in place and space, with our large Australian History course, 'The Australian Experience,' providing examples to global learners in the open MOOC course that provoke challenging questions about Australia's past as a nation built on colonialist political agendas. Later chapters in this book share examples of the course content for this course, and others, including the highly innovative creation of games, supporting learning connections for students, and tools to aid forms of teaching in disciplines often delivered in a workshop mode, such as creative writing.

Our project also sought to help develop critical thinking skills for students in the online environment, with Tathahira arguing that online learning may facilitate more active and critical perspectives in an asynchronous setting where students can review, reflect, and formulate views (Tathahira, 2020, p. 84). Other scholars agree, suggesting that the interactive elements are needed to enhance this critical thinking skill (Hussin, 2019, p. 9). Experts also posit that students must already be able to exercise their critical thinking capacity to effectively study in an online mode (Hussin, 2019, p. 9). In planning the weekly steps for both content and student engagement, this aspect was sharply articulated through the purpose of each learning step and its place in the development of students' insight. For example, students in the HASS1000 core course in their second week learning about visual epistemology and 'ways of seeing' are invited to watch and listen to dialogic interviews, read seminal literature, summarise and comment on their ideas, interact with a timeline of Australian art, discuss with peers, and then to offer reflections on whether their ideas have changed in the process of learning. They then repeat these steps with different content including a section on photography and an essay by Susan Sontag. Much of this content is also relatable to the everyday world around us, which is saturated by visual messaging.

The creation of masterplans of content and learning elements as steps was very different for our educators. It was literally a 'step change' in learning design, and many of us experienced trepidation about whether we knew how to do this work (Gormley, 2014, p. 21), which is not uncommon with online course design. To map large sections of courses, broken down into modules and weeks, was challenging and highly creative. It proved important to project manage the development of the degree. The leadership of the learning designers and project lead Dr Clare Lloyd in collaboration with FutureLearn staff proved invaluable to help maintain educator confidence, and group sessions as well as individual sessions kept staff on track with their course development. Some educators displayed resistance and expressed difficulty, which is not surprising; it was an enormous change and a great deal of work to develop the courses and degree over a period of many months, structured and staggered in a complex timeline, which meant there were constraints on the academics involved.

Conclusion: presence and absence, looking beyond the moment

BA degrees have been subject to a range of interventions in the past decade to ensure the currency of the humanities in higher education. During the delivery of the 3-week open-course modules, educators brought global and degree learners together at scale, at the same time improving and increasing their teacher presence and visibility as educators (Coleborne & Lloyd, 2019). The project achieved its aim of reinvigorating the curriculum, maintaining enrolments in the degree, and diversifying teaching practices for online environments, creating a strong capability during the COVID-19 pandemic. These ideas also started to inform a wider institutional strategy for digital and online learning. In May 2019, we ran a BA Online Showcase to present the innovative work achieved to the DVC Academic. We also participated as speakers at a FutureLearn Forum in Melbourne in November 2019 (see Coleborne & Lloyd, 2019).

As we consider the overall outcome of the process of designing a BA degree online, the student experience of online learning should be central to our reflections. A later chapter in this book considers the complexities in assessing the outcomes of the BA Online. We undertook a range of surveys with students in the early years of the degree such as qualitative survey data from open-course online learners. Over time, feedback has come from the Course Experience Surveys (formerly Student Feedback Courses), and (improved) student retention data. Significantly, after the degree was launched and delivered over time, educators continued to report they were taking their positive experience of learning design back into classroom teaching. They have introduced new formats for the teaching of Arts, Humanities, and Social Science subjects that are less 'content' oriented and involve interactive pedagogies. As part of this, they have also developed digital assets and activities that are being reused and repurposed in the classroom.[12] Many of the academic educators who were part of the BA reinvention and the development of the BA Online were able to make positive and convincing cases for professional advancement via the academic promotions process and also won teaching excellence awards. Some have also successfully applied for Fellowships and Senior Fellowships with Advance HE, UK. This shows that the professional development aspect of the BA Online, including the cross-unit collaborations between academic educators, professional staff, learning designers, studio experts, and editors has all amounted to a large investment in workforce development and in its diverse and intersecting skillsets in tertiary education delivery.

Overall, these skills gained by academic educators in the School arguably (and demonstrably) prepared them for two futures. The first of these was the period of time between 2020 and 2022 when universities were forced to offer remote learning experiences in place of in-person teaching during COVID lockdowns. The relatively well-informed approach to online teaching in the large School was widely shared with others, which meant that the use of short videos, online polls, quizzes, and similar interactive forms of engagement, as well as regular online interactions using digital educational tools, all became the mainstay of learning for students enrolled in the university (for more on the experience of emergency remote teaching, see Ruegg, 2023). The second future that educators were preparing for, perhaps without fully comprehending it, was continued disruption to educational delivery models in light of GenAI; this comes in tandem with new generational cohorts of students with increasingly different digital skills, as well as a need for human connection and meaning. They are also seeking relevance and value from their arts and humanities education.

Notes

1 Such perceptions persist despite evidence in the data collated by government surveys such as the Graduate Outcomes Survey (GOS) and the Employer Satisfaction Survey (ESS) showing strong employment rates and employer satisfaction for BA degree graduates over time. These are widely disseminated via the government-funded Quality Indicators Teaching and Learning (QILT) data: see https://qilt.edu.au/ (Department of Education, Australian Government, 2024, URL accessed 10 November 2024).
2 Bachelor degrees in Australia vary mildly in their structures and number of units or 'points' that constitute the degree program as a whole. There is no standardised approach to the structure aside from ensuring degrees meet volume of learning thresholds and proscribed quality measures over 3 years, meeting the requirements for a bachelor's degree mapped to the Australian Qualifications Framework (AQF) as set out by the Tertiary Education Quality and Standards Agency (TEQSA). However, most degrees meet the expectation of depth in a disciplinary major in terms of AQF Level 7: see https://www.teqsa.gov.au/how-we-regulate/acts-and-standards/australian-qualifications-framework (Tertiary Education Quality Standards Authority, 2024, URL accessed 10 November 2024).
3 These include an interview with Catharine Coleborne by presenter James Valentine on 7 June 2022, 'Arts degrees qualify you for nothing and everything': https://www.abc.net.au/listen/programs/sydney-breakfast/arts-degrees/13918520 and by Christine Anu, ABC Radio, 10 June 2023, 'What's the future of higher education in Australia?' https://www.abc.net.au/listen/programs/weekendevenings/higher-education-in-australia/102453578.
4 See Catharine Coleborne, 'Three big Issues in higher education demand the new government's attention,' *The Conversation*, May 23, 2022, https://theconversation.com/3-big-issues-in-higher-education-demand-the-new-governments-attention-183349
5 Several research projects were conducted over time including the value of the BA, the nature and identity of the degree, enrolment trends and patterns, and WIL in the degree: https://dassh.edu.au/research/
6 These definitions are all used in the Australian higher education sector but are also critiqued by experts in equity and higher education, including Penny-Jane Burke; see Burke et al., 2016.
7 Internal document circulated to staff, University of Newcastle, 2018.
8 Summary of feedback on proposed BA Cores, consultation meetings, 16–30 August 2017.
9 See the University of Newcastle archived newsroom story: https://www.newcastle.edu.au/newsroom/current-staff/first-year-ba-students-offer-opinions-on-their-future-in-the-workplace

10 MOOCs were made popular by online learning platforms including American platform edX, and promised 'democratic' forms of education for global learners that was predicted to disrupt higher education provision in the late 2000s/
11 See the FutureLearn press release in 2019: https://www.futurelearn.com/info/press-releases/futurelearn-and-university-of-newcastle-australia-partner-to-deliver-online-arts-degree
12 This work was profiled in learning and teaching expert Sally Kift's online series published in *Campus Morning Mail*: see Coleborne and Lloyd (2022).

References

Bell, F. (2009). *Connectivism: A network theory for teaching and learning in a connected world*. University of Salford.

Bennett, A., Motta, S. C., Hamilton, E., Burgess, C., Relf, B., Gray, K., Leroy-Dyer, S., & Albright, J. (2018). *Enabling pedagogies: A participatory conceptual mapping of practices at the University of Newcastle, Australia*. Centre of Excellence for Equity in Higher Education, University of Newcastle.

Boud, D., Choen, R., & Sampson, J. (Eds.). (2014). *Peer learning in higher education: Learning from and with each other*. Kogan Page Ltd.

Burke, P. J., Crozier, G., & Misiaszek, L. (2016). *Changing pedagogical spaces in higher education: Diversity, inequalities and misrecognition*. Routledge. https://doi.org/10.4324/9781315684000

Coleborne, C. (2023, April 13). Why arts degrees and other generalist programs are the future of higher education. *The Conversation*. https://theconversation.com/why-arts-degrees-and-other-generalist-programs-are-the-future-of-australian-higher-education-203046

Coleborne, C., & Lloyd, C. (2019, November 25). *A step change in learning online: The FutureLearn bachelor of arts*. Asia-Pacific Partners' Forum at Graduate House, University of Melbourne.

Coleborne, C., & Lloyd, C. (2022, May 1). Online learning transforms humanities teaching. *Campus Morning Mail*. https://campusmorningmail.com.au/news/on-line-learning-transforms-humanities-teaching/

Crawford, R., & Jenkins, L. (2017). Blended learning and team teaching: Adapting pedagogy in response to the changing digital tertiary environment. *Australasian Journal of Educational Technology*, *33*(2), 51–72.

Department of Education, Australian Government. (2024). *Quality indicators learning and teaching*. https://qilt.edu.au/

FutureLearn. (2018, October 3). *FutureLearn and University of Newcastle partner to deliver online arts degree*. https://www.futurelearn.com/info/press-releases/futurelearn-and-university-of-newcastle-australia-partner-to-deliver-online-arts-degree

Gannaway, D. (2015). The Bachelor of Arts: Slipping into the twilight or facing a new dawn? *Higher Education Research and Development*. *34*(2), 298–310. https://doi.org/10.1080/07294360.2014.956689

Gormley, C. (2014). Teaching the principles effective online course design: What works? *Irish Journal of Academic Practice*, *3*(1), article 3.

Harvey, A., & Luckman, M. (2014). Beyond demographics: Predicting student attrition within the Bachelor of Arts degree. *The International Journal of the First Year in Higher Education*, *5*(1), 19–29. https://doi.org/10.5204/intjfyhe.v5i1.187

Huang, H. (2002). Toward constructivism for adult learners in online learning environments. *British Journal of Educational Technology*. *33*(1), 27–37.

Hussin, W. N. T. W., Harun, J., & Shukor, N. (2019). Online interaction in social learning environment towards critical thinking skills: A framework. *Journal of Technology and Science Education*, *9*(1), 4–12.

Lloyd, C., & Devine, A. (2019, November 25–26). *Partner-led discussion: The future of higher education and the role of FutureLearn as strategic partner*. Asia-Pacific Partners' Forum at Graduate House, University of Melbourne.

Lloyd, C., Herb, A., Kilmister, M., & Coleborne, C. (2021). Partnerships and pedagogy: Transforming the BA Online. In *Seventh international conference on higher education advances (HEAd'21) proceedings* (pp. 925–932). http://dx.doi.org/10.4995/HEAd21.2021.13001

Mestan, K. (2016). Why students drop out of the bachelor of arts. *Higher Education Research & Development, 35*(5), 983–996. https://doi.org/10.1080/07294360.2016.1139548

Ruegg, R. (2023). "It's a pain, but it's not like the end of the world": Students' experiences of emergency remote teaching. *Australasian Journal of Educational Technology, 39*(2), 33–46.

Stone, C. (2022). From the margins to the mainstream: The online learning rethink and its implications for enhancing student equity. *Australasian Journal of Educational Technology, 38*(6), 139–149. https://doi.org/10.14742/ajet.8136

Tathahira, T. (2020). Promoting students' critical thinking through online learning in higher education: Challenges and strategies. *Englisia: Journal of Language, Education and Humanities. 8*(1), 79–92.

Tertiary Education Quality Standards Authority. (2024). *Australian qualifications framework*. https://www.teqsa.gov.au/how-we-regulate/acts-and-standards/australian-qualifications-framework

Tubman, P., Oztok, M., & Benachour, P. (2016). Being social or social learning? A sociocultural analysis of the FutureLearn MOOC platform. In *IEEE 16th international conference on advanced learning technologies*.

3 Reflections on the partnership between FutureLearn and a regional Australian university

An ecological perspective

Monty King

Introduction

Universities globally face a number of interacting challenges in the post-COVID era, not least of which is meeting the changing needs of students. Students are busy people, often in full-time employment, and the on-campus experience no longer holds the same attraction. Online learning options offer a more flexible alternative, giving students agency to study when and where they want, but conversely students can be wary of poor-quality online learning experiences, typified by interminable lecture capture recordings, and 'death' by PowerPoint, Zoom, and various other online delivery tools.

Well-designed learning activities can enhance the learning experience, yet there is ample recent evidence of hastily conceived, poorly executed online higher education programs (Ives, 2021; Newton, 2022) giving rise to the neologism 'panicgogy' (Spinks et al., 2023) and concerns of the 'Disneyfication' of learning as entertainment (Clarke, 2022). During the pandemic and its resulting lockdowns, many students found online participation easier than in-person interactions and appreciated the flexibility in asynchronous online learning and the opportunity to learn at a pace that suited them (Shankar et al., 2023). A study of the online student experience in Dutch universities during the pandemic found that "a larger number (70%) of the students graded the virtual learning experience as sufficient and better, and that the majority would like to partially follow virtual lessons even after social distancing" (Suleri, 2020, p. 91). Conversely, a study in the United States cited lower student engagement and motivation due to lower-quality teaching and learning online during the pandemic (Ives, 2021). In the United States, there has been rapid growth in demand and supply of online higher education but generally negative student persistence and performance, with online students 3%–15% more likely to withdraw from study before graduation (Xu & Xu, 2019).

Higher education observers such as Peter Bryant (2022) have noted an inflection point in higher education since the pandemic, as universities have an opportunity to 'learn forward' from the lessons of rapid transitions to online learning during COVID restrictions or 'snap back' to pre-lockdown practices

DOI: 10.4324/9781003505785-4

and assume business as usual. Institutions adopting the former approach can benefit from taking a considered, integrated approach to online and blended learning as a design activity rather than a reproduction of old teaching modalities (Goodyear, 2015; O'Donnell & Schulz, 2020). As universities compete for resources and students, more established universities have generally been less inclined to invest in online learning provisions, whereas newer institutions have been more open to exploring this channel as an opportunity to increase enrolments (Salama & Hinton, 2023).

Many universities, particularly late adopters looking to mobilise quickly and add their course offerings to the ever-swelling online higher education marketplace, have invested in online programs produced in partnership with third-party Online Program Managers (OPMs), who provide the initial capital and infrastructure to produce online courses and associated services (Springer, 2018). While OPMs provide a path for universities to fast-track entry to the online higher education market, they also require outsourcing one of the core functions of the university. A report by Australian EdTech Holon IQ noted an increase in 'insourcing'; that is, resourcing internal online learning design and production teams to develop programs (Holon IQ Education Intelligence Unit, 2019). It is also worth noting that these partnerships are not always successful, and by the end of 2023, 10 UK universities had ended 10 partnerships with OPMs (Mosley, 2023).

The online Bachelor of Arts degree partnership between the University of Newcastle and FutureLearn is an instructive case study of a collaboration between a university and a learning experience platform (LXP) which began before the COVID-19 pandemic and benefitted from being designed and produced well before the pressures of the pandemic were brought to bear. As universities globally consider the future of their teaching and learning provision and the role of online education in the broader higher educational landscape, the partnership between FutureLearn and UON Australia demonstrates the benefits of doing the work of ideating, designing, and producing online courses employing an interdisciplinary team 'in house,' rather than looking to an OPM to take on the bulk of the intellectual, technical, and creative labour required.

Contemporary universities in an 'ecological situation'

> An ecological situation is a situation in which there is present one or more ecosystems. Ecosystems are dynamic – but fragile assemblages of entities having some unity and sets of interconnections.
>
> (Barnett, 2020, p. 272)

Ronald Barnett's seminal work on higher education, *The Ecological University; a Feasible Utopia* (2018) offers a vision for contemporary universities in, of, and for the world, entangled within a series of ecosystems connecting institutions and individuals globally. Barnett first focuses on the ecological framing of knowledge, social institutions, people, the economy, learning ecologies, culture, and the natural environment, which together constitute a university's ecological profile. These are important ecological elements of a global higher education system, while concurrently discussion of the digital university (Peters & Jandrić, 2018) has also recently emerged. Barnett recognises that other ecologies may be added to their preliminary grouping, citing the digital environment as a possible additional ecological element (Barnett, 2020).

Cope and Kalantzis (2017) have adopted an ecological metaphor in advancing the idea of e-learning ecologies to describe the increasingly important role of digital technology in mediating connections between learners, teachers, and knowledge and the transformation of higher education that has resulted. Through their publications (and accompanying massive open online course [MOOC] on the Coursera platform) they investigate the new, innovative ways in which learning communities form and interact online and the pedagogic configurations and patterns which emerge from them. Ellis and Goodyear (2019) recognise the work of Barnett, Kalantsis, Cope, and others in advancing an ecological conceptualising of higher education. They propose adopting

> educational ecology as an applied science – useful for understanding educational activities and outcomes and also for producing actionable knowledge – knowledge that is useful in designing, creating and managing those elements of educational ecosystems that are susceptible to such leadership work and understanding the relationships between what can be designed/managed and what emerges and evolves.
>
> (p. 12)

These applications of an ecological metaphor, and the various entanglements among the ecological spheres of the university, provide a useful conceptual tool for exploring and better understanding developments in higher education, focusing in this chapter on the partnership between a university and a learning experience platform.

This chapter provides an account of the ideation and design phases of the first modules produced for the University of Newcastle Bachelor of Arts degree hosted on FutureLearn from a partnership manager's perspective. It describes the early collaboration between the two organisations, the challenges faced in developing an online degree, and how the university was well-placed to tackle them. The chapter includes reflections on the degree development process framed through an educational ecologies lens and its implications for the contemporary ecological university. It concludes that online education provision is a core business for all universities and that expert, multidisciplinary digital learning design and production teams are crucial to creating learning experiences, which embody the identity of that university.

A BA on FutureLearn

I began working as a partnership manager (PM) at FutureLearn in early 2018, shortly after migrating to the United Kingdom from Western Australia. PMs at this time were responsible for the day-to-day operational relationship and quality assurance reviewer for the MOOCs produced by their partner institutions. My professional background was in teaching and academic support for university students, whereas most of my fellow PMs came from a publishing background, but there was a collective wealth of knowledge and experience both within this team and the FutureLearn degrees product team working together toward a vision to create a quality learning experience on the FutureLearn LXP. I began taking on partnerships with British, Australian, South African, and New Zealand universities, as well as institutions throughout East Asia.

The FutureLearn LXP was founded by the Open University UK and was designed specifically with social learning 'baked in' to the platform. The approach to learning is grounded in social learning pedagogy Conversation Theory, developed by Gordon Pask and Diana Laurillard (Sharples et al., 2014). As part of the social learning experience at scale, "[t]he more people who engage with the course, the faster the discussion flows and the more the content is expanded with different perspectives" (Sharples et al., 2014, p. 19). The platform was designed around three foundational pedagogical principles: *telling stories*, *provoking skills,* and *celebrating progress*. Each principle played an important role in the Bachelor of Arts degree developed by the University of Newcastle, Australia.

The first postgraduate degrees on FutureLearn were launched by Coventry University in the United Kingdom in mid-2018, with Deakin University in Australia committing to postgraduate degrees soon after (Shah, 2017). According to a FutureLearn press release at the time of launch:

> Online students will learn at the same time as campus-based students, and as part of this move by Newcastle, they will offer flexible study options to their campus-based students by allowing them to choose online versions of their modules where available.
> (FutureLearn, 2018)

The opportunity for on-campus students at UON to study modules on FutureLearn offered a key point of difference in study options. For students living out of town or travelling for work, it allowed them to complete parts of their degree wholly online, reducing travel and requirements to attend the physical campus. This flexibility is central to the value proposition of digital learning ecologies, offering 'nomadic' students opportunities to learn and become 'adaptable experts' (González-Sanmamed et al., 2020, p. 94).

The announcement that the University of Newcastle was planning to launch an online degree, albeit a 'slice' of the full on-campus offering, was first met with a degree of surprise within FutureLearn, as some wondered how the relatively short MOOC format of 3–6 week courses would extend across a 3-year learning journey with modules offered across multiple majors, but there was a genuine curiosity within the Newcastle management and a commitment to explore how best to conceive and create an online Arts degree. There was a tight timeframe for design and production, with the first semester of modules due to be launched in February 2019, less than 6 months after the degree partnership announcement. The degree planning process at the university was well under way by this time, but to assist in expediting course production, I travelled to Newcastle for 3 weeks in October 2018 to support the development of the opening tranche of first year modules.

FutureLearn was developed to host short (generally 3–6 week-long) MOOCs, and so an early question became determining how to use the conventional FutureLearn MOOC format to structure a series of 12-week, semester modules. Some degree partners chose to organise semester modules into a single 12-week course, with the advantage of being able to make the entire semester available to students. At Newcastle, the decision was made to group modules into four 3-week courses, with the first course of each module being offered as an open, 'taster' MOOC for all learners on FutureLearn to access. The four courses were 'nested' into a module structure, and students enrolled in the Bachelor of Arts degree then continued seamlessly into the next course in the module, while the learners on the taster course could proceed no further than the first 3 weeks without enrolling in the degree.

The FutureLearn course taxonomy divides a week of learning – starting on a Monday morning and finishing on a Sunday night (following British time standards). Each week then consists of broadly 3–7 activities. These are groups of steps: articles with text and images, video, audio, polls, quizzes, peer review activity steps, and dedicated discussion steps. Almost all FutureLearn step types include a comments feed for learners to contribute to a conversation, post a reflection, or ask or answer a question. In discussion steps, the prime focus of that learning activity is to prompt students to contribute to discussions.

There was resistance to teaching courses in a FutureLearn-style MOOC format in some quarters of the faculty, with some academic staff understandably concerned about their workloads as they took on the task of co-designing and producing content specifically for the FutureLearn platform. This was mitigated partly by clarifying that staff would retain the rights to reuse content, so that video and other resources produced could be repurposed in on-campus teaching as part of a blended teaching and learning approach. Other academic staff expressed concerns around supporting first year students and the unique challenges of maintaining student engagement on a wholly online degree. Their concerns were mitigated partly by ensuring student support via access to student study support was communicated throughout the modules, and through various means of establishing and maintaining educator presence, as explained in more detail later. Additionally, there was the challenge of hosting an undergraduate Arts degree, with its emphasis on discussion, generative knowledge, and reflection, which had not previously been attempted on a course of this scale. These last two challenges were in part countered by creating what could be termed e-learning ecologies: using FutureLearn's social learning functions to foster a supportive online learning community and maintain educator presence by ensuring module tutors regularly monitored discussions and answered student questions in the course comments.

Another early challenge concerned the opposition of one senior academic to the open enrolment model proposed in the MOOC taster course. The academic fundamentally objected to the idea of enrolled students having the same learning experience as other non-University of Newcastle learners signed up to do the taster. They believed the student cohort should feel part of a more intimate, supportive cohort, not a massive open social learning experience, and despite attempts to argue the potential benefits during the first weeks of the module, the academic declined to be involved. While other teaching staff felt the pressure of time constraints and competing teaching, research, administrative and other commitments, we were able to make the most of limited time for proposition design, drafting, filming, and other course production tasks, as we were ably supported by the Newcastle learning design and production team.

The University had one considerable advantage in looking to rapidly develop an online degree. Importantly it had prior experience designing and producing MOOCs, notably the successful *Drawing Nature, Science and Culture: Natural History Illustration 101* on the edX MOOC platform. As a result, an interdisciplinary Online Learning Initiatives production team, although small, was already in place. This meant they were ready to commence the ideation and design phase as soon as the agreement was signed. Ellis and Goodyear (2019) stress the importance of collaborative relationships between academic and professional staff within a university educational ecology, the latter including learning designers and learning technologists. UON had an established Online Learning Initiatives team with extensive experience in online course production.[1] The Callaghan campus was equipped with an impressive film studio, making the need for an OPM partner in course production redundant as the expertise and tools were already available in-house. As an example, the team was already well aware of the importance of sourcing and creating illustrative images to enrich the learning experience, and they had a dedicated graphic designer in the production team to create or find and obtain the rights to the thousands of images required for the degree modules as part of their tasks.

We began working on a core humanities module designed to be taken by all students in the first semester, entitled 'What does it mean to be human?' We broadly agreed on a weekly structure that provided a template of good practice to adopt across different subjects, and which was flexible enough to avoid repetition in the overall learning experience. This structure became an exemplar design pattern (Laurillard, 2012), which could then be adapted to other modules. This consisted of an introductory activity group of steps welcoming students to the week, recapping the content covered the previous week, and previewing the week to come. This would usually end with a discussion prompt or poll to prompt conversation and orientate students to the work ahead. The next activities were then organised around weekly intended learning outcomes, with the final activity a chance for students to share reflections, ask outstanding questions to the learner cohort and lecturer, and often to complete a concept-check quiz aligned to the week's intended learning outcomes. Throughout the early module design and production phases, the UON team adopted FutureLearn's pedagogic principles, and some of the ways in which they were used to enrich the learning experience are detailed next.

Telling stories

As noted in the introduction, the FutureLearn platform was designed based on social constructivist educational principles, notably Diana Laurillard's Conversational Framework (Laurillard, 2012). One method for developing an engaging narrative in any learning environment is through the use of 'big questions,' posed to help frame and direct the learning, promoting active inquiry within the learning experience (O'Donnell & Schulz, 2020). One of the biggest big questions became the opening focus of one of the core courses: 'What does it mean to be human?' This laid the basis for the study of Arts and Humanities and provided a clear, engaging framework for students to situate their learning.

Throughout the modules, the lecturer generally assumed a narrator role, establishing educator presence, which has been found to increase student engagement in online learning and foster learning communities (Tuffnell, 2021). Course videos, including introductions to the module and each week, as well as lecture-style presentations, were filmed either in the campus studio or in the lecturer's office and generally involved some element of a presentation to the camera. Written textual content (called 'articles' on FutureLearn) similarly focused on developing the teacher's presence, helping establish a connection to the lecturer, which was then strengthened through any online synchronous tutorials. A clear advantage here is that students who have difficulty with a particular concept can replay or reread sections of the resources and conduct their own research, and ask clarifying questions in synchronous tutorial sessions and via step comments on FutureLearn.

An innovative feature of one of the modules was the use of the University of Newcastle Callaghan campus environment as a resource. The university is one of a number of 'bush campus' university spaces in Australia, developed in the post-World War II expansion of higher education (Holden, 2021). In the module "What does place mean to us?", students are introduced to one of the university's lecturers and Indigenous advisers, Dhanggati/Gumbayngirr man Raymond Kelly. He explains some of the cultural significance of the Callaghan campus has to the local Awabakal people. In one course video (see Figure 3.1), he accompanies fellow academic, Murri woman Brooke Collins-Gearing, on a walk along a section of the Birabahn Trail, which runs through the campus, pointing out and explaining places of cultural and historical significance. This video is a powerful pedagogic tool, grounding the learning experience in the physical campus space. The online activity shows students the connection between land and the story of the local Indigenous people, giving those studying off campus a strong link to the campus environment. It is also a powerful means of representing Indigenous Knowledge online, contributing an Awabakal perspective on what place can mean within a regional knowledge ecology.

Another early Australian FutureLearn degree partner, and a university with a bush campus, Deakin University in Geelong, adopted a similar approach in its courses, making the campus space a central element of the learning experience. For example, in their MOOC Professional Resilience (https://www.futurelearn.com/courses/professional-resilience), Adjunct Professor Doctor Marcus O'Donnell addresses students in many of the course videos from bush locations on the campus grounds and encourages students to take time each week to spend in nature, as a way of recharging and refreshing after work. Deakin and Newcastle's approach to incorporating the campus into the online learning experience establishes a connection with the physical university that is often missing from the online learning experience. Just as establishing educator presence is a key principle of online learning (MacKenzie et al., 2022), campus presence can enrich and build on the narrative thread woven through the learning experience.

Figure 3.1 A screenshot from a course step video 'Journeying the Birabahn Trail' in the course "What does place mean to us?" Presented by Dr Raymond Kelly and Dr Brooke Collins-Gearing.

Provoking conversations

Another core FutureLearn pedagogic principle encourages course authors to 'provoke conversations' through massive social online learning, and this was a feature Newcastle was keen to leverage in their online BA. These conversations are facilitated through the use of polls and discussion steps, which include an explicit prompt for students to reflect, debate, collaborate, critique, and generally engage with discussion on a given topic, but they can also be found across almost all step types, resulting in a multitude of sites for students to learn through various forms of exchange.

The provocation to encourage students to contribute to conversations can often be controversial. In the Australian history course early in the first week includes an open debate on the controversy in Australia around the celebration of Australia Day. The week continues exploring 'contested issues' around Australian history, posing the question 'When does the history of Australia start?' (see Figure 3.2). Learners are invited to choose the answer which they believe is correct.

> **Bearing this debate in mind, where should we start a history of Australia?**
>
> **Earlier, we said we'd explore contested issues in Australian history. The first of these is *when does Australian history start?***
>
> - In 1770 'Captain' James Cook first set foot in Botany Bay. Is this where we need to begin?
>
> - Or in 1607 with the arrival of the first white men - the Dutch explorers and navigators searching for Terra Australis (the unknown south land)?
>
> - Or some 50,000-120,000 years ago. Is it impossible to locate a clear beginning?
>
> - How about 1788, the year that the British began their colonisation of Australia. Is this where we should start our journey?
>
> - Perhaps we need to bring the date forward to 1901, the year Australia's colonies federated?
>
> - And, I'm sure you've heard it stated before that it was through bloodshed that Australia became a nation in its own right. If this is the case, maybe the Gallipoli Campaign in 1915 provides a possible date?
>
> - Or suggest your own in the comments below.

Figure 3.2 A screenshot from a poll question in the first week of the University of Newcastle *Great South Land: Introducing Australian History* course on FutureLearn.

Source: Karageorgos et al. (2019). https://www.futurelearn.com/courses/great-south-land

Once learners make a choice, the following feedback appears on the screen next to the profile photo and name of the lead educator (see Figure 3.3). The pink text in the response hyperlinks to an article detailing archaeological evidence to support the scientific estimate of 65,000 years of prior Indigenous habitation of Australia and presents a perspective to add to an ecology of knowledges proposed by Santos (2016) and others. The conversation provocations sometimes bordered on the controversial, and inevitably given the scale of interaction on the open taster courses, some offensive comments were reported by learners and deleted from the comments area. FutureLearn's reactive moderation feature (FutureLearn, n.d.) allows moderators to review step comments that have been 'flagged,' and they can delete comments that fail to meet platform standards.

Effie Karageorgos | Lead Educator

Until quite recently, Aboriginal history has not had a place in 'national' history, so it has been easy to point to other dates as the starting point for Australian history. Yet, we know from archaeological evidence that the Indigenous peoples of Australia have lived on the Australian continent for at least 50,000-120,000 years. **Indeed, we need to begin before the British started their colonisation.**

Figure 3.3 A screenshot of the feedback that appears after learners choose a response to the poll question shown earlier.

Source: Karageorgos et al. (2019). https://www.futurelearn.com/courses/great-south-land

Some enrolled University of Newcastle students reported feeling overwhelmed in contributing to step discussions during the first 3-week open course, where comment feeds could run into the hundreds. By contrast, once the taster ended and the second course in the module began with only other enrolled students on the course, the number of comments dropped significantly. It was often necessary for tutors and facilitators on the course to step in and comment early in the second course, reassuring and encouraging students to contribute. The creation of learning communities, strengthened by facilitation, is an important element of e-Learning ecologies proposed by Cope and Kalantzis (2017), and the pedagogic affordances of social learning, including online interactions between student peers, are central to the conversational approach adopted by the University of Newcastle on the FutureLearn platform.

Celebrating progress

Online study can be perceived as an isolated learning experience, particularly if it is not mitigated against by design (MacKenzie et al., 2022) and so the third FutureLearn pedagogic principle of 'celebrating progress' took on further importance in a 3-year undergraduate degree. Undergraduate student retention, in both online and in-person delivery modes, remains an important issue for universities globally, particularly given the consistent evidence of low MOOC engagement and low completion rates. As such, marking milestones throughout the course experience is a means of recognising even small successes and providing some extrinsic motivation. On the FutureLearn platform, simple functions such as the ubiquitous pink 'mark as complete' button on course steps, the course progress bar, and the end-of-week celebration are small ways in which learner progress is celebrated.

Within the University of Newcastle degree modules, this celebratory element was enhanced through regular messages of encouragement from lecturers and tutors within the courses, and by providing opportunities for students to acknowledge personal progress through activities such as reflective tasks. In one first year Film, Media, and Cultural Studies course, the creation of small online collaborative cohorts within modules – an extra step type on degree courses which creates a collaborative space for students to work on problems together – also created spaces for students to support each other and recognise achievements within an e-learning ecology.

Another small but important feature of celebrating success on the platform is the requirement that formative quizzes include instructive feedback on both correct and incorrect responses. This feedback is delivered by the educator, whose name and platform profile picture appears as the deliverer of the feedback (similar to the feedback provided on poll steps as in Figure 3.3). This provides an opportunity to congratulate students on a correct answer with a brief explanation of why the answer is correct or to point out why it is incorrect and prompt the student to review their learning and try again. While this may seem like a small element of the learning experience, it is a crucial opportunity to maintain educator presence through feedback and encouragement.

In late 2019, just a few months before the start of the COVID-19 pandemic, I transitioned to a new role as a learning designer at FutureLearn, and I had no further direct involvement with the BA Online project team, but I remained in touch to offer advice and awaited FutureLearn updates at staff meetings with interest. The success of the collaboration between the University of Newcastle and FutureLearn provides some salutary lessons in the task of successfully ideating, designing, marketing, and launching an undergraduate degree on an online learning platform, which are discussed next.

Discussion

Perhaps the most important factor in the success of building an engaging, active, social learning experience in an online BA was the pre-existence of a multidisciplinary online module development team of learning designers, graphic designers, learning technologists, and other members with a clear remit to work with often very busy academic staff to develop innovative approaches to module development. Whether it was adapting existing content, designing and building activities to encourage social learning, or simply sourcing a set of illustrative images to enrich the learning experience, the team stepped up and delivered. The fact that the team had already worked on MOOCs for another platform definitely aided this process, and team members worked to tight deadlines to produce resources of excellent quality.

There was also a strong shared sense of what 'good' looked like. By developing clear design patterns and working with FutureLearn's pedagogic principles to the fore, the modules had a consistency of look and feel, and a commitment to telling stories, provoking conversation and celebrating progress. The modules adopted a distinctly Newcastle pedagogic approach, innovating in various ways depending on the topic. The use of poll and discussion steps to facilitate debate, as shown in the 'When should Australian history begin?' activity, is one example of ways in which the affordances of the platform were leveraged to create an engaging social learning experience.

The use of the University of Newcastle campus in the bush campus tradition as an element of the online learning experience was another noteworthy feature. Goodyear (2015) in his paper on 'teaching as design' explains a process of "shaping the landscape across which students walk. It involves the setting in place of epistemic, material and social structures that guide, but do not determine, what students do" (p. 34). This has interesting implications for the design of online learning, in this case through regional Australian bush campus environments, where the learning experience encourages students to follow (digitally, if not literally) in our footsteps. There is an opportunity for all universities, be they regional or central, urban or bush, to cast the campus as a key element of the learning experience.

The partnership between the University of Newcastle and FutureLearn has broader implications and applications for universities looking to expand into the provision of online degrees. In applying an ecological lens to the partnership with FutureLearn, it is clear that Newcastle embraced the potential for online learning to radically transform teaching and learning practice, and their approach to producing and circulating knowledge. The Bachelor of Arts degree presents a local epistemic perspective to a global audience, increasing its academic reach and drawing student perspectives into an actively social learning experience, which is an instructive example of an e-learning ecology. Beyond a focus on sustainability, the Callaghan campus is a teacher, linking the natural, knowledge, and learning ecologies of the university through a digital medium. For the contemporary university, creating and nurturing digital learning ecologies as part of the shift to online teaching and learning is fast becoming part of core business and an important means of 'productive entanglement' with wider ecosystems. The example provided by the University of Newcastle shows this is not a job to be outsourced, but rather insourced to a dedicated multidisciplinary team with a remit to create engaging, active, social learning experiences which reflect in a sense the personality, the particularities of a place, and the knowledge produced within it.

Conclusion

The experience of working with the University of Newcastle to host a Bachelor of Arts degree on FutureLearn was one of the most interesting and rewarding course development projects I have been involved with. Although this is an example of a successful Australian online degree program, the insights do not apply just to this context; online degrees are ripe for innovation, and using technology to nurture e-learning ecologies has potential for all universities looking to branch into this area. Adopting an ecological disposition to higher educational research enables a deeper inquiry into the individual ecological patterns exhibited by a university, including their approaches to innovation in online and blended learning, in providing the king of flexible, quality learning experience students seek.

While OPMs may assist institutions in starting their journey into online education, ultimately, the investment in internal teams has clear advantages, not least of all the opportunity to innovate with technology to create learning experiences with a clear institutional identity, incorporating resources such as the campus and educator presence. The decision to host a Bachelor of Arts degree on FutureLearn may have at first seemed surprising, but there was in fact an inherent logic to the partnership. FutureLearn's social learning approach complemented Newcastle's vision for creative, innovative learning experiences that could expand their reach whilst maintaining a distinctly Newcastle vision for quality online higher education, and the success of the degree is a direct result.

Note

1 The Online Learning Initiatives team later became integrated with the Learning Design and Teaching Innovation (LDTI) Unit (see Chapter 1).

References

Barnett, R. (2018). *The ecological university; a feasible utopia*. Routledge.
Barnett, R. (2020). Realizing the world-class university: An ecological approach. In S. Rider, M. E. Peters, M. Hyvönen, & T. Besley (Eds.), *Evaluating education: Normative systems and institutional practices*. Springer. http://www.springer.com/series/11809
Bryant, P. (2022, November 4). '. . . and the way that it ends is that the way it began': Why we need to learn forward, not snap back. *Peter Bryant Blog Page*. https://peterbryant.smegradio.com/and-the-way-that-it-ends-is-that-the-way-it-began-why-we-need-to-learn-forward-not-snap-back/

Clarke, D. (2022). *Learning experience design: How to create effective learning that works*. Kogan Page.

Cope, B., & Kalantzis, M. (Eds.). (2017). *E-learning ecologies: Principles for new learning and assessment*. Routledge.

Ellis, R. A., & Goodyear, P. (2019). *The education ecology of universities: Integrating learning, strategy and the academy*. Routledge.

FutureLearn. (2018, October 3). FutureLearn and University of Newcastle Australia partner to deliver online arts degree. *Press Release*. https://www.futurelearn.com/info/press-releases/futurelearn-and-university-of-newcastle-australia-partner-to-deliver-online-arts-degree

FutureLearn. (n.d.). *Code of conduct*. Terms and conditions. Retrieved June 5, 2024, from https://www.futurelearn.com/info/terms/code-of-conduct

González-Sanmamed, M., Sangrà, A., Souto-Seijo, A., & Blanco, I. E. (2020). Learning ecologies in the digital era: Challenges for higher education. *Publicaciones, 50*(1), 83–102. https://doi.org/10.30827/PUBLICACIONES.V50I1.15671

Goodyear, P. (2015). Teaching as design. *HERDSA Review of Higher Education, 2*, 27–50. www.herdsa.org.au/herdsa-review-higher-education-vol-2/27-50

Holden, S. (2021). Parallel narratives of disciplinary disruption: The bush campus as design and pedagogical concept. In E. Couchez & R. Heynickx (Eds.), *Architectural education through materiality: Pedagogies of 20th century design* (1st ed.). Routledge.

Holon IQ Education Intelligence Unit. (2019, February 13). *The anatomy of an OPM and a $7.7B market in 2025. Part 1. Deconstructing the online program management model. How we got there, where it's at and where it might lead*. https://www.holoniq.com/notes/the-anatomy-of-an-opm-and-a-7-7b-market-in-2025

Ives, B. (2021). University students experience the COVID-19 induced shift to remote instruction. *International Journal of Educational Technology in Higher Education, 18*(1). https://doi.org/10.1186/s41239-021-00296-5

Karageorgos, E., Ariotti, K., & Cushing, N. (2019). Where should we start a history of Australia? In *Great south land: Introducing Australian history*. University of Newcastle. https://www.futurelearn.com/courses/great-south-land

Laurillard, D. (2012). Teaching as a design science: Building pedagogical patterns for learning and technology. In *Teaching as a design science: Building pedagogical patterns for learning and technology*. Routledge.

MacKenzie, A., Bacalja, A., Annamali, D., Panaretou, A., Girme, P., Cutajar, M., Abegglen, S., Evens, M., Neuhaus, F., Wilson, K., Psarikidou, K., Koole, M., Hrastinski, S., Sturm, S., Adachi, C., Schnaider, K., Bozkurt, A., Rapanta, C., Themelis, C.,. . . Gourlay, L. (2022). Dissolving the dichotomies between online and campus-based teaching: A collective response to the manifesto for teaching online (Bayne et al. 2020). *Postdigital Science and Education, 4*(2), 271–329. https://doi.org/10.1007/s42438-021-00259-z

Mosley, N. (2023, October 20). Exploring the changing online education company landscape in UK higher education. *Neil Moseley Blog*. https://www.neilmosley.com/blog/exploring-the-changing-online-education-company-landscape-in-uk-higher-education

Newton, D. (2022, March 31). Another bad report card for remote, online learning. *Forbes*. https://www.forbes.com/sites/dereknewton/2022/03/29/another-bad-report-card-for-remote-online-learning/

O'Donnell, M., & Schulz, L. (2020). Learning design meets service design for innovation in online learning at scale. In S. McKenzie, F. Garivaldis, & K. R. Dyer (Eds.), *Tertiary online teaching and learning: TOTAL perspectives and resources for digital education* (1st ed., pp. 45–60). Springer Nature. https://doi.org/https://doi.org/10.1007/978-981-15-8928-7

Peters, M. A., & Jandrić, P. (2018). *The digital university: A dialogue and manifesto*. Peter Lang. https://doi.org/10.3726/b11314

Salama, R., & Hinton, T. (2023). Online higher education: Current landscape and future trends. *Journal of Further and Higher Education, 47*(7), 913–924. https://doi.org/10.1080/0309877X.2023.2200136

Santos, B. S. (2016). *Epistemologies of the South: Justice against epistemicide*. Routledge.

Shah, D. (2017, August 7). FutureLearn and Coventry university to roll out 50 online degrees. *Class Central*. https://www.classcentral.com/report/futurelearn-coventry-university-roll-50-online-degrees/

Shankar, K., Arora, P., & Binz-Scharf, M. C. (2023). Evidence on online higher education: The promise of COVID-19 pandemic data. *Management and Labour Studies, 48*(2), 242–249. https://doi.org/10.1177/0258042X211064783

Sharples, Mike., Adams, A., Ferguson, Rebecca., Gaved, M., McAndrew, P., Rienties, P., Weller, M., & Whitelock, D. (2014). Innovating pedagogy 2014: Open University innovation report 3. *OPEN*. https://ou-iet.cdn.prismic.io/ou-iet/4df5aa6b-4777-4737-b454-5401b8e1bf1a_innovating-pedagogy–2014.pdf

Spinks, M., Metzler, M., Kluge, S., Langdon, J., Gurvitch, R., Smitherman, M., Esmat, T., Bhattacharya, S., Carruth, L., Crowther, K., Denton, R., Edwards, Ordene, V., Shrikhande, M., & Strong-Green, A. (2023). 'This wasn't pedagogy, it was panicgogy': Perspectives of the challenges faced by students and instructors during the emergency transition to remote learning due to COVID–19. *College Teaching, 71*(4), 227–243. https://doi.org/https://doi.org/10.1080/87567555.2021.2018395

Springer, S. (2018). One university's experience partnering with an online program management (OPM) provider: A case study. *Online Journal of Distance Learning Administration, XXI*(1), 1–14.

Suleri, J. (2020). Learners' experience and expectations during and post COVID-19 in higher education. *Research in Hospitality Management, 10*(2), 91–96. https://doi.org/10.1080/22243534.2020.1869463

Tuffnell, C. (2021). Faculty learning communities: Supporting the development of online educators. *Studies in Technology Enhanced Learning*. https://doi.org/10.21428/8c225f6e.2191c396

Xu, D., & Xu, Y. (2019). *The promises and limits of online higher education: Understanding how distance education affects access, cost and quality*. American Enterprise Institute. https://files.eric.ed.gov/fulltext/ED596296.pdf

Part 2
Case studies in online teaching and assessment

4 FutureLearn as a learning environment

Striving for a community of inquiry

Mitchell J. Taylor and Julia Cook

Introduction

Higher education pedagogies are increasingly informed by the constructivist claim that social interaction is an essential element in deep and meaningful learning. In line with the research literature, which suggests that interaction can promote higher levels of satisfaction, retention, and academic performance (Sadera et al., 2009; Reinhart, 2010; LaBarbera, 2013), social presence has become a key point of focus for many educators, and we see a growing interest in strategies to cultivate community and connection. Fostering these sentiments can, however, be challenging for educators working in online environments – particularly in the context of massive open online courses (MOOCs) (Poquet et al., 2018). Despite the influence of constructivist pedagogy, many digital education platforms – especially those developed for the provision of MOOCs – continue to follow a transmission model of learning, in which knowledge is passively received by students from an authoritative source (usually in the form of recorded video lectures) (Ferguson & Sharples, 2014; Sun et al., 2021, p. 138).

Recognising this limitation, some platforms have sought to incorporate insights from constructivist pedagogies. One such platform is FutureLearn, a joint initiative of several UK universities. FutureLearn was created to challenge the dominance of US-based MOOC platforms such as Coursera and edX (Shaw, 2012). The design of FutureLearn is explicitly underpinned by a constructivist approach to learning and is directly informed by the Conversational Framework developed by Laurillard (2002). According to this framework, teaching must be a "dialogic process": a "continuing iterative dialogue between teacher and student" (Laurillard, 2002, p. 71). This approach stands in direct contrast to the transmission model of learning; rather than assimilating predefined knowledge, students are encouraged to take a "reflective, interpretative approach to their learning", and to construct knowledge by interacting with the course content, teachers and other students (Laurillard, 2002, pp. 71–72). Aligning with these principles, the FutureLearn platform presents each week of course content in multiple steps, and, in contrast to platforms such as Coursera or edX, which organise student interaction around

DOI: 10.4324/9781003505785-6

a central discussion forum, a discussion area is attached to each individual step. Learners are encouraged to share experiences and reflections and interact with each other, as well as with their instructor.

Despite these features, many scholars have questioned whether FutureLearn lives up to its pedagogical ambitions (Tubman et al., 2016; Ferguson & Sharples, 2014). This reflects a broader debate in the literature about the extent to which constructivist models of teaching and learning can be applied in online spaces and the ability of online education platforms to sustain the development of effective learning communities – particularly in MOOC settings (see Garrison et al., 2000; Poquet et al., 2018; Ferguson & Sharples, 2014). In this chapter, we reflect on our own attempts to apply constructivist pedagogies on FutureLearn. Specifically, we focus on our attempt to apply the Community of Inquiry (CoI) model developed by Garrison et al. (2000) while facilitating a number of sociology courses on the platform. We begin by addressing existing literature on the importance of interaction in current pedagogical thinking. We then reflect on our own experiences teaching on FutureLearn, considering the benefits and drawbacks of the platform with respect to the CoI model.

Interaction and pedagogy: reviewing the literature

The work of Vygotsky (1934/1986) has been highly influential in the field of pedagogy. Drawing attention to the influence of sociocultural factors on human development, Vygotsky (1934/1986) argued that the internalisation of social activities is central to the development of higher psychological processes. Opposing the transmission model of learning, Vygotsky instead focused on the activities and actions of students themselves, who should, he held, "not only learn to perceive, but also to respond" (1926/1997, p. 48). Vygotskian approaches to learning and instruction thus place a high emphasis on participant interaction, arguing that the "social environment is the true lever of the educational process", and that "the teacher educates the student by varying [this] environment" (Vygotsky, 1926/1997, p. 49). In other words, the belief is that "individuals learn – truly learn – by appropriating in an active, goal directed manner the practices of the thought community with which they are interacting" (Schallert & Hailey Reed, 2003, p. 103).

Claims of this kind, carried forward by a 'social constructivist' tradition of pedagogical thinking (see Jonassen, 1991), have been a prominent concern in research on distance learning environments, which are often thought to lack interactivity when compared with more 'traditional' classroom settings. As noted by Moore (1993, p. 22), distance education is not simply characterised by a 'geographic separation' of participants, but by a *pedagogic* separation: a 'transactional distance' between teachers and learners. This distance is, Moore (1993, p. 22) claims, "a psychological and communications space to be crossed, a space of potential misunderstanding between the inputs of instructor and those of the learner". Importantly, Moore (1993) argues that transactional distance increases when dialogue is low, suggesting that interaction can – when positive, synergistic, purposeful, and constructive – function as a means to bridge transactional distance.

A range of literature supports the claim that interaction – usually conceptualised with the aid of Moore's (1989) well-known distinction between learner-content, learner-instructor, and learner-learner relationships – is a crucial element in meaningful learning, and should be prioritised in distance learning design (Anderson, 2003; Schallert & Hailey Reed, 2003; Bates, 1990). For example, Swan's (2002) study of students participating in asynchronous online courses found that students who reported higher levels of perceived interaction with course materials, instructors, and peers also reported higher levels of both course satisfaction and perceived learning. Likewise, Northrup's (2002) research with graduate students in an online Master's program found that students perceive interaction with content, peers, and instructors as important elements in their online learning experience. From these and countless other research studies (see Bernard et al., 2009) has come a widely held belief that interaction can improve student outcomes by enhancing motivation, facilitating retention, and encouraging forms of higher-order thinking (such as reflection, critical thinking, and creativity).

For this reason, theoretical models of successful learning often stress the importance of communication, conversation, or community. One such framework is the CoI framework developed by Garrison et al. (2000). Drawing on Moore's work, as well as Lipman's (1991) concept of critical learning communities, the CoI model attempts to identify the "crucial prerequisites for a successful higher educational experience" (Garrison et al., 2000, p. 87). Three core elements are identified: cognitive presence, social presence, and teaching presence. Cognitive presence refers to the degree to which participants in a CoI are able to construct meaning through sustained interaction and dialogue (Garrison et al., 2000, p. 89). Social presence refers to the extent to which the participants in the CoI are able to present themselves as 'real people': to project their personal characteristics into the learning environment (Garrison et al., 2000, p. 89). Finally, teaching presence refers to "the design, facilitation and direction of cognitive and social processes for the purpose of realising personally meaningful and educationally worthwhile learning outcomes" (Anderson et al., 2001, p. 5). These elements, and their interrelationships, are thought to be essential to a "worthwhile educational experience" (Garrison et al., 2000, p. 88).

Despite the challenges of online learning, Garrison et al. argue that computer-mediated communication has "considerable potential to create a CoI for educational purposes" (2000, p. 87), and studies have shown that the three elements of the CoI model do appear to contribute to the success of online courses (including those run as MOOCs) (Holstein & Cohen, 2016). One must, however, consider how certain digital platforms will support this community to a greater or lesser extent. For example, Sun et al. (2021), specifically focusing on MOOC platforms, found that while indicators of cognitive, teaching, and social presence were evident on the five platforms studied (Coursera, FutureLearn, edX, iCourse, and XuetangX) certain platforms provided more elaborated functions with respect to these dimensions. While this suggests that certain platforms will be more effective than others for cultivating a CoI, research on this is scarce, and more reflection is needed on how specific features of platform design impact the ability of educators to create and maintain an effective CoI.

Communities of inquiry on FutureLearn

In light of the earlier discussion, this section presents some reflections on the effectiveness of FutureLearn with respect to the CoI framework, drawing on our experience of facilitating undergraduate sociology courses on the platform. While these courses were generally restricted to students enrolled in our Bachelor of Arts and Bachelor of Social Science degrees, one large first year course ran in a MOOC format for the first 3 weeks of semester, after which it ran as a closed course for enrolled students for a further 9 weeks. This meant that enrolled students were interacting with learners external to the university on the FutureLearn platform.

Students in closed courses were, however, still involved with FutureLearn. While an LMS was used to convey information about course administration and assessment (including the provision of feedback on assessment tasks), FutureLearn hosted all of the weekly course content. As such, it was the primary method of course delivery and the main site of student interaction. Though the LMS did contain tools for learner-learner interaction, we decided to prioritise FutureLearn in our attempt to create a CoI. This meant that students were encouraged to discuss and interact on FutureLearn, rather than using the discussion forums on the LMS. Students were expected to work through a series of FutureLearn steps (usually between 10 and 15) each week, with each step consisting of a video, a short written text, or a 'call to action' (for instance, a research activity or discussion prompt) or a quiz. In line with FutureLearn's design format and its broader pedagogical philosophy, all of the steps aside from the quizzes were designed for the students to leave comments or reflections, and essentially functioned as a set of asynchronous discussion forums.

In line with the CoI model, we were especially concerned with the development of social presence, it being well recognised that social presence can be difficult to cultivate in computer-mediated dialogue (Garrison et al., 2000). FutureLearn seeks to overcome this in a variety of ways. For example, all comments made on the platform are headed by both the name and profile picture of the student commenting. Students also have a personal profile, accessed by clicking on their name. This profile allows them to display a picture, a location, and short 'about you' text. By accessing these profiles, students can 'follow' other accounts and will receive a notification every time that account leaves a comment. While these tools help to individuate students, and are often a recommended feature of online learning platforms (see Fiock, 2020; Laurillard, 2002), we found that they were infrequently used. For example, the vast majority of students in our courses did not edit or personalise their profile, and simply kept the default picture: their initials on a coloured background.

Following the advice of Lapadat (2000), who describes personalising the learning environment by beginning with self-introductions and using personal anecdotes (cf. Garrison et al., 2000), as well as both Lapadat (2002) and Rovai (2001), who emphasise the importance of providing clear guidelines about the level of interaction, engagement, and collegiality expected in online spaces, we sought to cultivate social presence by beginning all of our courses with a step introducing ourselves as educators and sharing some details about our lives, often in the form of a short video. We also used this step to outline expectations around communication and invited students to introduce themselves in the comments. While many students did this, and while this did seem to function effectively as a means of cultivating social presence in our smaller, closed courses, we were often overwhelmed by the large number of comments in the courses which began as MOOCs. In addition, although we responded to each of these introductory comments – attempting to cultivate teacher presence in the online space – in our experience, these introduction pages generated minimal interaction between learners. This is perhaps due to the sheer volume of comments; it being unlikely that most students have the time or desire to read through several pages of introductory posts.

In general, the volume of comments in the MOOC portion of courses proved challenging for developing a CoI. While large courses provide ample opportunities for learner-learner interaction, previous research has established that social presence is more difficult to create in large cohorts (Poquet et al., 2018). Moreover, a larger cohort is likely to have a higher teacher-student ratio, leading to a lower level of teacher presence. As Garrison et al. (2000) note, student activity on online discussion boards is likely to be increased if students receive messages which recognise their contributions, provide further guidance, and facilitate critical discourse. Although we replied to the vast majority of comments, this was quite time-consuming and the volume of comments made creating novel responses difficult, often leading to repetitious interactions.

In the case of the MOOC courses, the number of comments also led to concerns about cognitive presence. Existing research has found evidence of a point of diminishing returns in online discussions and has noted that learners can become overwhelmed by the amount of interactions available to them (Castano-Munoz et al., 2013). In this respect, one of the key challenges of the FutureLearn platform is that it offers relatively few tools for instructors to curate student discussion or to minimise the impact of inappropriate or irrelevant comments (Chua et al., 2017). While instructors can 'pin' comments so that they appear at the top of a comment stream, and while students can sort comments so that they are listed from 'newest', 'oldest', or 'most liked' (as well as filtering them to include 'all comments', 'bookmarked' comments,

comments from people they follow, or their own comments), the default view is 'newest', in which comments simply appear in the order of posting. In this view, pertinent comments may gradually find themselves pushed down to the bottom of the page or into additional 'pages' that students have to click through. Importantly, there is no keyword search function that would allow students to find comments on topics of interest to them. As Tubman et al. (2016) point out, this means that finding valuable information in FutureLearn discussions can often become a matter of serendipity and luck.

These problems did not affect our non-MOOC courses, where enrolments were – simply due to the relatively low numbers of students enrolled in our sociology programs – typically between 30 and 50 students. While this supports the general belief that limiting class size is an important step when developing a CoI (see Fiock, 2020; Rovai, 2000), our experience suggests that with regards to FutureLearn, smaller is not always better. As outlined earlier, FutureLearn is structured according to weekly content that is broken down into 'steps', with each step having its own discussion area. In smaller courses, where there were generally between 10 and 15 'steps' each week, this meant that students' comments were often quite dispersed. In many cases, steps would have no comments or a single interaction between student and instructor. It appears that these courses failed to reach a 'critical mass' of students which may be necessary for FutureLearn – explicitly developed for the provision of MOOCs – to function as intended, and in this case, we may have simply been asking too much from the platform.

From a CoI perspective, the asynchronous nature of FutureLearn discussion offered both benefits and drawbacks. Although asynchronous formats are typically valued for their flexibility – something which is generally quite important to online students (Northrup, 2002) – they can also have a positive impact on cognitive presence. For example, Newman et al. (1996), comparing computer conferencing with face-to-face seminars, found that the former elicited a higher level of critical thinking. This was certainly evident in our FutureLearn discussions. Students often left comments that showed a thoughtful and reflexive engagement with the course content, particularly when prompts asked them to apply theories, themes, or sociological findings to their own lives. As Garrison et al. (2000, p. 90) argue, asynchronous, text-based discussion affords room for reflection, giving students more time to consider material and formulate their responses. In addition, it gives students time to engage with external material, and to incorporate this into their learning. This was also evident in our experience with FutureLearn. Students regularly took up our 'calls to action', which typically encouraged them to undertake additional research and share resources with the group. This created a useful pool of resources from which all students could draw.

Despite these positives, Garrison et al. (2000) also note that excessive flexibility will often frustrate the development of a CoI. For this reason, they suggest that asynchronous online discussion threads "should last a week or two at the most so as to avoid the build-up of large numbers of postings on the same topic" (Garrison et al., 2000, p. 97). Our experience of FutureLearn supports this assertion. In line with our students' preferences for flexible delivery, as well as the need for revision, course weeks were, once opened, available to students for the duration of the semester. While we encouraged students to follow the pace of the course, completing the content in the week it was assigned, they often lagged behind, meaning the cohort tended to be working across multiple weeks of course content at any given time. This reduced our ability to create sustained dialogue on a single topic, and to cultivate a sense of focused, collaborative inquiry. It also created challenges for teaching presence, as instructors were required to simultaneously monitor discussions across multiple course weeks. In addition, because instructors do not receive a notification when students leave comments on particular steps (unless they are following the student or are being replied to), comments left in the past weeks of the course were easily overlooked.

This speaks to another challenge of the platform. As discussed earlier, FutureLearn operates on a 'discussion in context' model inspired by Laurillard's (2002) Conversational Framework. Ostensibly, this fits in well with the CoI model, as the two approaches have a shared genesis in constructivist pedagogy. For example, Laurillard's (2002, p. 86) contention that dialogue is essential for cognition, comprehension, and understanding, clearly parallels Garrison et al.'s (2000, p. 89) claim that social presence is an essential feature of high-quality learning, and facilitates critical thinking in a community of learners. The implementation of these ideas on FutureLearn could, however, be improved. While Laurillard (2002, p. 71) stresses the importance of 'continuing iterative dialogue', the discussion in context model tends to silo interaction. Discussion is always embedded in individual steps, and students generally have little reason to revisit these steps after an initial engagement. In fact, FutureLearn encourages students to move on by placing a 'mark as complete' button at the end of each step (this updates a student's 'progress' page). While this feature did seem to motivate students, it also meant that students who completed steps early in the week would rarely return to interact with subsequent posters. Indeed, because students only receive a notification when one of their own posts receives a reply or a 'like', and thus only receive updates about conversations in which they have actively participated, students who do not follow others, and do not consciously decide to revisit earlier steps, may simply never see many of the comments posted to the platform (cf. Tubman et al., 2016).

Some other design limitations of the FutureLearn platform are worth commenting on from the perspective of the CoI framework. First, for Garrison et al. (2000), social presence is linked to emotional expression. Indeed, scholars generally consider 'socio-emotional communication' as a key target when developing a CoI (see Fiock, 2020). While such communication is harder to establish in the absence of visual cues, both Kuehn (1993) and Walther (1994) found that participants in computer-mediated communication will often overcome this by using emoticons and other kinds of symbolic displays to add affective elements to their dialogue. FutureLearn is, however, relatively limited in the kinds of communication options it affords students. For example, while students can write a text comment, FutureLearn does not support the rendering of emojis or the use of pictures in comments. This is despite the rapid growth in the use of emojis as a communication medium and the well-recognised benefits of emojis as a means of enhancing social presence and supporting constructivist pedagogies (Kaye et al., 2016; Doiron, 2018).

Second, while FutureLearn offers an open-ended space for peer interaction, the course content is presented in a relatively rigid manner, in a simple, linear progression of steps. There are few options for students to define individual learning goals or to create adaptive study pathways (Sun et al., 2021). From a CoI perspective, it can also be difficult to adapt the content to the needs of particular cohorts, or to encourage forms of student-driven inquiry. In our case, the course content was generally produced well before teaching began, with the support of learning designers. While this offered many benefits from the perspective of cognitive presence – allowing us to produce visually appealing videos and sophisticated learning materials – it nevertheless meant that making major changes in response to student feedback could be complex and difficult once courses had already begun. In light of the theory of transactional distance, which holds that programs high in 'structure' (i.e., those that have little "possibility of reorganising the programme to take into account inputs from learners") are high in the transactional distance (Moore, 1993, p. 26), this represented a potential weakness of our FutureLearn offerings.

Finally, while FutureLearn provides plenty of opportunities for discussion, it offers comparatively few tools for collaboration between students, limiting the development of social presence. As Garrison et al. (2000, p. 95) note, collaboration is more than a "simple interaction" or "information exchange"; rather "it must draw learners into a shared experience for the purposes of constructing and confirming meaning". In line with this view, the CoI framework encourages the use of activities to "build and sustain a sense of group commitment" (Garrison et al., 2000, p. 101; Fiock, 2020). FutureLearn is, however, relatively limited in its ability to facilitate group projects, as it does not provide facilities for smaller group discussion and does not have a messaging or chat function that would allow group members to communicate in a direct or synchronous fashion (see Sun et al., 2021). This was a challenge in our courses, which often incorporated group assignments as a way to enhance social presence (following Fiock, 2020). In these cases, we relied on the LMS to provide students with a space for group collaboration (namely via file-sharing and text-based discussion), though many groups transitioned into using third-party platforms such as Facebook, Teams, or Zoom. While this was an effective means of creating a social presence, it also meant that students were able to establish a more straightforward (and familiar) method of peer interaction outside of FutureLearn, which may have reduced their interest in discussions on the platform.

Conclusions

Overall, our efforts to apply the CoI framework on the FutureLearn platform met with mixed success. While we seem to have succeeded in establishing a high level of both cognitive and teacher presence, social presence – undoubtedly the most essential element in a *community* of inquiry – proved more difficult to accomplish. Despite our efforts to create iterative dialogue, few students replied to our comments, and even fewer responded to the comments of their fellow students. While we deployed a number of strategies from the pedagogical literature to try and address this deficiency (such as sharing personal stories, being active in discussion, being *less* active in discussion, using humour in comments, developing more open-ended questions, and mentioning the benefits of peer-interaction in course materials [Fiock, 2020]), instances of learner-learner interaction remained low across our courses. Interestingly, this remained the case even when we trialled making participation on FutureLearn a graded assessment, in which 'responding to other people's posts in an encouraging manner' was an explicit criterion point. In fact, it is possible that this move harmed the quality of discussion and interaction. Ke (2010) found that forcing online participation by making it a graded component may have adverse effects on collective inquiry and can lead to a lower level of 'knowledge-constructive' interactions. In our case, courses that assessed participation tended to generate interactions that were repetitive, performative, and for the most part superficial.

In light of our own experience, we have two recommendations for anyone who may be planning to embark on a similar project:

First, those developing online courses need to be acutely aware of the pedagogical implications of different learning technologies. As Garrison et al. (2000, p. 92) note, while "most technologies, skilfully employed, are sufficiently robust to meet a wide variety of desirable outcomes", we must also acknowledge that particular learning technologies will inevitably shape the way their users relate to one another, and will naturally lend themselves to different pedagogical aims. In the case of FutureLearn, it seems that despite being grounded in Laurillard's Conversational Framework, there are structural features of the platform which limit its ability to sustain iterative dialogue. Indeed, research on FutureLearn has consistently revealed a low level of learner-learner interaction. For example, Tubman et al.'s (2016) study of six distinct FutureLearn MOOCs found that less than half of enrolled students had left a single comment on the platform, and that 62% of 'conversations' contained only a post and one reply. Likewise, Chua et al. (2017), studying a single FutureLearn MOOC, found that only 33% of learners had left a comment and that 26% of posts never received a reply. As such, it seems that FutureLearn is, in its current form, relatively ineffective at generating high-quality forms of written interaction.

Second, we recommend that instructors continue to reflect on whether interaction is a necessary component of a successful online course. Although online instructors are often concerned about a lack of interaction between learners or frustrated in their efforts to engage the 'invisible' online student, our own experience suggests that we should not overemphasise the importance of interaction for online learners. As Sharp and Huett note, the type of learner who chooses to participate in online education courses may have "significantly different goals and preferences . . . that may not lend themselves well to learning communities" (2006, p. 7). While there is little consensus in the literature as to which forms of interaction are most important to distance learners, a number of studies have found that online students perceive learner-learner interaction to be less important to their learning than learner-instructor or learner-content interaction (Kyei-Blankson et al., 2019; Kelsey & D'Souza, 2004; Reisetter & Boris, 2004; Ke, 2010; Rourke & Kanuka, 2009), while others have failed to demonstrate a relationship between learner-learner interaction and perceived learning in online courses (Arbaugh & Benbunan-Fich, 2007). Indeed, despite the proliferation of theoretical models which advocate for conversation, collaboration, and reflexive dialogue, studies have found that students often see interaction as a burden and may deliberately seek out offerings in which it is minimised or avoided (May, 1993; Kramarae, 2003).

Considering this research, it seems reasonable to ask, following Sharp and Huett, whether "we are doing the right thing forcing learning communities on an audience that, quite possibly, neither desires nor needs them" (2006, p. 7). For example, Downing et al. note that students generally take a pragmatic approach to interaction, "disengaging when they feel they have all the information they need to complete the summative assessment tasks they are set" (2007, p. 212). Likewise, Gorsky et al. (2007) argue that the benefits of interaction are context-dependent and often related to the level of perceived difficulty in a course (with students in 'easy' courses generally preferring to study alone). In this sense, a lack of interaction should not necessarily be taken as a negative sign. In fact, it may be counter-productive to try to sustain a high level of online interaction for the duration of a course, particularly if this pushes one past the point of 'diminishing returns' (Castano-Munoz et al., 2013; Downing et al., 2007).

With this in mind, it is important to note that although we struggled to create genuine CoIs in our FutureLearn courses, this should not be taken as a negative evaluation of the platform as a whole. While FutureLearn could do more to support this particular pedagogical strategy (such as by giving the option to search and filter comments, providing some opportunities for centralised discussion, creating more tools for students to connect and collaborate, and expanding the ways students can respond to content), it still helped us achieve a range of positive learning outcomes, and was, in general, well received by students. Student retention and completion rates for FutureLearn courses were generally commensurate with those of their face-to-face versions, as were the student evaluation scores. Moreover, in qualitative course feedback collected via anonymous student surveys at the end of semester, students typically reflected positively on their experiences with the platform. For example, students generally enjoyed the self-paced nature of the content, the professionalism of the learning resources, the ease with which they could navigate and review course material, and the ability to ask questions about course material by simply commenting within 'steps'. Negative comments about the platform were extremely rare, and many students indicated that they were looking forward to doing further online courses in the FutureLearn format.

This suggests that interaction should not be taken as the only (nor even the most) important criterion when assessing learner engagement or judging the utility of an online learning platform. Although FutureLearn was intentionally designed to promote dialogue between learners, our experiences suggest that it can be a valuable learning platform even when this type of interaction is relatively minimal. In our own case, while many students did, in their end-of-course surveys, report that they appreciated the ability to engage with other students, most also felt that it was generally not required, and it was not something that they saw as a particularly valuable or noteworthy feature of FutureLearn as a platform. Instead, they spoke positively about the way in which the platform presented them with content, with many praising the division of material (which they felt was well segmented into manageable, 'bite-sized' pieces), as well as the quality and professionalism of the video content.

Ultimately, this feedback placed us into what Sharp and Huett well describe as a "philosophical and pedagogical conundrum" (2006, p. 7). As they note:

> Philosophically, one wants to believe in the value of dynamic learning communities; pedagogically, most educators have been trained to value collaboration and have often experienced the educational power of learning communities firsthand. However, the online learner is not the traditional student, and perhaps it is time researchers did a better job of acknowledging that and started thinking differently.
>
> (2006, p. 7)

Without denying the wealth of evidence supporting constructivist approaches, it does seem that we should continue to question our assumptions about the utility and necessity of interpersonal interaction in online settings (cf. May, 1993). We invite anyone who is about to embark on the project of developing online courses (whether on FutureLearn or otherwise) to consider such issues and to engage reflexively with the learning needs and priorities of their students.

References

Anderson, T. (2003). Getting the mix right: An updated and theoretical rationale for interaction. *International Review of Research in Open and Distance Learning, 4*(2), 1–14.

Anderson, T., Rourke, L., Garrison, D., & Archer, W. (2001). Assessing teaching presence in a computer conferencing context. *Journal of Asynchronous Learning Networks, 5*(2), 1–17.

Arbaugh, J. B., & Benbunan-Fich, R. (2007, January). The importance of participant interaction in online environments. *Decision Support Systems, 43*(3), 853–865. https://doi.org/10.1016/j.dss.2006.12.013

Bates, A. W. (1990). Interactivity as a criterion for media selection in distance education. *Annual Conference of the Asian Association of Open Universities*. ERIC Document No. ED329245

Bernard, R. M., Abrami, P. C., Borokhovski, E., Wade, C. A., Tamim, R. M., Surkes, M. A., & Bethel, E. C. (2009). A meta-analysis of three types of interaction treatments in distance education. *Review of Educational Research, 79*(3), 1243–1289. https://doi.org/10.3102/0034654309333844.

Castano-Munoz, J., Sancho-Vinuesa, T., & Duart, J. M. (2013). Online interaction in higher education: Is there evidence of diminishing returns? *The International Review of Research in Open and Distance Learning, 14*(5), 240–257.

Chua, S., Tagg, C., Sharples, M., & Rienties, B. (2017). Discussion analytics: Identifying conversations and social learners in FutureLearn MOOCs. In L. Vigentini, Y. Wang, L. Paquette, & M. L. Urrutia (Eds.), *MOOC analytics: Live dashboards, post-hoc analytics and the long-term effects* (pp. 36–62), CEUR-WS.org

Doiron, J. G. (2018). Emojis: Visual communication in higher education. *PUPIL: International Journal of Teaching, Education and Learning, 2*(2), 1–11.

Downing, K. J., Lam, T., Kwong, T., Downing, W., & Chan, S. (2007). Creating interaction in online learning: A case study. *Research in Learning Technology, 15*(3), 201–215. https://doi.org/10.3402/rlt.v15i3.10931

Ferguson, R., & Sharples, M. (2014). Innovative pedagogy at massive scale: Teaching and learning in MOOCs. *Open Learning and Teaching in Educational Communities*, 98–111. https://doi.org/10.1007/978-3-319-11200-8_8

Fiock, H. (2020). Designing a community of inquiry in online courses. *The International Review of Research in Open and Distributed Learning, 21*(1), 135–153.

Garrison, D. R., Anderson, T., & Archer, W. (2000). Critical inquiry in a text-based environment: Computer conferencing in higher education. *The Internet and Higher Education, 2*(2–3), 87–105.

Gorsky, P., Caspi, A., & Smidt, S. (2007). Use of instructional dialogue by university students in a difficult distance education physics course. *Journal of Distance Education, 23*(1), 1–22.

Holstein, S., & Cohen, A. (2016). The characteristics of successful MOOCs in the fields of software, science, and management, according to students' perception. *Interdisciplinary Journal of e-Skills and Lifelong Learning, 12*(2016), 247–266. https://doi.org/10.28945/3614

Jonassen, D. (1991). Evaluating constructivistic learning. *Educational Technology, 31*(10), 28–33.

Kaye, L. K., Wall, H. J., & Malone, S. A. (2016). Turn that frown upside-down: A contextual account of emoticon usage on different virtual platforms. *Computers in Human Behavior, 60*, 463–467.

Ke, F. (2010). Examining online teaching, cognitive, and social presence for adult students. *Computers & Education, 55*(2), 808–820.

Kelsey, K. D., & D'Souza, A. (2004). Student motivation for learning at a distance: Does interaction matter. *Online Journal of Distance Learning Administration, 7*(2), 1–10.

Kramarae, C. (2003). Gender equity online, when there is no door to knock on. In D. Moore & W. Anderson (Eds.), *Handbook of distance education*. (pp. 261–272). Lawrence Erlbaum.

Kuehn, S. (1993). Communication innovation on a BBS: A content analysis. *Interpersonal Computer and Technology*, *1*(2).

Kyei-Blankson, L., Ntuli, E., & Donnelly, H. (2019). Establishing the importance of interaction and presence to student learning in online environments. *Journal of Interactive Learning Research*, *30*(4), 539–560.

LaBarbera, R. (2013). The relationship between students' perceived sense of connectedness to the instructor and satisfaction in online courses. *Quarterly Review of Distance Education*, *14*(4), 209–220.

Lapadat, J. C. (2000). *Teaching online: Breaking new ground in collaborative thinking*. ERIC Clearinghouse on Information & Technology (ERIC Document Reproduction Service No. ED 443 420).

Lapadat, J. C. (2002). Written interaction: A key component in online learning. *Journal of Computer-mediated Communication*, *7*(4), JCMC742.

Laurillard, D. (2002). *Rethinking university teaching: A conversational framework for the effective use of learning technologies* (2nd ed.). RoutledgeFalmer.

Lipman, M. (1991). *Thinking in education*. Cambridge University Press.

May, S. (1993). Collaborative learning: More is not necessarily better. *American Journal of Distance Education*, *7*(3), 39–49.

Moore, M. G. (1989). Editorial: Three types of interaction. *American Journal of Distance Education*, *3*(2), 1–7. https://doi.org/10.1080/08923648909526659

Moore, M. G. (1993). Theory of transactional distance. In D. Keegan (Ed.), *Theoretical principles of distance education* (pp. 22–38). Routledge.

Newman, D. R., Johnson, C., Cochrane, C., & Webb, B. (1996). An experiment in group learning technology: Evaluating critical thinking in face-to-face and computer-supported seminars. *Interpersonal Computing and Technology*, *4*(1), 57–74.

Northrup, P. T. (2002). Online learners' preference for interaction. *Quarterly Review of Distance Education*, *3*(2), 219–226.

Poquet, O., Kovanović, V., de Vries, P., Hennis, T., Joksimović, S., Gašević, D., & Dawson, S. (2018). Social presence in massive open online courses. *The International Review of Research in Open and Distributed Learning*, *19*(3). https://doi.org/10.19173/irrodl.v19i3.3370

Reinhart, J. (2010). Graduate students' communication practices and perceived sense of community. *Quarterly Review of Distance Education*, *11*(4), 223–238.

Reisetter, M., & Boris, G. (2004). What works: Student perceptions of effective elements in online learning. *Quarterly Review of Distance Education*, *5*(4), 277–291.

Rourke, L., & Kanuka, H. (2009). Learning in communities of inquiry: A review of the literature. *Journal of Distance Education*, *23*(1), 19–48.

Rovai, A. P. (2000). Building and sustaining community in asynchronous learning networks. *Internet and Higher Education*, *3*, 285–297. https://doi.org/10.1016/S1096-7516(01)00037-9

Rovai, A. P. (2001). Building classroom community at a distance: A case study. *Educational Technology Research and Development*, *49*(4), 33–48.

Sadera, W. A., Robertson, J., Song, L., & Midon, M. N. (2009). The role of community in online learning success. *MERLOT Journal of Online Learning and Teaching*, *5*(2), 227–284.

Schallert, D. L., & Hailey Reed, J. (2003). Intellectual, motivational, textual, and cultural considerations in teaching and learning with computer-mediated discussion. *Journal of Research on Technology in Education*, *36*(2), 103–118. https://doi.org/10.1080/15391523.2003.10782407

Sharp, J. H., & Huett, J. B. (2006). Importance of learner-learner interaction in distance education. *Information Systems Education Journal*, *4*(46). http://isedj.org/4/46/.

Shaw, C. (2012, December 20) FutureLearn is UK's chance to 'fight back', says OU vice-chancellor. *The Guardian*. https://www.theguardian.com/higher-education-network/blog/2012/dec/20/futurelearn-uk-moocs-martin-bean

Sun, W., Schumacher, C., Chen, L., & Pinkwart, N. (2021). What do MOOC dashboards present to learners? In M. Sahin & D. Ifenthaler (Eds.), *Visualisation and dashboards for learning analytics* (pp. 117–148). Springer.

Swan, K. (2002). Building learning communities in online courses: The importance of interaction. *Education, Communication & Information*, 2(1), 23–49. https://doi.org/10.1080/1463631022000005016

Tubman, P., Oztok, M., & Benachour, P. (2016). Being social or social learning: A sociocultural analysis of the FutureLearn MOOC platform. In *2016 IEEE 16th international conference on advanced learning technologies (ICALT)* (vol. 1).

Vygotsky, L. S. (1986). *Thought and language* (A. Kozulin, Trans.). MIT Press. (Original work published 1934).

Vygotsky, L. S. (1997). *Educational psychology* (R. Silverman, Trans.). Saint Lucie Press. (Original work published 1926).

Walther, J. B. (1994). Anticipated ongoing interaction versus challenge effects on relational communication in computer-mediated interaction. *Human Communication Research*, 20, 473–501.

5 Creating engaging videos for online teaching

Sacha E. Davis and Adam Khamis

Introduction

Strategy-driven video content provides a key means of engaging with students online, presenting course material, demonstrating key academic skills, and conveying instruction for assessments, providing a great deal of flexibility in how content is presented (Gedera, 2021). In this chapter, we – a teaching historian and a learning media producer with extensive industry experience – reflect on the experience of producing over 250 videos across three different courses, for the online learning platforms FutureLearn and edX, and learning management system Canvas.

Literature has established the value of video for learning and ways of making video more accessible, for example, captioning and guidelines on the length of video to maximise engagement (Seidel, 2024). One strand of this literature is the value of 'instructor presence' for engagement, but there is a dearth of advice on how to achieve authentic instructor presence or how to give educators the skills to produce compelling learning videos. Learning media production practices especially remain largely opaque. This chapter will bring to light the 'behind the scenes' experiences that make engaging learning videos possible. Next, we outline our stages of video production, from initial planning to post-production. Our aim is to outline a production methodology and practical, hands-on advice that can be applied in a variety of contexts, whether in a small studio or just with a smartphone and a tripod, to create educational content that maintains longevity and relevance. We will provide our reflections on this process to share our experience in creating online course material.

We have written this chapter through a process of collaborative autoethnography, a qualitative research method that aims to be simultaneously collaborative, autobiographical, and ethnographic (Chang et al., 2013). Autoethnography was originally conceived as a self-reflexive means of understanding cultures through autoethnographic epiphanies, which Ellis et al. (2011) define as "remembered moments perceived to have significantly impacted the trajectory of a person's life" (p. 275). Here, we capture the relationship between academic and media producer in the production of content.

DOI: 10.4324/9781003505785-7

We begin our analysis by each reading and reflecting on our own written reflections on the learning design, planning, filming, and editing processes, which have been born out of a working relationship that has lasted years and has had an enduring impact on our professional practice. We then share each other's reflections and reflect on the common themes and experiences, moving beyond descriptive summaries of pedagogical and filmmaking practice to highlight underlying principles. As such, uniquely to the literature, this chapter is also a reflection of 'third space' collaboration between academic and professional staff, that has shaped our approach to video content production (Veles et al., 2023).

Who we are and what we set out to do

Between 2019 and 2021, we converted three in-class undergraduate history courses to fully online delivery through the FutureLearn and edX platforms. These ranged from introductory to capstone level, were all 12 weeks in length, and delivered in the lecture-tutorial model.

- *Europe and the World*: A big-picture survey of world history from the dawn of the European age of exploration to the present. Aimed at students with little/no prior experience of tertiary-level history.
- *Reading the Past*: A survey of historiographical theory and methodology aimed at students with at least 1 year of tertiary level history education.
- *Fascism, War and Genocide*: An in-depth exploration of fascism in the first half of the 20th century, aimed at advanced-level undergraduate students. This was a 20-unit course, with double the expected lecture hours than a standard 10-unit course.

Each course provided its own challenges: the need for very clear and structured content in *Europe and the World*, finding engaging ways to present challenging theoretical content in *Reading the Past*, and providing an appropriate depth of engagement in *Fascism, War and Genocide*. Since completion of filming, the courses have undergone periodic revisions.

As professionals, we brought distinct skill sets to the process of online content production. Sacha says:

> I am a cultural historian, focusing on the history of Central Europe from the mid-eighteenth to the mid-twentieth centuries. Over the last sixteen years, I have taught a wide range of courses at multiple universities, from undergraduate to master's level. These have included broad 1st year survey courses as well as in-depth courses aimed at upper-level students. Before commencing the conversions for the online BA, I had prior experience of synchronous and asynchronous online teaching, but I had never produced online videos before.

Adam says:

> I have been a Learning Media Producer at the University of Newcastle since 2018. In addition to my work with Sacha, I have produced, filmed, directed and edited over 1000 videos across other courses with various academics from many specialities. Utilising 20 years of experience in the film, television and advertising industries in Sydney, including special effects on feature films at Fox and Disney Studios.

Working together had immense value for our professional development. We each brought skills to the table that were reflected in the calibre of work we produced. We also benefited from the support of a learning designer and other members of the university's Learning Design and Teaching Innovation (LTDI) team. Most of the principles we present here are scalable to collaborative efforts in departments or institutions.

What we created

Together, we have created more than 200 videos over the three courses (62 for *Europe and the World*, 57 for *Reading the Past*, 102 for *Fascism, War and Genocide*), most of which are 5–7 minutes in length. Videos took many forms, including straight to camera, speaking over slides, composite image in frame, and on location. We filmed in a fully equipped studio with cinema cameras, extensive lighting, a green screen, and broadcast quality sound and post-production setups. The videos were very well received by students, as anonymous feedback shows:

> Sacha's videos were my favourite part of the course. They were very informative and assisted with learning the content, but the reason that they were my favourite part of the course was because of how engaging and entertaining they were. I really appreciate the effort Sacha has put in to making education yet entertaining videos with props, accents and backgrounds.[1]

(Student feedback consistently credited Sacha for what was in fact very much a team effort. This is testament to the successful establishment of instructor presence.)

Next, we discuss the theoretical and methodological principles that guided our approach.

Pedagogical considerations in online video content

Videos need to be carefully designed and developed, integrating pedagogical techniques and elements to create interactive learning moments (Gedera,

2021). This is a core value we applied with instructor videos for meeting the challenges of the online learning environment. Central to our approach is fostering instructor presence, 'richness' in video content, and media production practices.

Instructor presence

The 'social presence' of instructors in online teaching, Lim et al. (2021) argue, is of particular importance in maintaining student satisfaction, especially in relatively 'unstructured' disciplines in the humanities where content is not by nature fixed, cumulative, or dictated by accrediting bodies, but must be repeatedly revisited to draw out new levels of meaning, requiring a higher level of facilitation. Videos featuring the instructor provide social presence in the online teaching environment equal to that of traditional lectures, reinforced by 'richness' of verbal and non-verbal cues (Luckhardt, 2023), such as vocal tone, gaze, and gestures (Korving et al., 2016; Lim et al., 2021; Pi et al, 2020; Rosenthal & Walker, 2020). Wang and Antonenko (2017) found that

> instructor presence [in online videos] produced a significant positive effect on participants' perceived learning, satisfaction, and mental effort, which are essential factors that contribute to learner motivation and engagement in the autonomous and self-regulated online learning environment.
>
> (p. 88)

We found that students drew similar conclusions in their anonymous course feedback, with one student asserting: "I learned a huge amount of information I didn't know before. Sacha E. Davis presented excellent video content."

Many students identified the videos as their favourite part of the course, with one student reporting:

> This course was incredibly engaging! My favourite part of the course was how passionate Sacha was in getting the content across to us in an engaging way. Even though it was online, I was equally if not more engaged in this course than if I was to go on campus and participate in a lecture and tutorial.

Learning media production practices

In implementing rich instructor presence, we were also guided by media production practices. Learning media producers aid academics in applying pedagogical principles through multimedia and immersive technologies, fostering inclusion, and engaging students in their digital learning environments (University of Western Sydney, 2017). Most importantly, they assist "instructors to find the most effective production method for their content" (Central Michigan University, n.d.). At the University of Newcastle (UON), on-site studio facilities enable interviews, demonstrations, simulations, lightboard recordings, drone shots, 360-degree video, animation, and graphic design.

While dedicated video production resources allow increased variety, engaging videos are still possible with a smartphone in their absence. We find the key is making the most effective use of available resources. Where possible, we emphasise the importance of collaborative relationships between academics and professional staff, bringing distinctive skills to pre-production, on-camera performance, and post-production. The more these processes are practiced, the more streamlined content creation becomes. We next outline our principles for doing so.

Sacha says:

> I've often frequently recorded course videos on my phone: on-the-spot interviews, a location shoot while travelling, and especially when the first Covid lockdown in New South Wales struck midway through the teaching semester, requiring a sharp transition to online teaching across all courses while preventing access to the studio. In each case, I benefited from the techniques learned in studio – and from being able to draw on Adam and the learning design team for input.

Planning video content

The first step is deciding which course material should take video form, as opposed to written text, exercises, and so on. Luckhardt (2023) urges the 'chunking' of course material into different media types guided by the natural rhythm of online engagement, with segmentation into short videos, written texts, comments, and so on. In addition to variety and maintaining social presence across the course, chunking enables consideration of what material would most benefit from being in video form. In our case, Sacha and a learning designer 'chunked' the content and identified material to be converted to video, consulting with Adam on the creative possibilities and how to execute each one. Furthermore, while high-quality video content is more time-consuming to produce, it can result in an enduring pedagogical asset that can be reused repeatedly over multiple offerings of a course. In this section, we consider some key uses of video, including introducing expert testimony, demonstrating key skills, explaining difficult content, and maintaining engagement through 'hero' videos. We end with a consideration of the importance of scripting.

Adam says:

> Video Content strategy was something we discussed in detail. I wanted to look at the 'peaks and troughs' of engagement in a course visually,

to identify where a standout 'hero' video or some other approach to the content was needed to boost the visuals as opposed to a straightforward piece to camera with images. My previous experiences taught me to look deeper or think differently about creating content, so applying the same principles to online course content seemed natural. It was important to take a 'forest for the trees' perspective to see where students may drift off or find the content lacking in engagement – or simply to identify better ways to deliver the material.

Expert testimony

A priority for us in content planning was to bring the expertise of the broader research community into the virtual classroom. Guest lecturers on their area of specialty or emerging research provided an excellent resource, especially in *Europe and the World*, which has a global focus beyond the expertise of any one historian. This material also generally has longevity and can be used across multiple courses. For example, the late Lyndall Ryan recorded a video on the Colonial Frontier Massacres in Australia project for a unit on the Australian History Wars in *Reading the Past*.[2] In addition to bringing research expertise into the virtual classroom, such videos also highlighted the contemporary research, as well as the possibilities for further study.

Teaching key skills

Video is excellent for highlighting key skills, and guiding students through primary sources (Luckhardt, 2023). This was particularly important in *Fascism, War and Genocide*, which has a strong 'material culture' component, culminating in an assignment in which students co-produce a virtual "Museum of Fascism" (Davis et al., 2023). A video in which Sacha 'read' Weimar Hyperinflation-era stamps, and a bank note modelled source analysis skills. Object-based learning has been shown to reinforce student engagement, even when the artefacts are viewed virtually (Ellinghaus et al., 2021; Schultz, 2018). We extended these skills further with museum curators at the Sydney Jewish Museum (SJM), with whom we produced course content that also served as models for how to present a physical artefact to a museum audience.

Video also provides an invaluable means of explaining dense or difficult concepts. For example, in *Reading the Past*, the video scaffolded key concepts around the problem of bias. Historians recognise that there are no 'objective' sources; they always reflect the values, concerns, and viewpoints of their creators. Less experienced students, however, tend to treat bias as rendering a source unusable, as opposed to seeing it as an entry point to better understanding the source's author and context. Consequently, we produced a video modelling how to 'read' a simple source (a salt sachet) to draw out the implicit value assumptions in its labelling (see Figure 5.1).

Figure 5.1 'A pinch of bias:' reading a salt sachet.

Sacha says:

> The salt video is one of my favourite learning exercises. We shot the video with me sitting at a table in a virtual cafe. The salt packet was a very natural object in that context, with its one-word label ("Salt") having a clear and obvious meaning. The exercise then gets the students to break down the cultural assumptions in the label – privileging sodium chloride as the definitive salt, privileging the salt content over the air content in the packet, and over the packet itself, and so on, highlighting the assumptions inherent in even the simplest texts.

Hero videos

Many other videos might be best described as normal lecture content (alternating between Sacha as on-screen narrator and image slides). However, we strategically chose lecture segments that lent themselves to enhancement, for example, through props, location, green screen, and other effects. We describe these as 'hero' videos: material designed to make a memorable impression, requiring a higher level of preparation, filming, and post-production than can be given to all course content (Cameron, 2023). For example, to emphasise the spatial and geographical dimensions of *Fascism, War and Genocide*, we filmed the introductory video from above and placed Sacha on a green screen, upon which we projected a map of Europe beneath his feet in post-production (see Figure 5.2). It allowed us to demonstrate the scope of the course in an exciting and engaging fashion. This could not be done in a classroom and fosters greater engagement.

66 *Moving Your University Course Online*

Figure 5.2 Introduction to *Fascism, War and Genocide*.

Figure 5.3 Filming in a cinema: before.

We also made strategic use of location shots. For example, when filming with the SJM curators, as discussed earlier, we did a day shoot in the Museum's storage space to create a 'behind the scenes' view of museum practices. For *Europe and the World*, we shot a film about World War I Propaganda in the university archive, which served the secondary function of raising awareness of the value of archival research. Using a green screen in the studio and some lighting (see Figure 5.3), we placed Sacha in a cinema discussing film

Figure 5.4 Filming in a cinema: . . . and after.

history to great effect (see Figure 5.4). These videos always aimed to deepen engagement by presenting the material in an interesting way.

Scripting

A careful scripting process accompanied the 'chunking' of the courses. Sacha's existing lecture notes, honed through frequent face-to-face delivery, were revised to take advantage of the video medium (such as through props that would be cumbersome to take to a face-to-face class). Furthermore, the online medium required adaptations. For example, while students (ideally) attend an entire face-to-face lecture, viewing the material in one sitting, videos and other chunks must stand independently, allowing students to pause or leave a lesson and return to it later (Luckhardt, 2023). Consequently, we inserted greater framing of material, clearer introductions and conclusions, and calls back and forward to material already presented or coming up in the future. Furthermore, Luckhardt (2023) suggests that effective videos will focus on the ideas and skills that apply directly to the course learning outcomes. In line with this, we made greater effort to signpost the relevance of material to course themes, as well as drawing out explicit connections to assignments. As Sacha reflects

> Critically revisiting course content with an eye to how best to present it was an invaluable activity in and of itself. In addition to determining the best medium for presentation, it led me to reconsider – and make more explicit to my students – the purpose of each section. This has led me to adopt clearer signposting in both my online and in-person delivery.

These efforts were appreciated by students, according to their anonymous feedback, with one student noting: "Videos and breakdowns were great, and the way the course progressed felt smooth." A further factor in creating enduring assets is performance to camera, discussed next.

Performing to camera

Maintaining social presence is more challenging on screen than in a face-to-face environment, something that academics often only realise when first watching their own recordings. Good delivery, coupled with techniques such as varying vocal tone, facial expression, rate of speech, and body language help reinforce social presence (Lim et al., 2021). The goal in creating course content should be longevity, so that videos can be reused or repurposed for several course offerings. In preparing video content, we benefited from Adam's extensive film industry experience, enabling him to identify several factors that could be improved upon to increase the effectiveness of on-camera performance. Next, we outline those factors.

Preparation

It is important that instructors come prepared for the video shoot. This includes rehearsing the material beforehand – even if it is drawing from lectures that have been given before or using a teleprompter. As Adam highlights

> The way academics deliver their material is crucial to creating engaging content. If the academic is going 'through the motions' or giving a flat performance, students will disengage pretty quickly. If academics show their own passion and interest for the material, it will always yield better results.

Sacha highlights the importance of practise from the academic's perspective.

> While a confident lecturer, I initially approached online filming with some trepidation. It has, however, been a very positive experience. Rehearsing – that is, reading through the scripts a few times the morning before the recording session – helped considerably, even where I had presented the same material in face-to-face lectures multiple times.

It is best to read the script out loud, to make apparent any cumbersome or awkward phrasing before filming, and to provide a chance to correct the language. Practicing enabled us to make many small improvements throughout the courses, as well as saving time by reducing the number of takes required.

Posture and delivery

Both posture and delivery of your script need to be considered to enable an engaging performance. Adam says:

> Be aware of your own body language when onscreen. Maintain a straight posture and eye contact with the lens (that is, with your virtual audience). Do not be afraid to use your hands; gestures can be powerful when emphasising a point. Slightly enhance your natural delivery for greater engagement and to make a connection despite the distancing effect of the small screen. Remember to breathe! A robotic or monotone delivery will not be as effective (unless it is for comedic effect). It is important to watch out for the 'flat tyre' effect, where after a while, your shoulders can start to hunch and the energy in your delivery can deflate . . . like a flat tyre. It is useful to take a brief break at that point.

Following these guidelines greatly reinforces instructor presence, as student feedback highlights: "Sacha E. Davis is an excellent and engaging lecturer, even as an online student I found this to be true," and "Sacha E. Davis is a fantastic lecturer, it is obvious that he is knowledgeable and enthusiastic about the topics." Practise goes a long way in building confidence in front of the camera and making the recording process more rewarding. Developing camera skills is also important, as discussed next.

Filming

While the previous section was written primarily for the on-camera instructor, this section is predominantly written with a learning media producer in mind. In many cases, the instructor may record their own content, but whether you are a media producer working in the studio or a sole academic filming with your smartphone and a lapel microphone, the principles of creating an effective engaging content remain the same.

Preparation

Once again, preparation and planning are key. If you are working in a team, meet with your collaborators. Once the course has been designed and material to be converted to video identified, request scripts or bullet points for the filming component. This requires a strategic approach. Plan where to shoot, whether in a studio, lecture theatre, or on location, and plan a production schedule. This is also a time to decide upon which are 'hero' videos and which are more straightforward pieces to camera, lightboards, interviews, or other kinds of material. Shooting may need to be spaced around the academic's other commitments, and there is no need to record all videos in one go.

We were fortunate to be resourced to shoot each course completely across a semester, but filming might equally be completed over several course iterations, starting with an introduction and a few assessment 'explainers.' If there are any assets, images or links to videos, it is better to have these before filming, to save time in post-production and determine integration into the scripts.

Recording equipment

With the constant rapid advancement of cameras, software, lighting and sound technology, there is limited utility in anchoring this chapter in any particular equipment. The advice provided here applies to a broad spectrum, from a smartphone to a fully equipped film studio. Smartphones have capable cameras and, complemented by a simple tripod and/or lapel microphone, are a great way to get started. Sound is vital, and it is important not to ignore this or give it less attention, as Adam says, "Always test your gear before you shoot."

> There are differing opinions on this, but for me, sound is a little more important than the visual. You can get away with a bad shot, you cannot do the same with bad sound. The main thing is to treat each as equally important and ensure both are as good as your resources allow. Terrible sound will kill your vision. A completely out of focus interview will not help you either, but at least you can still turn it into a podcast! Lighting is also important as you don't want the video to be too dark or overexposed unless it serves a purpose to the content.

Overall, it is not about the equipment you have so much as about how you utilise what you have available.

Framing

Start by framing your subject in an evenly lit environment. If you do not have a studio or any lights or sound equipment, choose a quiet room, preferably with natural light and carpet, so that it does not have an echo. When positioning the speaker, avoid shooting directly against a wall by having at least 2–4 metres separation from your background. Keep the shot simple for delivery so the instructor can use their hands to emphasise points and if you have a camera that has enough resolution, you can 'crop into' 'close ups' to break up the video. 'Midshots' (from the waist to just above the head) fill the space and permit the capture of body language (see Figure 5.5). Avoid too much negative space unless it is serving a purpose, such as leaving space for an image.

Scripts and teleprompters

Some academics like to film without a script which is fine – if they can stay on topic without drifting away from other subject matter. A teleprompter

Figure 5.5 Using hand gestures and body language for emphasis.

allows the academic to focus on their delivery instead of finding the right words to say. Sacha almost always recorded with a script in front of a teleprompter and found it very helpful in keeping on topic and concentrating on delivery.

Directing

Be confident in directing the academic. Ensure their delivery is clear, well-paced, and in line with the principles outlined earlier. Observe whether they are conveying their enthusiasm for the material or losing steam. Redo any sections that did not work or contain too many errors and stumbles, so you have enough strong takes for a solid product. If you are a sole academic recording your own videos, you will need to be mindful of these things yourself. In this case, it is even more important to be prepared.

Adam says:

> Don't be shy to give the academic feedback and to cut the take. They may need a full script warm up first or a few paragraphs, whereas other academics do their best work on the first take. It's a case-by-case basis. An example of direction can be – "Your tone is great, but the pace is a little fast. You're flying through the sentences. Take a breath and please slow down a little." Once you have developed a shorthand with your talent, I can say to Sacha – 'Sacha, 20% up on the delivery and slow it down a little." Or "Flat Tyre is settling in, have a quick breather." Don't be afraid! You are there to create great content for the academic that you're both happy with and most importantly that the students, find engaging, connect with and enjoy learning from.

Sacha says:

> Receiving feedback was very helpful when my delivery was too flat, or when I was speaking too fast. Also, don't be afraid to deliver material a couple of different ways, to take more than one take, and see what works.

Bringing content to life with visual effects and props/artefacts

The video medium also allows educators to use visual effects, especially in hero videos, to reinforce student attention and learning. In face-to-face teaching, such techniques can be cumbersome or impossible. Many of these can be achieved on screen with relative ease, using props or audiovisual assets. Others are more complex, requiring the use of greenscreen and post-production visual effects. Rapidly advancing technology is making these effects increasingly accessible and intuitive to use. We discuss these next.

Intercutting film footage

In addition to static images and slides, we utilised historical film footage that is increasingly available online, especially for *Fascism, War and Genocide*. Much of this footage was in the public domain or could be used for educational purposes under Australian copyright law. We deployed these assets in varying ways, such as interspersed with Sacha talking or with his comments as voiceover. On occasion, we also inserted Sacha into the footage, as discussed next. Footage from multiple sources could be interwoven into a video at a standard too complex to reproduce 'live' during a face-to-face lecture. We also used audio material without footage, such as for content on the uses of oral history in *Reading the Past*.

Props

Physical objects provide a simple and effective way of adding materiality to a video and fostering deeper engagement, as discussed above. Material objects can also make broader processes concrete to students. For example, in *Europe and the World*, we wished to illustrate how the Columbian Exchange of plant and animal species between Eurasia and the Americas and the mass production of plantation commodities had transformed the world, shaping the lives of students today. We did so by sitting Sacha at a table with the products of the commodities trade – a cotton tablecloth, coffee which he sweetened with sugar, tobacco and a pipe, and so on. It was a simple exercise that would be inconvenient to reproduce in the face-to-face classroom but that worked effectively to illustrate the materiality of the commodities trade and the everyday nature of its consumer products.

Props were also used to give embodiment to audio recordings lacking visual content. A video about the use of oral history for *Reading the Past* included cut aways to a reel-to-reel tape player during excerpts of oral history interviews. Props do not have to be physically present; Sacha discussed Otto Dix's triptych *Metropolis for Fascism, War and Genocide* in front of a large-screen video display of the painting, allowing him to point out salient features and providing a further example to reinforce source analysis skills.

Green screen

We shot against a green screen curtain in the UON studio to create a number of backgrounds, locations, scenarios, and visual effects. At the most basic level, we used a green screen to place Sacha in front of static images, such as in front of crowds at a Nazi rally in *Fascism, War and Genocide*. Other uses were more ambitious. Sacha was inserted as a reporter at the Nuremburg Trials, making asides about the process of justice. He was colour-graded black and white to better blend into the scene and provide the content in an engaging way.

We also shot the introduction to the same course with Sacha standing on a map of Europe. We used a green screen carpet, coupled with a raised tripod, to look down on Sacha as he delivered to the camera. Knowing the map layout beforehand was essential so Sacha knew where to gesture and move his hands to match the map moving around underneath his feet (Figure 5.2). We shot a far simpler 'time travel' video for *Reading the Past*, which had Sacha sitting in an office chair up against a green screen, swiping left and right like a dating app, but instead of selecting partners, he would go through time; appropriate historical footage and 'B movie' special effects were green screened in in post-production. Both videos had the effect of setting out the (geographical and temporal) scope of the relevant courses and of creating an exciting introduction designed to foster engagement. It is not, however, necessary to have access to a professional studio to use greenscreen. The increasing sophistication of readily available AI apps now makes it possible to replace your background without a green or blue screen.

Students responded very positively to the range of content and effects in their anonymous feedback. For example, one student opined: "the videos were very engaging and comprehensive. I found them easy to watch and very informative, I loved the multimodal aspect with captions, photos, and songs incorporated, and the use of humour to poke fun at fascists."

Conclusion

In developing online videos for our courses, we benefited from being able to work together as a team, as well as from strong support from LTDI. An unpredicted benefit of developing online teaching materials was the resilience provided by multiple forms of delivery, as we discovered during the COVID-19 lockdowns. *Europe and the World* and *Reading the Past* were already being taught in parallel face-to-face and online streams, allowing us to simply make a version of the online material available to the (formerly) on-campus cohort. The quality of material produced for the BA Online was greatly appreciated by students suddenly forced into the online learning space. *Fascism, War and Genocide*, conversely, had not yet been prepared for online teaching. As a consequence of working with Adam, Sacha was able to solo produce videos during the pandemic that provided good educational outcomes.

The proliferation of AI platforms such as image and video generators, as well as voice cloning and avatar generators, further expand the range of tools for educational video production and seem to offer new opportunities for sole content creators to achieve something closer to a studio-quality product. We did not use these AI platforms in the production of these courses, as they had not yet achieved the necessary maturity for course creation. Furthermore, we were particularly concerned not to create 'realistic' reproductions that might be confused with authentic historical material.

The process of video creation that we adopted is reflected in many ways in the auto-ethnographic approach of this article; it was a collaborative, reflective process in which we applied our skill sets to produce outstanding educational video content. While we were privileged to have access to excellent resources, our real strength lay in that collaborative process, in determining the best material to take to video format and in exploring the ways that video might best be presented. The process of necessity took preparation and planning, but it paid significant dividends.

Appendix: Checklist

Planning video content

Select content that will best benefit from the video format:

- expert testimony;
- demonstrating key skills;
- difficult content; and
- hero videos.

Script in advance, taking the online learning environment into account:

- practice scripts out loud and
- rehearse before recording.

Wardrobe:

- pick a simple colour palette;
- avoid stripes and patterns; and
- avoid green when recording before a green screen.

Posture and delivery:

- maintain a straight posture;
- maintain eye contact with the lens;
- use gestures and facial expression; and
- watch out for the 'flat tyre' effect.

Your voice:

- take some deep breaths before you start;
- find a comfortable pitch and projection; and
- reset, stretch, walk, and breathe.

Branding:

- identify your own style and develop it.

Preparing for filming

- plan your filming ahead of time;
- consider location and lighting and do reconnaissance;
- trial effective framing of your footage; and
- take test footage to check before recording.

Bringing content to life with visual effects and props/artefacts

Select appropriate effects and tools that:

- reinforce key content;
- demonstrate key skills;
- maintain engagement;
- are realistic given the skills and resources available to you; and
- look at the multiple online tutorials to assist you in applying the technology.

Notes

1 We have not corrected punctuation in student feedback.
2 Colonial Frontier Massacres in Australia, 1788–1930. University of Newcastle. https://c21ch.newcastle.edu.au/colonialmassacres/

References

Cameron, J. (2023). Content marketing ideation: How to generate and manage creative concepts. In A. Krowinska, C. Backhaus, B. Becker, & F. Bosse (Eds.), *Digital content marketing* (pp. 31–60). Routledge. https://doi.org/10.4324/9781003346500-3

Central Michigan University. (n.d.). *Learning media production services and examples.* https://www.cmich.edu/offices-departments/curriculum-instructional-support/select-or-develop-materials-and-tools/multimedia/learning-media-production-services-and-examples

Chang, H., Ngunjiri, F., & Hernandez, K.-A. C. (2013). *Collaborative autoethnography*. Routledge.

Davis, S., Kilmister, M., Mereles, A., & Khamis, A. (2023). Exhibiting history: OBL assessment online. *Public History Weekly, 11*(1). https://dx.doi.org/10.1515/phw-2023-21035

Ellinghaus, K., Marsden, B., McIlvenna, U., Moore, F., & Spinks, J. (2021). Object-based learning and history teaching: The role of emotion and empathy in engaging students with the past. *History Australia, 18*(1), 130–155. https://doi.org/10.1080/14490854.2021.1881911

Ellis, C., Adams, T. E., & Bochner, A. P. (2011). Autoethnography: An overview. *Historical Social Research, 36*(4), 273–290. https://doi.org/10.12759/hsr.36.2011.4.273-290

Gedera, D. S. P. (2021). A practical guide to video-making for teachers: Key principles and tools. In D. S. P. Gedera & A. Zalipour (Eds.), *Video pedagogy theory and practice* (pp. 229–239). Springer.

Korving, H., Hernández, M., & De Groot, E. (2016). Look at me and pay attention! A study on the relation between visibility and attention in weblectures. *Computers & Education, 94*, 151–161.

Lim, J. R. N., Rosenthal, S., Sim, Y. J. M., Lim, Z. Y., & Oh, K. R. (2021). Making online learning more satisfying: The effects of online-learning self-efficacy, social presence and content structure. *Technology, Pedagogy and Education, 30*(4), 543–556.

Luckhardt, C. (2023). Dynamic video content in the online history classroom. In S. K Stein, & M. MacLeod (Eds.), *Teaching and learning history online: A guide for college instructors* (pp. 85–93). Routledge.

Pi, Z., Xu, K., Liu, C., & Yang, J. (2020). Instructor presence in video lectures: Eye gaze matters, but not body orientation. *Computers & Education, 144*, 103713.

Rosenthal, S., & Walker, Z. (2020). Experiencing live composite video lectures: Comparisons with traditional lectures and common video lecture methods. *International Journal for the Scholarship of Teaching and Learning, 14*(1), A08.

Schultz, L. (2018). Object-based learning, or learning from objects in the anthropology museum. *Review of Education, Pedagogy, and Cultural Studies, 40*(4), 282–304. https://doi.org/10.1080/10714413.2018.1532748

Seidel, N. (2024). Short, long, and segmented learning videos: From YouTube practice to enhanced video players. *Technology, Knowledge and Learning, 29*(4), 1965–1991. https://doi.org/10.1007/s10758-024-09745-2

University of Western Sydney. (2017). *Teaching and learning procedures – multimedia production and use*. https://policies.westernsydney.edu.au/view.current.php?id=00298

Veles, N., Graham, C., & Ovaska, C. (2023). University professional staff roles, identities and spaces of interaction: Systematic review of literature published in 2000–2020. *Policy Review in Higher Education, 7*(3), 127–168.

Wang, J., & Antonenko, P. D. (2017). Instructor presence in instructional video: Effects on visual attention, recall, and perceived learning. *Computers in Human Behavior, 71*, 79–89.

6 Teaching screen and cultural studies online

Hamish Ford and Rebecca Beirne

Introduction: teaching screens and culture online

> What would a post-Gutenbergian film studies text look like?. . . . [It] would be a three-dimensional, online immersive environment that would not try to imitate the linear sequentiality of a paper-based textbook but would exploit the hypertextual as well as electronic media's multimedia (audio, video, animated graphics) potentials: in other words, it would be a hypermedia environment that subordinates verbal text to highly visual and tactile formats [. . .] Film studies still requires the structured environment of the expert in order to continue teaching the discipline's fundamental core concepts, and therefore still needs to promote deep learning (which cuts across the traditional/progressive divide), but those concepts need to be embedded in today's electronic environment if they are to actively engage the twenty-first-century student and continue to provide an elective learning experience.
>
> (Buckland, 2012, p. 554)

Warren Buckland's 2012 provocation about what 21st-century film studies' pedagogical texts might, or should, be like is pertinent to considering the benefits and challenges of teaching screen and cultural studies online. Neither Screen Studies nor Cultural Studies are 'traditional' disciplines. Although they have been around for well over half a century as dedicated academic subject areas, each has at its outset embraced new, very diverse kinds of texts and definitions thereof, at the heart of which is often new ways of seeing, with special (if also often critical) attention given to the role of popular culture. Screen and Cultural Studies have both been 'impure' areas of study from the start, emanating, drawing from, and impacting an array of scholarly fields with little heed given to traditional disciplinary boundaries. Long before such language became ubiquitous in the academy, they have always been truly interdisciplinary, progressive endeavours.

With some of the 'primary texts' – films, television programs, or other audiovisual media – that screen studies scholars want students to engage with can be difficult to access, weekly screenings have long been a key part of such courses. In the case of film studies, the oldest form of screen studies,

DOI: 10.4324/9781003505785-8

this has also been in the interest of replicating a cinema-type communal experience and plays an important role in the discursive pedagogical process in subsequent class discussions. While film studies traditionally incorporate such screenings, despite more than half a century of such teaching and learning practice, university lecture spaces and timetabling constraints are often not particularly suited to this special need that sits outside of traditional lecture/workshop/seminar formats as defined by older, more established academic disciplines. Cultural studies, meanwhile, with its interrogation of contemporary culture and the ways that it operates with a keen eye for the diverse political ramifications thereof, also sits rather uniquely within the academy due in part to having origins outside it, at least in Australia and the United Kingdom, notably in the field of adult education (Grossberg, 1994). Asking students to think critically about diverse 'texts' (now much more broadly redefined beyond the written word), cultural processes, and societal structures we take for granted requires an extremely careful, interactive approach. This is palpably so in our current era, with emotions running high regarding hot button issues of increasingly global culture and politics. This is all to say that in considering how to adapt from a face-to-face teaching environment into an online one, when it comes to Screen and Cultural Studies, it is not quite a matter of undoing perfection and trying to make it anew in a virtual space, for inherently interdisciplinary areas have never fit quite neatly into a traditional academic format. Rather, the creation of an online version of our major provides an opportunity to further utilise and engage the already multimedia, screen-based textuality and pedagogy well suited to our courses and to think therefore about creating rather simply transferring them to a fully online format. Throughout the process, we have sought to keep in mind Buckland's mutually reliant questions: How might we "exploit the hypertextual," so that we "actively engage the twenty first century student" (2012, p. 554)?

This chapter addresses the benefits and challenges of asynchronous online learning in the context of Screen and Cultural Studies, a diverse interdisciplinary major taught at the University of Newcastle (UON). The pedagogical approaches to teaching both screen studies (Buckland, 2012; Creely et al., 2021; Kannas et al., 2022; Kessler, 2015; Liu, 2022) and cultural studies (Giroux & Shannon, 2013; Grossberg, 1994; Steinberg, 2012) are very much discussion based. These areas value plurality of interpretation, analysis, and critique, and constructive arguments heavily dependent on the varying contextual knowledges and skills of contributing scholars, teachers, and students. Additionally, both screen studies – in our case, as elsewhere, primarily focused on film and television studies as well as incorporated selection of other screen-based media – and cultural studies involve the presentation and analysis of multiple textual forms subject to intellectual property laws and educational provisions in terms of copyright that are more complex when it comes to reproducing material online than it is in the classroom.

In considering how to create our courses for an online format, we thought it crucial to maintain and even extend the role of students in extensively discussing and debating their ideas as prompted by those they encounter through their learning via a carefully curated set of lecturer-provided videos, text prompts, images, clips, and larger audiovisual and literary texts designed to spark their intellectual curiosity and analysis. The commercial third-party platform initially chosen by UON offered much potential in this respect through a format wherein weekly topics are divided up into a series of smaller 'steps' in which each diverse learning element (comprising one or more of the above text or media type) is typically paired with a comment section in order to stimulate students' engagement with course content, as well as in-site quizzes, embedded 'Padlets' and other tools to add variety to the learning experience. We were helped throughout by the University's excellent learning designers to oversee the construction of each course, professional video production personnel, and a team of specialised technical staff. As the two full-time ongoing academics responsible for the Screen and Cultural Studies major, writing and teaching seven of its nine dedicated online courses since 2019, ahead we explore both the challenges and generative, discipline-appropriate aspects of teaching film, television, and other audiovisual media asynchronously online. Taking in the macro considerations for teaching screen-based areas and the micro experience of writing and delivering specific courses in this context, two of which will be explored ahead in the form of entry-level and upper-level examples, the chapter charts our 6-year experience of teaching our major online.

Launching in 2019, the redesigned UON Bachelor of Arts (BA) featured a fully online version of the program, within which Screen and Cultural Studies would be one of four majors available. This new online degree option and revitalised face-to-face BA were born of extended and highly collaborative work by a large School committee throughout 2016–2018 (for more on which, see Chapter 2 of this book). Our discipline area, newly renamed Screen and Cultural Studies, had in fact taught several subjects online going back to 2008 prior to the BA Online's development, which meant we had more existing online experience than many of our colleagues from other disciplines as we transitioned to designing and teaching the online version of the degree. Previously taught via the Blackboard learning management system, we had been concerned that our courses, built around readings, slides, and discussion boards, did not adequately engage students. Moving to the new social media-based platform in 2019 and writing our courses for this radically different format, we wanted to engage students in more diverse, exciting ways while retaining the core substance and learning principles we value as screen and cultural studies scholars and teachers in keeping with the principles and ideal re-imagining as previously outlined by Buckland (2012). Being a featured part of the new BA Online as one of only four majors available gave us this opportunity, developing digital teaching materials featuring professionally shot and edited videos, clean and appealing design aesthetics, and a welcoming platform loosely based on social media formats. As of 2025, these same principles are being embedded in a new in-house platform built within Canvas, with further enhancements based on what we have learned throughout the BA Online process.

Using an asynchronous online platform

Early in the BA Online's development, the decision was made to partner with FutureLearn, a UK-based social media-style platform, then specialising in MOOCs for masters and postgraduate courses. Founded by the Open University in 2012 in partnership with top-ranked UK Universities (Parr, 2012), the platform has been owned by for-profit education firm Global University Systems since 2022 (Williams, 2022). UON's BA was the first undergraduate program hosted on the platform, indicating the partnership's innovative nature. The social learning model embodied by FutureLearn proved to be well-suited for the purposes of our Screen and Cultural Studies major, which comprises an interdisciplinary mix of subject areas and emphasises both a plurality of scholarly perspectives and consistently high levels of student engagement – both essential for teaching our subject areas and, research suggests, absolutely crucial for successful online learning (Gherghel et al., 2023). As active screen and cultural studies researchers and experienced lecturers, we have long utilised the capacity of online video and other multimedia, web-based sources in our course creation and delivery in the 'synchronous' teaching context. In many cases, adapting to an optimal form of fully online teaching and learning offered us the opportunity to further utilise and properly extend this aspect of our courses and their delivery to greater, more efficient effect, the platform and technology now aligned with the pedagogy we had long sought to practice. At the same time, challenges inevitably emerged, particularly regarding the availability of films and television programs via streaming – which can be acute in Australia when it comes to regional restrictions – and the issue of screen media copyright in online learning.

Shi et al. (2019) note that "FutureLearn employs a social constructivist approach, inspired by Laurillard's Conversation Framework, which describes a general theory of effective learning through conversations (or social interactions)" (p. 476). With our interdisciplinary humanities-based backgrounds, we have always put a premium on active classroom learning and critical thinking when it comes to student responses to audiovisual texts, their socio-historical context, and scholarly accounting. The FutureLearn platform appeared well-suited to encourage discussion of the production, consumption, and scholarly analyses of films, television programs, and other screen-based media. Following the large-scale collaborative work of the 2016–2018 BA renewal committee, which sought to maintain or even strengthen critical thinking as a core skill taught in both the new face-to-face and online degrees, it was vital to ensure such focus and skills development were maintained and even enhanced via the diverse potential offered by cutting-edge asynchronous teaching and learning practice. (For more on critical thinking in the online environment, see Hussin et al., 2019, and Tathahira, 2020.)

The social media-based model has proven an ideal platform for our major's encouragement of student learning, both when it comes to direct interaction between student and teacher and in the form of the potential for bespoke peer-to-peer learning. The asynchronous format potentially enables such peer-to-peer learning more easily and automatically than a traditional offline context via the discussion fields in the multiple steps of a course's given week. In a typical face-to-face environment, the teaching academic is typically not only directing, encouraging, and interacting with class discussion, but the finite duration of a timetabled class of necessity also curtails the length and diversity of conversational responses to a topic, screening, or reading, and thereby the capacity of students to substantially initiate as well as participate in such discussion. (For more on this, see Gherghel et al., 2023.) In contrast, each step of a social-learning-based online course offers rich potential for extended discussion via a healthy mix of academic-student and peer-to-peer interaction in the form of primary threads and sub-threads – a valuable form of more informal learning for both students and teaching staff, as Kessler (2015) and Boud et al. (2014) suggest.

The asynchronous, social media-style online format also allows us as course designers and teachers to structure each week of a course so that students can take it at their own speed. This depends not only on how efficiently they are able to cover course material (set screenings, readings, and academic-provided content steps spanning text, video, and other modes) but also the extent to which students engage in and generate discussion throughout the week. The longer time frame allows instructors greater capacity to gear the conversation around points of potential student interest and comparison, leading to superior pedagogical outcomes (Gherghel et al., 2023; Kessler, 2015). This is especially important for our diverse cohort when it comes to the stage of life, academic and class background, and commitments outside the university. Herein lies the primary ongoing appeal of online learning: to make tertiary education available to people no matter their various personal and professional situation, background, identity, personal obligations, health, and age, and to best design courses and pedagogies in light of this reality. (For more on this, see Archambault et al., 2022; Miller, 2015; and Steele et al., 2019.) The potential learning experience offered by a quality online platform utilised to its fullest is such that students can in no way be said to have a lesser-quality university education experience compared to their face-to-face counterparts. At the same time, it has also become increasingly apparent, especially when it comes to assignments, that some students desire or need some level of real-time interaction with their lecturers in the form of well-timed synchronous video sessions throughout the course. Even if these may often not be very well attended, our students have indicated via feedback (via online comments, emails, or official University-administered course evaluations) that they appreciate having the option of such interaction every few weeks.

While welcoming the potential for diversity of teaching materials and format, including a rich array of created and curated online video and other media as central to our teaching, the freedom of an asynchronous environment when it comes to learning pace and potential for increased student-generated discussion (Gherghel et al., 2023; Kessler, 2015; Serdyukov, 2015) and fostering of critical thinking (Hussin et al., 2019; Tathahira, 2020), we were also presented with a variety of designing and teaching challenges. One of these has been that our online courses need to remain in close proximity to their existing face-to-face versions regarding overall content and the Screen and Cultural Studies major. This has meant working out how to deliver key learning outcomes via bite-size 'steps', featuring a mix of text- and video-based content and interactive material and discussion in line with well-established research into online learning (Archambault et al., 2022; Baran et al., 2011; Gormley, 2014; Steele et al., 2019), and our particular teaching areas (Buckland, 2012; Liu, 2022). With a view to offering more specific insights, we will now discuss two representative courses from our suite of online offerings, one entry-level and one upper-level, as case studies through which to address in more detail the process of designing, teaching, and evaluating our experience of running the Screen and Cultural studies online major since 2019.

A first-year online media literacy course: SCRN1000 *Media Literary*

SCRN1000 *Media Literary* responds to the ever-greater need for media literacy education. The 21st century is increasingly rich, complex, and challenging when it comes to media and information, and discerning the reliability, biases, persuasive techniques, and means of such communication is crucial for empowering citizens with the ability to think for themselves. Media literacy education is, thereby, a form of applied critical thinking, using a set of lenses and dynamic processes of analysis to navigate our increasingly screen-based, global, virtual world. To learn these skills, however, students don't just need to be told about them. They need to witness and engage with their specific application and try to apply it for themselves, developing, adapting, and applying such skills. In a face-to-face classroom, this is typically done through small and larger group discussions such that even those who do not actively contribute get to hear their peers doing so and the teacher's responses. Moving to an online context, given that such courses often have only a small proportion of students taking the step of posting their analysis or ideas (Archambault et al., 2022; Steele et al., 2019; Liu, 2022), the importance of building interactive engagement has been even more important for Screen and Cultural Studies.

A refocused update of our previous introductory Screen and Cultural Studies course, SCRN1000 *Media Literacy,* was launched in February 2019 along with the BA Online. Once the pandemic arrived a year later, it became clear that the need for skills-based media literacy training was more vital than ever, and students were invited to turn their newfound skills to verifying and debating the accuracy of and discourses surrounding mass and user-generated media coverage about vaccines, masks, and other contentious issues. This flexibility was enabled by the online version of the course having been devised as much less focused on imparting information than building a conversation that welcomed students to take part as equals, bringing their own knowledge and experience of the media into play (Kessler, 2015; Pelz, 2010; Serdyukov, 2015) and echoing longer cultural studies principles of education (Grossberg, 1994). All learning videos for the course were conversational in style, highlighting that there is no one 'right way' of understanding texts and culture, as well as asking specific questions as to how students might apply insights contained in the videos to examples from their own media diets and experiences. Although usually coming from different disciplinary contexts, research into the length of lecture content videos in terms of student completion and engagement suggests that students are less likely to watch the entirety of videos lasting 10 min or more (Manasrah et al., 2021). As with all our online courses, for SCRN1000 the vast majority of the videos are thereby under 10 min for both pedagogical reasons (maintaining student engagement) and the practical motivation (the inclusion of multiple media examples that would date before longer videos are redone).

As has been observed from comments for MOOCs (Miller, 2015; Swinnerton et al., 2017), we have found that even in an enrolment-only environment, a small proportion of students contribute regularly substantively to online course discussion, and some do not comment at all. This can even occur in cases where official student satisfaction scores are high. The lack of response can lead to great disappointment for educators and learning designers who put significant thought and resources into course design and teaching. Given that "[p]revious research has shown that interaction with instructors, as well as collaboration between participants in online courses, improve satisfaction and perceived learning" (Gherghel et al., 2023), we made the decision to assess student posts in a selection of weeks for this course. Students would not be assessed for the technical quality of their writing, but rather on engagement with instructors and peers. Although not recommended by the learning design team for its principle of enforcing student engagement, a sharp increase in participation for the course following this change has been beneficial for student engagement and morale and is also designed to establish good habits for subsequent courses' participation (irrespective of whether it remains graded). Notably, once students start posting, they continue doing so in weeks for which they are not assessed. They also engage with each other more because the course has specified that this is important. As their posts are open-ended reflections engaging with both the course materials and peer discussion, the engagement still needs to be active, thoughtful, and considerate. In a period when students are increasingly busy and stressed, making a small extrinsic measure reward available that specifically values their engagement helps make *them* value engagement and prioritise it.

Initially, the first 3-week module was available simultaneously to UON students enrolled in the course and worldwide users as a MOOC. There were issues, however, in mixing our existing undergraduate cohort within a MOOC environment. As communicated via emails to the lecturer as well as comments in the discussion threads (especially after this initial three-week period was over), some students felt intimidated by the fast-paced addition of comments, many of which originated in the United Kingdom and thus would happen en masse overnight for those in Australia. In addition, during a case study of LGBTQ+ representation in the third week of the course, comments by some of the global FutureLearn participants often devolved into homophobia and transphobia rather than interrogating the overall concepts of representation and stereotyping. Although dissenting opinions and perspectives are always welcome in our classes and indeed are part of the tertiary education learning process, in a face-to-face context such comments can be immediately engaged with and potentially reframed into a learning opportunity. The nature of asynchronous teaching does not always allow this to happen, especially when it comes to the mass contribution of a global cohort. Some of our students were understandably upset to be faced with bigoted discussion in their learning environment. Course staff wrote to students to encourage civility and kindness towards one another and notified learning support staff of posts that required deletion. The course coordinator also wrote to UON students separately via the LMS to reassure them, and fortunately this was the final week of the open section of the course before it was closed off to UON students exclusively. While the initial open component has since been disbanded across our offerings, more reflection and research on the potentially different values and accountabilities between enrolled and MOOC students (Miller, 2015; Swinnerton et al., 2017) in responding to content would be useful.

From the outset of the course design, it was initially made clear that we would only be able to substantially update online course materials every few years, beyond very minor corrections and changes. While this would be rather unusual for academics teaching in a regular face-to-face context, it was especially difficult for an online course about media literacy such as SCRN1000. In its face-to-face version, examples, statistics, and trends can be easily updated on a week-by-week basis so that students can engage with and respond to the media they are experiencing, which is in constant flux, 'in real time' through the use of live online sources in the classroom. This is crucial to students honing their skills, becoming empowered in relation to the media around them, and seeing the relevance of the concepts in their everyday lives in a quickly changing image-saturated environment. As of 2025, the University's LDTI (Learning Design and Teaching Innovation) staff are migrating all content from FutureLearn (which required centralised updating) to the university-wide LMS Canvas. This means that all elements can potentially be altered at any time by the relevant teaching academic, with technical support still available. This brings the updateability of the online courses in line with the alteration and updating of slides, discussion points, sources, and data used in the face-to-face version of the course.

A particular challenge for this course, in light of its need for regular updating of courses and examples, has been the application of copyright for educational purposes, an especially fraught issue in the online context. Due to the difficulties in determining the limits of fair use provisions for media literacy education in the United States, scholars in that country have developed a 'Code of Best Practices in Fair Use for Media Literacy Education,' in which it is observed that "educators involved in media literacy feel uncertain in this new environment of heightened commodification" (2008). While the code offers some brief guidance as to including copyrighted material within the curriculum posted to a website, it is otherwise mostly focused on classroom spaces. Furthermore, US Fair Use provisions are different from Australian Fair Dealing laws (for more on this, see Aishwarya, 2020). In our case, such uncertainty is further complicated by what can easily appear as a lack of clear information regarding the legal requirements and precedents under Australian copyright law for the online education context, which results in problematic complexity when it comes to the reproduction and distribution of audiovisual material. One need only look at the guidance issued to Registered Training Organisations by the Australian Skills Quality Authority on copyright in education regarding how to avoid copyright breaches and that copyright licensing is managed across three different organisations (ASQA, 2019) to see the complexity of creating an online course that is primarily about copyrighted materials and using them in a way that is appropriate. While copyright limitations are a potential challenge in other online teaching and learning contexts, for our courses – and especially SCRN1000 – it is particularly acute.

An upper-level online screen studies course: SCRN3200
Documentary Cinema

For our second case study, we have chosen a representative from the major's film studies courses, thereby speaking to the challenges of teaching this subject area online and discussing the development of an upper-level course in this context. Reflecting on their experience at Monash University, Creely et al. (2021) observed that the transition to online teaching, which always involves changes to curriculum and materials in all disciplinary contexts, has some "considerations specific to film studies as a discipline" (n.p.). One of these is the importance of "students and educators gathering communally to view films" (2021, n.p.) – a point that can be extrapolated to television and other audiovisual media studies and to which we will return in more detail later. In the context of Monash's COVID-necessitated wholesale transition to the online space, Creely et al. write about attempting "to maintain a pedagogical approach for our community of students that preserved our sense of cinema's capacity to be socially meaningful in different ways – personally, politically, intellectually" (2021, n.p.). A few years earlier, the UON Screen and Cultural

Studies discipline and major (then called Film, Media, and Cultural Studies) was facing similar challenges, although on a very different timeline, as we prepared a fully online version of our major in the Bachelor of Arts, the preparation and launch of which took place before the pandemic's outbreak.

As part of our online suite of courses spanning the different subject areas and specialisations of an interdisciplinary major, the dedicated third-year screen studies course selected for online creation was SCRN3200: *Documentary Cinema: Rendering the Real*. We felt this course would be less negatively impacted than other upper-level courses in the major by both the restriction on regular wholesale changes and the issue of films' and television programs' availability via streaming platforms thanks in part to the less overtly commercial, often more 'educational' nature of documentary cinema. An additional, more overtly positive motivation for creating an online version of the course was to make it as accessible as possible for a diverse cohort spanning multiple backgrounds, age ranges, and career interests as well as academic specialisations, appealing to students studying areas such as History, Sociology, Education, and Politics.

While our implementation of the online Screen and Cultural Studies major pre-dated and was perfectly timed for COVID-era restrictions, accounts, and research from other universities' experience of online teaching enforced by the latter can help analyse the realities of teaching screen studies online. Such accounts deal in some detail with perhaps the most overt challenge in creating and teaching an online film studies course, screenings. If a long and valuable tradition for such courses involves students watching films on a large screen in a darkened room together as a group, with the move to online, this is of necessity replaced with watching films at home in very different circumstances (Creely et al., 2021; Kannas et al., 2022; Kessler, 2015). In addition to choosing topics and films in light of the need for ongoing streaming access – ideally via university-supplied services such as Kanopy and ClickView that are free to students, or, where necessary, commercial subscription-based platforms – the move to online involves a radically different screen type and spectatorial environment whereby students watch a course's primary material, changing their fundamental experience and perhaps even meaning of such set audiovisual texts and thereby that of the subject itself. (This key difference in the online environment is not faced, for example, by English Literature courses that have always relied on students completing set texts outside of timetabled class times.)

In their own research following the wholesale COVID-era shift to at-home learning at RMIT University via a series of focus groups, Kannas et al. (2022) report something of a mixed response to the move online, emphasising the radical difference in how films are watched. They note how most students of necessity watched courses' primary films on laptops, typically in bedrooms and only occasionally with family or friends on a larger screen. While the use of smaller screens to watch films (a process in fact dating back to the 1950s mass proliferation of television) and solo viewing is already a fundamentally different context compared to the darkened lecture hall and large screen approximating a cinema-like environment, an even bigger change involves watching films on an interactive personal computer and browser page thereof while very often being concurrently involved in another screen activity. Kannas, Douglas, and Thompson report students engaging in a mix of other university work and researching the film while watching it, as well as pleasure browsing, social media participation, and communication via direct message, thereby only partially paying attention to the film set for study purposes. Using the binary formulation of their study's title, students in this online spectatorship environment are thereby 'glancing' rather than 'gazing.' In a small number of cases, they add, participants reported private messaging as a two-or-more process of commenting on a film while watching it 'together' (2022). As if such a personalised spectatorial context is not radically different enough, as compared to a traditional screening, the RMIT study also cites extensive accounts of pausing the film at will and watching it over multiple sessions, sometimes spanning days (Kannas et al., 2022). This is echoed by anecdotal reports we have received (via email, online discussion, in person, and via official course feedback) from students.

The move to online when it comes to core audiovisual screen studies texts remains a challenge cited by many students both in the available research and in our experience. Most respondents in the RMIT study reported that watching films in this personalised, multi-screen or window environment "was not conducive to their enjoyment, understanding of, or engagement with, course films" (2022, p. 50). This majority sentiment is echoed by the feedback we have received. This chimes with the long-held view that watching feature films in a traditional setting – a darkened room on a single, large screen either alone or with others without any competing screens or windows – is a special (sometimes even described as sacred) 'gazing' experience, the gradual loss of which has long been lamented by 'cinephile' commentators – for example, three decades ago, Sontag (1996) – who see more distracted modes of spectatorship as demonstrating a broader, gradual cultural shift endemic of late capitalism. Yet the reported student experience of watching of films and television programs online at home is not unambiguously negative, for very important and timely reasons. Despite the majority sense of loss with the move to watching films online, Kannas, Douglas & Thompson report: "For a small group of students, however, second screen use appeared to bolster levels of cognitive engagement" (2022, p. 50). They note that the multi-screen/browser window context can actually involve a more interactive mode of spectatorship not only familiar to everyday viewers of diverse video-based audiovisual texts marking what can be seen as the 'YouTube-ization of culture,' but that has also in fact been essential to screen studies almost since its very inception. Hence, rather than pejoratively distracted 'glancing,' in this understanding, the viewer potentially becomes *more* engaged with the audiovisual text through having much more control, pausing and playing at will, being able to rewind or fast-forward, and taking notes via a separate screen or window, which some of Kannas, Douglas, and Thompson's respondents report doing (2022). Initially enabled by the advent of home video and the remote control, as evoked by Laura Mulvey (2006), then further enhanced in both efficacy and quality by subsequent digital formats (following Mulvey see Fischer, 2017, and Ford, 2007), and now streaming, rather than entirely new, this mode of spectatorship and engagement has in reality largely driven film and television studies since the 1970s in allowing limitless close studying of individual films and programs – a process reaching its potential apotheosis in the online learning environment.

SCRN3200 students and those of other courses in the major suggest a similar challenge with watching films alone at home on a laptop, as described earlier and reported by Kannas et al. (2022). The latter research is also echoed by the occasional student (typically those that are especially engaged across the course elements) who has noted the advantages of 'delayed viewing' (pausing, etc., at will) and close analysis potentially enabled by watching films alone at home. The radically altered nature of spectatorship for online learning is a topic that warrants further research and investigation for our courses and beyond. A possibility worth exploring, one reported as having some success – if with fairly small numbers of participants – in the 2022 RMIT study, is to schedule voluntary 'live' screenings whereby students press play at the same time, incentivising the watching of films without pausing, while also adding the potential for opt-in private messaging. This enables a hybrid mode of highly participatory viewing that incorporates aspects of single- and multi-screen spectatorship.

Beyond the central film studies issues of streaming availability and spectatorial context, other challenges regarding how best to deliver non-filmic 'content' also emerged as SCRN3200 was developed online. Like our other second and third year-directed offerings, in addition to a dedicated screening, the face-to-face incarnation of this course features a combined, interactive seminar model centred around extensive discussion rather than lecture material. Based on the same films and readings, pedagogical 'framing' content was thereby built from the ground up for the online version of the course when it came to structuring the 'steps' comprising each week and the linear structure thereof. Even so, as with its face-to-face version, the focus remains on interactive discussion of set screenings and readings, rather than extensive 'content' in the form of lectures broken up in the online context. Instead, a diverse array of learning modes (sometimes featuring brief independent research tasks) was created to build and sustain the narrative of each week and three-week module, with short text and video material contextualising the primary content. Students could thereby concentrate on watching the set films and curated clips, completing the set readings, and discussing all this in response to an array of prompts, plus a handful of filmed interviews, polls, and Padlets. Student feedback (via email, online comments, official course evaluation, or in person) shows that this approach has proven effective.

A key question for this course, as with all our online offerings (in particular upper-level ones), was how to approach set readings. Be it face-to-face or online, an overall increase in what could be called challenging reading at both quantitative and qualitative levels can be expected as students travel undergraduate course offerings within their degree. Reflecting the highly mixed, 'impure' nature of screen studies when it comes to interdisciplinarity as evidenced in published commentary and analysis within and beyond the academy, across all levels our courses feature a truly diverse array of sources spanning short reviews, blogs, video pieces, and news reports, interviews, and industry surveys, through to traditional academic literature, medium-dedicated and more general humanities-oriented theory, and scholarly video essays. This principle applies even more for online courses such as SCRN3200 so that students read a variety of types of sources to help experience, appreciate, and analyse the genuinely diverse nature of analysis devoted to screen production, reception, and culture, and its scholarly accounting.

For SCRN3200's online version, one the handful of occasions where it was felt appropriate to set challenging, lengthy journal articles or chapters featuring difficult theoretical writing, dedicated videos were created to explicate the key concepts of material students may find difficult. In one sense, these videos effectively replicate parts of what an academic may do in a lecture or seminar when seeking to frame and explain a particularly challenging reading and related concepts, but the online environment offers much more potential regarding effective and visually engaging communication thereof. So, rather than just watching the lecturer speak at some length, in these more detailed, 'explication' videos, students are treated to carefully curated images and clips in addition to slides featuring bullet points and key quotations. The viability of such videos, as with those described earlier for SCRN1000 featuring concurrent analysis of clips being shown on screen, would be potentially impacted by stricter copyright crackdown. Such effective and sophisticated pedagogical material offers one of the clearest examples whereby the potential for online teaching of screen studies-based courses can be fully realised in a way entirely 'authentic' to the subject area, where students can enjoy bespoke, high-level audiovisual production. Both casually and formally (via official course evaluations), many have indicated their appreciation for such videos.

Conclusion: the online future of screen and cultural studies

Optimal online course design and teaching offer much potential, even in some important ways possibly exceeding that of face-to-face learning, while also bringing into sharp relief some ongoing limitations and challenges. It is also important to remember that asynchronous online learning suits some students (most obviously those unable to come onto campus due to other life commitments and mobility considerations) much more than others who continue to strongly prefer traditional synchronous learning in a classroom.

In our experience, both preferences are reported across a wide demographic range spanning school-leavers and mature-age students.

We have in many ways been satisfied with the results of our efforts in creating a vibrant Screen and Cultural Studies major in the UON BA Online, and student responses have overall been positive. University-administered course assessment surveys show that our online courses match or sometimes exceed their face-to-face siblings in overall satisfaction, and anecdotal feedback has also been particularly good. It is, however, important to emphasise the ongoing challenges involved with online teaching and learning for our group of subject areas. Streaming availability and copyright restrictions remain substantial issues. Meanwhile, the pragmatic limitation of not being able to make wholesale changes for each new run of a course (as can be easily enabled in the case of face-to-face offerings) promises to be eased as our university moves to an in-house, Canvas-based online learning format in 2025. Hopefully, this will also enable the overcoming of another, more minor, frustration whereby to make even small corrections or changes, we need to communicate these to LDTI staff rather than being able to directly edit course steps ourselves.

We have found that online learning can be incredibly successful if done well via an optimal, social media-like platform. At the same time, asynchronous content delivery, taking in different issues discussed earlier involving access to and watching films and television at home, remains an area of both challenge and opportunity, suggesting the need for ongoing experimentation and research. We look forward to further honing how our Screen and Cultural Studies courses are taught online, seeing more research in this and related areas, and optimising the potential for a virtual teaching and learning environment. After all, such an environment is hardly an alien one for both our major and the increasingly global 21st century reality in which we live, work, learn, and play: a world exponentially rendered by, comprised of, and analysed through, screen-based communication and culture.

References

Aishwarya, V. V. (2020). Legal regulation of fair dealing and fair use in India, Australia and the United States. *International Journal of Law Management & Humanities*, 3, 986–995.

Archambault, L., Leary, H., & Rice, K. (2022). Pillars of online pedagogy: A framework for teaching in online learning environments. *Educational Psychologist*, 57(3), 178–191.

Australian Skills Quality Authority (ASQA). (2019). *Registered training organisations*. https://www.asqa.gov.au/rtos

Baran, E., Correia, A., & Thompson, A. (2011). Transforming online teaching practice: Critical analysis of the literature on the roles and competencies of online teachers. *Distance Education*, 32(3), 421–439.

Boud, D., Choen, R., & Sampson, J. (Eds.). (2014). *Peer learning in higher education: Learning from and with each other*. Kogan Page Ltd.

Buckland, W. (2012). Film and media studies pedagogy. In R. Kolker (Ed.), *The Oxford handbook of film and media studies* (pp. 527–556). Oxford University Press.

Center for Media and Social Impact. (2008). *Code of best practices in fair use or media literacy education*. https://cmsimpact.org/code/code-best-practices-fair-use-media-literacy-education/

Creely, L., Letizi, R., Monaghan, W., Russell, G., & Troon, S. (2021). When Zoom replaces the cinema: Reimagining Film Studies online during Covid-19 through collaborative teaching and community building. *Journal of Cinema and Media Studies*. https://quod.lib.umich.edu/j/jcms/18261332.0060.802/-when-zoom-replaces-the-cinema-reimagining-film-studies?rgn=main;view=fulltext

Fischer, L. (2017). Laura Mulvey's "delaying cinema": Delayed thoughts on a resonant text. *New Review of Film and Television Studies, 15*(4), 431–434.

Ford, H. (2007). A new gaze via remote control. *RealTime, 77*, 16.

Gherghel, C., Yasuda, S., & Kita, Y. (2023). Interaction during online classes fosters engagement with learning and self-directed study both in the first and second years of the COVID-19 pandemic. *Computers & Education, 200*(104795), 1–9. https://doi.org/10.1016/j.compedu.2023.104795

Giroux, H. A., & Shannon, P. (2013). *Education and cultural studies: Toward a performative practice*. Routledge.

Gormley, C. (2014). Teaching the principles of effective online course design: What works? *Irish Journal of Academic Practice, 3*(1), article 3, 1–30. https://arrow.tudublin.ie/cgi/viewcontent.cgi?article=1024&context=ijap

Grossberg, L. (1994). Introduction: Bringin' it all back home: Pedagogy and cultural studies. In H. I. Giroux & P. McClaren (Eds.), *Between borders: Pedagogy and the politics of cultural studies*. Routledge.

Hussin, W. N. T. W., Harun, J., & Shukor, N. A. (2019). Online interaction in social learning environment towards critical thinking skills: A framework. *Journal of Technology and Science Education, 9*(1), 4–12.

Kannas, A., Douglas, L., & Thompson, J. (2022). Gazing or glancing? Mapping student engagement when film studies moves online. *Convergence: The International Journal of Research into New Media Technologies, 29*(1), 47–60. https://journals.sagepub.com/doi/10.1177/13548565221148102

Kessler, K. (2015). Finding the face-to-face when you have no face: Fostering student-student and student-professor engagement in the online media classroom. *Cinema Journal: The Journal for the Society of Cinema & Media Studies: Cinema Journal Teaching Dossier, 3*(1). https://teachingmedia.org/finding-the-face-to-face-when-you-have-no-face-fostering-student-student-and-student-professor-engagement-in-the-online-media-classroom/

Liu, Y. (2022). Research on online and offline mixed teaching practice based on college film and television literature course. *Scientific Programming*, special issue: Scientific programming for fuzzy system modelling of complex industry data. https://doi.org/10.1155/2022/3336282

Manasrah, A., Masoud, M., & Jaradat, Y. (2021). Short videos, or long videos? A study on the ideal video length in online learning. In *2021 international conference on information technology (ICIT)* (pp. 366–370).

Miller, S. L. (2015). Teaching an online pedagogy MOOC. *Journal of Online Learning & Teaching, 11*(1), 87–102.

Mulvey, L. (2006). *Death 24x a second*. Reaktion Books.

Parr, C. (2012). *FutureLearn picks league table stars for debut line-up*. https://www.timeshighereducation.com/futurelearn-picks-league-table-stars-for-debut-line-up/422182.article

Pelz, B. (2010). (My) three principles of effective online pedagogy. *Journal of Asynchronous Learning Networks, 14*(1), 103–116.

Serdyukov, P. (2015). Does online education need a special pedagogy? *Journal of Computing and Information Technology, 23*(1), 61–74.

Shi, L., Cristea, A. I., Toda, A. M., & Oliveira, W. (2019). Social engagement versus learning engagement an exploratory study of futurelearn learners. In *2019 IEEE 14th international conference on intelligent systems and knowledge engineering (ISKE)* (pp. 476-483). https://doi.org/10.1109/ISKE47853.2019.9170438

Sontag, S. (1996, February 25). The decay of cinema. *The New York Times*, Section 6, 12.

Steele, J., Holbeck, R., & Mandernach, J. (2019). Defining effective online pedagogy. *Journal of Instructional Research, 8*(2), 5–8.

Steinberg, S. R. (2012). Critical pedagogy and cultural studies research: Bricolage in action. *Counterpoints, 422*, 230–254.

Swinnerton, B., Hotchkiss, S., & Morris, N. P. (2017). Comments in MOOCs: Who is doing the talking and does it help? *Journal of Computer Assisted Learning*, (33), 51–64. https://doi.org/10.1111/jcal.12165

Tathahira, T. (2020). Promoting students' critical thinking through online learning in higher education: Challenges and strategies. *Englisia: Journal of Language, Education and Humanities, 8*(1), 79–92.

Williams, T. (2022, November 30). "Deal done" for global university systems to buy FutureLearn. *Times Higher Education*. https://www.timeshighereducation.com/news/deal-done-global-university-systems-buy-futurelearn

Part 3
Challenges and opportunities in adaptation

7 Designing a history course for online and face-to-face delivery

'The Australian experience'

Michael Kilmister, Kate Ariotti and James Bennett

Introduction

This chapter examines two interrelated challenges likely familiar to educators working in the 'post' COVID-19 pandemic university where digitally enhanced practice has a greater presence than before 2020. The first challenge is translating face-to-face teaching to online; the second is designing learning that appeals to students from a wide range of backgrounds while ensuring core disciplinary concepts are still taught and assessed. This chapter explores these challenges through a case study of a large first-year survey course at the University of Newcastle, Australia: The Australian Experience. Across the period 2018–2019, the authors were tasked with translating the course from face-to-face to online delivery – while simultaneously enhancing the on-campus version – as part of the University's plan to reinvigorate its Bachelor of Arts (the 'BA Online'). While each course in the BA Online ran parallel to its face-to-face counterpart, the Australian Experience was distinct due to its size and the makeup of its cohort, predominantly comprised of Teacher Education students who had uneven experiences of History education at the secondary school level. In other words, most students were 'conscripts,' not History students by choice.

Teaching Australia's past to university students who do not want to pursue a career in the field of History poses distinct challenges. Students' attitudes towards the subject are informed by their experiences in school. Australian secondary school students report being 'bored' in History classes and experiencing "narrow historical and educational approaches" from teachers sometimes not trained in the discipline (Clark, 2009, p. 758). The nation's secondary schools are experiencing declining enrolments in non-compulsory History subjects, suggesting young people increasingly perceive the subject to be less relevant to their futures (Cairnes & Garrard, 2023). Creating teaching that challenges these negative views of the discipline is an increasingly urgent task. Crotty (2024) suggests History departments in Australia, which are currently experiencing "a sharpening decline in staff numbers and an alarming decline in enrolments" (p. 523), might find respite by teaching in the programs of other disciplines. The reach of History can also be extended by digital offerings, for online learning can increase access to higher education (Moloney & Okley, 2010).

DOI: 10.4324/9781003505785-10

There is surprisingly little literature on designing effective asynchronous online learning.[1] This chapter helps to address this shortcoming through a case study in translating large class teaching in History for asynchronous delivery while maintaining the face-to-face mode. The chapter will address these overlapping topics through a co-authored reflection from the course coordinators – James coordinated the face-to-face mode and Kate the online version – and the learning designer (Michael), who collaborated closely with the teaching team. These reflections will underscore the value of engaging in collaborative discussions and curriculum design processes with students and colleagues, as well as developing interactive, student-centred learning activities that balance the development of skills with core content knowledge. The chapter will first explain the context of the course and the rationale for its redesign, followed by an overview of the collaboration that underpinned the curricula redesign. The operationalisation of learning design decisions and how students experienced the redesigned course in both the in-person and online formats will be illustrated by examples and student feedback. The chapter closes with implications for History programs.

About the course

The Australian Experience is the University's flagship History course, running continuously for over two decades.[2] It was originally devised by Nancy Cushing and offered initially only at the University's satellite campus at Ourimbah, located halfway between Newcastle and Sydney. As a small commuter campus where first classes commenced in 1989, circumstances made the School of Humanities interdisciplinary from the start, with James' office and the offices of the other historians situated adjacent to staff in the School of Education. This proximity to faculty in cognate disciplines led to productive collaborations, including an interdisciplinary seminar series and a teaching grant that spawned collegial conversations. A culture of interdisciplinarity laid the groundwork for collaborative activities.

At the time of the redesign in 2018, the Australian Experience was simultaneously delivered at three on-campus locations. A first-year survey course, it focuses on the histories of Australia from Aboriginal deep time history to the present day. Topics are updated regularly to accommodate changes in staffing, new scholarships, and developments in the school syllabus, but the following gives a flavour of what is covered over the 12 weeks of the course:

- pre-contact and post-contact Aboriginal society, including relations between Indigenous and non-Indigenous peoples,
- the British colonisation of Australia and its background,
- development of land use, economy, and political systems,
- the nation's involvement in war in the 20th century,
- social and cultural changes including land rights, the Stolen Generations, and reconciliation.

Interwoven into these topics are the skills used by historians in the practice of their craft, for example, source analysis. While convened by a single member of staff at each location, the course was also team-taught by Australianists in the discipline, with each member of the team giving a lecture most related to their expertise. Team teaching predated the redesign. Apart from reducing the workload for the course coordinator, team teaching can facilitate learning by exposing students to 'experts' (Yanamandram & Noble, 2006). Having different voices at the lectern talking to their expertise also afforded opportunities to promote upper-year electives and identify pathways to further study or vocational outcomes.

For 2019 (the year of this case study), the Australian Experience attracted almost 700 students in a single semester and across all modes of delivery; it continues to attract a similar enrolment. This makes it the largest History course offered by the university. The course can accommodate these large numbers by being delivered concurrently across two campuses and in the online mode. It attracts enrolments from over 20 programs, including a significant number of overseas exchange students; the majority of students are from two Bachelor of Education degrees for whom this is a compulsory course. This is due to the state's accrediting body for school teachers, the NSW Education Standards Authority, which requires pre-service teachers to take a series of courses associated with 'key learning areas' in the Australian Curriculum, including History. Students enrolled in the Bachelor of Education programs encounter the course in the first semester of their first year, which means staff on the course need to establish the significance of learning Australian History in the context of their broader studies and professional training (Ford et al., 2019).

Navigating the challenges

The makeup and size of the cohort make for unique challenges from a learning design perspective. Staff observations and surveys of students in the course have revealed their preference for learning experiences beyond the traditional lecture-tutorial model (Kilmister et al., 2017). Above all, students were looking for a structured, scaffolded learning experience and the prioritisation of core concepts and competencies directly mapped to their studies and employability. Beyond attitudes, the cohort often enters higher education with lower tertiary entrance scores compared to their counterparts at Group of Eight institutions,[3] creating a demand for academic skills support, particularly during the first year of study. Compounding the need for additional support is the proportion of students enrolled in the course from underrepresented backgrounds. The university has high enrolments of mature-aged students and students from low socio-economic, first-generation, or other disadvantaged backgrounds. These groups of students are underrepresented in Australian higher education and are more likely to experience educational disadvantage due to several factors, including missing the social and cultural knowledge to navigate university-level study (Patfield et al., 2022). The team recognised the opportunity to redesign the course as part of the BA Online project, which offered a means to better address the learning challenges these students faced and to make scheduled teaching more productive and enjoyable for colleagues and students alike.

Collaboration was vital for addressing these complexities. Michael was brought on early in the redesign process (late-2018) to advise on the redesign of the course, especially with respect to online learning design. He had his own personal experience with the course, both as a trainee teacher at the university and as a tutor and marker for several years. Michael drew on this long association to inform his role in the project: a critical friend who fostered a flexible dialogic approach between stakeholders. He also brought with him awareness of developments across the BA Online, to ensure the Australian Experience would align with teaching and assessment decisions elsewhere in the program. The authors worked together closely in the early stages to 'onboard' critical stakeholders. Their aim was to develop a structured, time-sensitive, and iterative curriculum design process that maximised colleagues' autonomy while ensuring consistency of the student experience across the different locations where the course was offered.

One of the first steps in their collaborative approach was to convene a meeting with the School of Education, which was accredited and primarily responsible for delivering the university's teacher-education program. This meeting was to identify their requirements. Alongside building assessment and study skills literacy that would serve students across the degree, requirements included students being conversant with key historical concepts and skills like analysing sources and evidence, developing empathetic understanding of the past, and to construct and communicate logical arguments.

Following this meeting, Kate and Michael organised a workshop with the permanent History teaching team to constructively align the course. This involved discussing and co-designing the course outline, the learning outcomes, the scope of the content, and assessment. To ensure constructive alignment (Biggs, 1996), summative assessments and due dates were made identical or equivalent across all modes of delivery. These were a set of learning exercises on the learning management system (LMS), an essay plan task, a major essay, and an end-of-semester test that incorporated multiple choice questions alongside short answer and longer form responses. The synchronicity in the assessment design ensured equivalency of assessment experiences and efficiencies, including the ability for assignment information and support to be duplicated across delivery locations.

Given the needs and motivations of the student cohort were a major driver of the redesign, it was decided early in the design process to hire a student partner. In alignment with the principle of recognising and rewarding partnership contributions (Healey et al., 2014), Kate and James successfully applied for an internal Teaching Investment Grant to employ a student to consultatively develop a set of week-by-week learning resources. The student partner brought to this role the perspective of having been a former student in the course and was also studying a postgraduate degree in Education. Being a postgraduate, better placed to engage with this work when the course design and development was occurring, that is, outside semester time. The partner led on creating interactive and student-centred experiences in scheduled learning sessions, with the authors periodically reviewing and offering feedback. This collaboration led to the development of different activities to complement discussions of the readings, including discussion questions, cloze passage activities, and timelines. The activities were also designed to be adaptable to a wide audience to enable Teacher Education students to draw on them in their future teaching.

In the interests of sustainable learning design and parity of experience regardless of delivery mode, the learning materials were adapted for the online version. An example will illustrate this design decision. In Week 6 of the course, which covers the federation of the Australian colonies and the new nation's immigration anxieties, students read articles on immigration policy including the dictation test immigration officials administered to immigrants at their discretion in the early 20th century. The intent of the test was to prohibit the entry of people considered 'undesirable.' Students took an example dictation test and discussed their experience and results in a discussion board. (They generally concluded they would not be admitted into Australia under this test!) For the in-person classroom, the activity was the basis of a small-group or whole-class discussion. This example demonstrates that the activities in either mode were usually identical in design but, as anticipated, were experienced differently.

Designing the online course

Like other courses in the BA Online, the online version of the Australian Experience was to run on FutureLearn and was split into four 'modules' comprised of 3 weeks, with 12 weeks of taught content in total (see Chapter 1). The recommended workload matched the face-to-face version (10 hours each week): students were expected to spend 3 hours engaging with the structured online activities and 7 hours on self-directed study. Content was released weekly to ensure that students were not overwhelmed and would progress at a pre-determined pace, which would also maximise interaction in the discussion boards. However, weekly content remained accessible for 'catch up' and revision purposes. Modules were given titles intended to encapsulate the main theme that cohered the module:

1. 'Great South Land: Introducing Australian History' – covers pre-contact Aboriginal societies through to the end of convict transportation in the mid-19th century.
2. 'Forging a Nation' – from the gold rushes during the mid-19th century to federation of the separate colonies in 1901.

3. 'Division and Defence' – takes the course through the world wars up to the end of the 1950s.
4. 'Global Australia' – from the 1960s to the present day.

The modularised structure was mirrored in the face-to-face version. The content for these modules was drawn from the face-to-face course – mainly its lecture notes, the textbook and the tutorial lesson plans and resources. Michael supported the team to organise content into sequences of meaningful learning activities designed to help students meet the intended learning outcomes for the week. Online lectures were broken into separate topics or themes, allowing discussions of set readings and other activities to happen in context rather than occurring in a tutorial following the lecture. The design applied Laurillard's (2012) Conversational Framework and her concept of 'learning types,' which describe the learning process.[4] In practice, this meant the authors created a 'storyboard,' breaking weekly content into activities comprised of consecutive learning 'steps,' for example, text articles supported by archival images, video, quizzes, and discussions (see Figure 7.1). It is relevant to note that fitting all learning types into the curriculum, or 'variety for variety's sake,' was not the goal. As Laurillard (2007) clarifies, the learning variety afforded by the Conversation Framework engages the

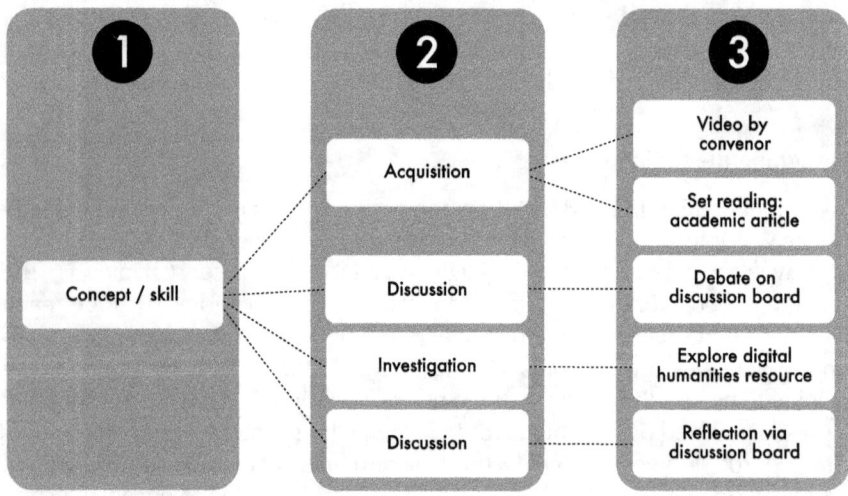

Figure 7.1 Three-stage example of how the authors used the Conversational Framework: (1) core concept or skill, constructively aligned to the learning outcomes; (2) learning types that support students to learn the concept or skill; and (3) how the learning types are experienced by students. This process was documented on spreadsheet software, which acted as a digital storyboard and project management tool. Note: labels in each column are intended to be read vertically, from top to bottom, that is, students would engage with the activities sequentially.

"student explicitly in tasks that elicit the kind of cognitive activity it takes to learn that idea, concept or skill" (p. 168). To ensure consistency, Michael met each guest lecturer to introduce them to the learning design methodology and co-design their week of the course.

Video served multiple purposes in the online course. A systematic review of videos in higher education finds several advantages, including allowing students to control their cognitive load and to fit learning around their other commitments (Noetel et al., 2021). Informed by good practice, videos were generally restricted to less than 10-minutes in length.[5] Topics that were turned into videos were selected deliberately to leverage a lecturer's expertise, enliven a 'dry' topic, or to utilise rich archival imagery to vividly illustrate the content. Studies have demonstrated that teacher enthusiasm in video lectures has a positive effect on student engagement, self-efficacy, and performance (Huangfu et al., 2022), and multimedia that presents words and pictures simultaneously are more effective for learning (Noetel et al., 2021). Short videos from Kate were also embedded at the beginning of each module to provide an overview of what students could expect over the next few weeks.[6] It was intended for these videos to demonstrate the teaching team's commitment to guiding students through the material and 'checking in' at key moments rather than just letting them 'muddle through.' Indeed, videos featuring the teaching team – including interview-style conversations and set pieces to camera – were essential for establishing instructor presence because there were no synchronous weekly sessions. Greater instructor presence via video is supported by research on online and blended learning, which finds it has a positive impact on retention and learning motivation (Beege et al., 2023).

Designing the face-to-face course

Learning variety and the scaffolded approach students experienced online was also a feature of the teaching in the face-to-face version of the course. While scheduled learning time remained unchanged from previous years (2-hour lecture; 1-hour tutorial over 12 weeks), changes were made to accommodate more interactivity. Many students fear taking History survey courses as they expect to have to sit and listen to long lectures (Hoover, 2006). As such, lectures in the course already had a history of featuring documentary films and other video clips to diversify the delivery of content and concepts (Kilmister et al., 2017). Before the redesign, each lecture was comprised of two major topics, a product of the 2-hour lectures – the first topic of the week would be presented for 50 minutes, then a 15-minute break followed by the next topic. The presentation of each topic typically followed a familiar formula: an initial overview including background and context, then discussion of major debates, key events, actors, and themes, and a conclusion linking the topic to the overall course and/or assessment regimen. To this, the lectures were enhanced with new modalities that enabled a more 'lectorial-style' approach, including live interactive polling and quizzes. While polling activities increase engagement, enliven lectures, and enhance learning (Sedghi et al., 2021), in the Australian Experience they offered instantaneous feedback to gauge students' understanding of key concepts. For example, in Week 6, the lecture began with a series of polled questions to ascertain students' knowledge of Federation and to act as a conversation starter. This activity was replicated in the asynchronous mode.

The co-designed learning resources became the central structure for the 50-minute group tutorials,[7] which were rebranded 'learning labs.' Inspired by the idea of social laboratories and their enhanced emphasis on experiential study (Hassan, 2014), the learning labs moniker was selected to represent a shift away from the traditional History seminar format based on the Socratic method and towards more active, collaborative teaching. The sets of resources for the learning lab sessions – which were designated as 'worksheets' – were both a lesson plan for tutors and a tangible study resource for students. For accessibility, they were formatted as plain documents and available for download from the LMS in advance of the week's learning. Rather than devoting the 1 hour tutorial time to Socratic discussions, the discussion of readings was compressed or utilised as a means for skills development. This new emphasis allowed the integration of exercises such as a weekly pop quiz and academic referencing practice. Designing content to include embedded support is critical for underrepresented students who may not have the confidence, sense of deserving, or time to request support (O'Shea et al., 2017). The variety of learning modalities also catered to diverse learning styles, from those learners who prefer individual classwork to those who like lively debate. Overall, the new approach provided implicit feedback on skills development relevant to assessment, something that had not really been possible with the previous tutorial model.

Reflections

Although further research is needed to determine whether the redesign met the aim of supporting students enrolled in non-History programs, trends in course evaluation data suggest a highly positive impact on the student experience. The online cohort was asked to respond to an optional survey. In response to an optional evaluation survey across the period 2020–2024, 92% of respondents (*n* = 39) either 'strongly agreed' or 'agreed' that learning materials used an 'appropriate mix of text, videos, and interactive features.'[8] The videos were similarly well received, with 90% strongly agreeing or agreeing they were 'informative and engaging.' Trends in answers to an open response question – "what were the best aspects/favourite part of this course?" – suggest target student groups benefitted from the changes. Students remarked positively on ungraded quizzes, with one noting they "forced me to complete the readings, which is something I struggle with because I am more of a hands-on, visual learner." They also appreciate the balance of multimedia texts: "The readings that were small articles, videos and pictures were really helpful to shape my understanding, as I sometimes lose meaning in texts." The coherency of the course, including the option for students to move largely at their own pace and interact in the discussion boards, were singled out in some responses. However, due to institutional restrictions on reporting routine evaluation survey data externally, it is only possible to report generalisable trends for the face-to-face course. Numerous students commented positively on the learning labs, especially the value of quizzes to track learning progress. The value of the changes to all modes of the course was recognised by a competitive institution-wide 'Educator Innovation and Impact Award' in 2019.

Developing a sense of community was critical to the success of the online course. It is well understood in the literature that educators' engagement in asynchronous discussions plays a crucial role in shaping students' learning outcomes (Xie & Correia, 2024), especially for Teacher Education students who strongly value social and caring pedagogies (Cain et al., 2024). In the Australian Experience, students received regular reminders from Kate to engage with the material and contribute to discussions within the 7-day period between one week's content opening and release of the next.[9] Kate spent approximately 30 minutes daily from Monday to Friday responding to comments and questions, and monitoring student progress. She found her input generated the most interaction when she extended conversations and learning or added relevant anecdotes. Some sensitive or surprising topics, for example, the internment of enemy 'aliens' in Australia during the First World War, generated more engagement than others – also a common experience in face-to-face teaching – and required extra monitoring or input. While the literature argues open-ended prompts generate higher-order responses (Xie & Correia, 2024), the authors found presenting too many prompts resulted in reduced engagement compared to discussions focused on one or two prompts.

Engaging a student partner to co-design learning activities was innovative in the authors' context. Nonetheless, there were perhaps opportunities to open the possibilities of partnership. According to Bovill and Bulley's (2011) ladder of student participation, students were given control of a prescribed area of the curriculum design in the Australian Experience. There are more 'steps' in the ladder, however, including 'negotiating' the curriculum in partnership with students. Given an aim of the redesign was to meet the diverse needs of the students, further pedagogic consultancy opportunities could have yielded additional benefits. However, the degree of partnership must depend on contextual factors. In this case study, a compact development timeline outside semester time reduced opportunities to engage undergraduates. Healey et al. (2014) stress Bovill and Bulley's ladder is not for determining the quality of the partnership but for exploring practice. Nichol et al. (2023) find student partnership in online learning improved the student experience, but advise there needs to be structure to support this activity to avoid tokenism. In the authors' redesign, temporary funding was needed to employ a student consultant representative of the wider cohort and to overcome the lack of partnership infrastructure. As Healey et al. (2014) conclude, it is not possible in every context to adopt partnership. However, wrestling with the challenges and exploring the potential partnership opportunities is a worthwhile enterprise for strengthening the student experience.

Just as robust scholarship demands a historian to draw on multiple sources and ask questions of those sources from different angles, multiple perspectives are essential to good curriculum design. The high degree of consultation discussed here is arguably unusual for the History discipline. Historians are traditionally not trained to research and write collaboratively (Chesterton, 2014), nor do they usually open their classrooms to collaborators, especially from outside the discipline (Parham, 2013). While History has proven instructional traditions that can effectively translate to online learning environments – such as small group exercises where students analyse primary sources (Irving, 2021) – the knowledge and experience with technologies is often missed, requiring input of professional staff with relevant expertise. By providing "full-course design support, professional development opportunities, content development, learning management system training and support, and multimedia creation in partnership with faculty experts" (Hodges et al., 2020, para. 15), professional staff play a crucial role in developing online learning.

Conclusion

This chapter has discussed how the authors used the opportunity offered by a strategic teaching and learning project to simultaneously enhance engagement in a face-to-face course and translate this design for asynchronous delivery. Although creating online learning is labour intensive, the process was made more sustainable by utilising the curriculum of the face-to-face version as 'the spine' of the course. A more student-centred teaching approach was enabled through consultatively identifying core competencies and priorities, enabling collaborative design mechanisms, and embedding activities that responded not only to student interests and needs but also taught them *how to learn* in History and developed their teaching practice. As evidenced by student feedback and recognition, the aims of the redesign were largely met. The project's success reflects both the value of engaging diverse voices to establish a collective sense of direction for curriculum design and offering flexibility in how students engage in History courses. The authors hope this chapter prompts History programs to consider asynchronous online education and the flexibility it can afford students as a potential answer to falling enrolments.

Notes

1 Exceptions are teaching with digital history (Guiliano, 2022), coverage of broad principles and use of different technologies (Stein & MacLeod, 2023), flipped

learning (Sendiziuk & Buchanen, 2018), and synchronous online modes (Shannahan & Fredericks, 2022).
2. The course was originally devised as a single-campus course only and evolved as a multi-campus offering over time.
3. The Group of Eight consists of Australia's most research-intensive universities.
4. There are six learning types: acquisition, investigation, practice, discussion, collaboration, and production.
5. A study of 6.9 million video-watching sessions shows that student engagement steadily declines when watching videos longer than 6 minutes (Guo et al., 2014).
6. Welcome videos are now embedded in every week in the face-to-face and online course. Comments in evaluation data reveal this is a welcomed change.
7. At UON, tutorials typically accommodate student numbers up to 30.
8. This is an ongoing survey implemented alongside the university-wide course evaluation surveys intended to gather student views particular to online delivery. The data covers the period 2020–2024. This data can be reported as it was approved by the Research Ethics Committee (QA186).
9. Reminders were in the form of messaging on FutureLearn and email.

References

Beege, M., Schroeder, N. L., Heidig, S., Rey, G. D., & Schneider, S. (2023). The instructor presence effect and its moderators in instructional video: A series of meta-analyses. *Educational Research Review, 41.* https://doi.org/10.1016/j.edurev.2023.100564

Biggs, J. (1996). Enhancing teaching through constructive alignment. *Higher Education, 32*(3), 347–364.

Bovill, C., & Bulley, C. J. (2011). A model of active student participation in curriculum design: Exploring desirability and possibility. In C. Rust (Ed.), *Improving student learning. global theories and local practices: Institutional, disciplinary and cultural variations* (pp. 176–188). The Oxford Centre for Staff and Learning Development.

Cain, M., Sheehan, H., & Taouk, S. (2024). 'It doesn't really like we've had the chance to really connect': The crucial need for social presence in fully asynchronous teacher education. *Teaching and Teacher Education, 152*, 1–10. https://doi.org/10.1016/j.tate.2024.104789

Cairnes, R., & Garrard, K. A. (2023). 'Learning from history is something that is important for the future': Why Australian students think history matters. *Policy Futures in Education, 22*(3), 369–382. https://doi.org/10.1177/14782103231177615

Chesterton, B. A. (2014, October 1). Historians writing collaboratively. *Perspectives on History.* https://www.historians.org/perspectives-article/historians-writing-collaboratively-october-2014/

Clark, A. (2009). Teaching the nation's story: Comparing public debates and classroom perspectives on history education in Australia and Canada. *Journal of Curriculum Studies, 41*(6), 745–762. https://doi.org/10.1080/00220270903139635

Crotty, M. (2024). Addressing the decline of academic history in Australia. *History Australia, 21*(4), 522–525. https://doi.org/10.1080/14490854.2024.2415501

Ford, M., Bennett, J., & Kilmister, M. (2019). Challenging Anzac myths in tertiary teaching: Engaging preservice teachers. (2019). *Journal of University Teaching and Learning Practice, 16*(5). https://doi.org/10.53761/1.16.5.5

Guiliano, J. (2022). *A primer for teaching digital history: Ten design principles.* Duke University Press.

Guo, P. J., Kim, J., & Rubin, R. (2014). How video production affects student engagement: An empirical study of MOOC videos. In *L@S '14: Proceedings of the first ACM conference on learning @ scale conference* (pp. 41–50). https://doi.org/10.1145/2556325.2566239

Hassan, Z. (2014). *The social labs revolution: A new approach to solving our most complex challenges*. Berrett-Koehler Publishers.

Healey, M., Flint, A., & Harrington, K. (2014). *Engagement through partnership: Students as partners in learning and teaching in higher education*. HEA.

Hodges, C., Moore, S., Lockee, B., Trust, T., & Bond, A. (2020). The difference between emergency remote teaching and online learning. *Educause Review, 27*. https://er.educause.edu/articles/2020/3/the-difference-between-emergency-remote-teaching-and-online-learning

Hoover, D. S. (2006). Popular culture in the classroom: Using audio and video clips to enhance survey classes. *The History Teacher, 39*(4), 467–478. https://doi.org/10.2307/30037067

Huangfu, Q., Li, Hong, Tang, S., Wang, J., Liu, Q., & Chen, G. (2022). How teacher enthusiasm affects students' learning of chemistry declarative knowledge in video lectures. *Chemistry Education Research and Practice, 23*, 898–912. https://doi.org/10.1039/D2RP00095D

Irving, H. (2021, February 3). Teaching history online in lockdown. *Social History Society*. https://socialhistory.org.uk/shs_exchange/teaching-history-online-in-lockdown/

Kilmister, M., Bennett, J., Ford, M., & Debenham, J. (2017). Treading on sacred ground? Confronting the Anzac myth in higher education. *History Compass, 15*, e12395. https://doi.org/10.1111/hic3.12395

Laurillard, D. (2007). Pedagogical forms for mobile learning: Framing research questions. In N. Pachler (Ed.), *Mobile learning: Towards a research agenda* (pp. 153–175). WLE Centre.

Laurillard, D. (2012). *Teaching as a design science: Building pedagogical patterns for learning and technology*. Routledge.

Moloney, J. F., & Okley, B. (2010). Scaling online education: Increasing access to higher education. *Online Learning, 14*(1), 55–70. https://doi.org/10.24059/olj.v14i1.1639

Nichol, D., Mulholland, K., Anderson, A., Taylor, S., & Davies, J. (2023). 'How was it for you?' The impacts of student-staff partnerships in developing online teaching and learning. *Journal of Further and Higher Education, 47*(9), 1276–1287. https://doi.org/10.1080/0309877X.2023.2241393

Noetel, M., Griffith, S., Delaney, O., Sanders, T., Parker, P., del Pozo Cruz, B., & Lonsdale, C. (2021). Video improves learning in higher education: A systematic review. *Review of Educational Research, 91*(2), 204–236. https://doi.org/10.3102/0034654321990713

O'Shea, S., May, J., Stone, C., & Delahunty, J. (2017). *First-in-family students, university experience and family life: Motivations, transitions and participation*. Palgrave Macmillan.

Parham, V. (2013). Learn something new everyday: One history professor's journey through online education. *Interface: The Journal of Education, Community and Values, 12*, 19–24.

Patfield, S., Gore, J., & Weaver, N. (2022). On 'being first:' The case for first-generation status in Australian higher education equity policy. *The Australian Educational Researcher, 49*, 23–41. https://doi.org/10.1007/s13384-020-00428-2

Sedghi, N., Limniou, M., Al-Nuiamy, W., Sandall, I. Al Ataby, A., & Duret, D. (2021, January). Enhancing the engagement of large cohorts using live interactive polling and feedback. *Developing Academic Practice*, 31–50. https://doi.org/10.3828/dap.2021.6

Sendiziuk, P., & Buchanen, T. C. (2018). Delivery: Relics of the past? Rethinking the history lecture and tutorial. In J. Clark & A. Nye (Eds.), *Teaching the discipline of history in an age of standards* (pp. 89–111). Springer.

Shannahan, J., & Fredericks, V. (2022). Transitioning into and improving online history teaching. *Journal of Classics Teaching, 23*(46), 138–146. https://10.1017/S2058631022000046

Stein, S. K, & MacLeod, M. (Eds.). (2023). *Teaching and learning history online: A guide for college instructors*. Routledge.

Xie, J., & Correia, A.-P. (2024). The effects of instructor participation in asynchronous online discussions on student performance: A systematic review. *British Journal of Educational Technology, 55*, 71–89. https://doi.org/10.1111/bjet.13350

Yanamandram, V., & Noble, G. (2006). Student experiences and perceptions of team-teaching in a large undergraduate class. *Journal of University Teaching & Learning Practice, 3*(1). https://handles.figshare.com/10779/uow.r.jutlp_vol3_iss1_6

8 Teaching challenging material
Technological affordances of staggered asynchronous online learning

Jessica Ford

Introduction

In the week prior to a face-to-face class on online pornography, I gave the students in my third-year Digital Cultures course a warning of sorts. I let them know that in next week's class, we would be discussing online pornography as a kind of digital labour, through which we could interrogate a range of issues: precarious labour, spreadability of digital media, individualisation of media diets, global versus local working conditions, and content ownership. I stated that although we would not be watching pornographic material or discussing personal consumption, we would be approaching pornography as a kind of digital sex work, taking the approach that sex work is work. This is not a particularly controversial position in Australia, where sex work is largely decriminalised; however, the production and distribution of pornography largely remain prohibited by law (Stardust, 2016, p. 1; Bartle, 2023). Despite the measured and delicate classroom approach, adhering to best practice on how to "lay the groundwork" for "controversial topics" (Burkstrand-Reid et al., 2011, p. 679), only about half of the enrolled students attended the so-called 'online porn' week. Although those who showed up were engaged, thoughtful, and productive, the mass 'opt-out' was not the ideal pedagogical scenario. My experience recalls Keith Barton and Alan McCully's argument that the "benefits of engaging students in controversial issues discussion" can easily "deteriorate into unproductive free-for-alls on the one hand, or thinly veiled recitations with occasional student comments on the other – and neither is likely to lead to the benefits envisioned for open discussion" (2007, p. 13). This research and my own experience were front of mind when approaching the design and delivery of media and cultural studies courses for a wholly online Bachelor of Arts in Australia.

Media and cultural studies are growing and changing fields and as such there is a consistent evolution of theoretical and conceptual approaches. What is considered a controversial topic today may no longer be so in just a year or two, thanks to emerging scholarship that demystifies how we use and understand emerging technologies and their impact. The same can be said of learning technologies with new tools, platforms, and environments

DOI: 10.4324/9781003505785-11

entering the already crowded marketplace. As such with change being one of the only constants, we need to focus not on the technologies themselves, which are being sold to us with increasing fervour and promises of radically reformulating learning and teaching but rather concentrate on what technology allows us to do. Here, I work through the opportunities and affordances of asynchronous digital learning to highlight how flexibility, asynchronicity, physical anonymity, and self-directed learning are particularly useful for exploring sensitive topics. These affordances are deliberately generic and do not belong to specific tools but rather accessible across many digitally enabled educational tools.

In media and cultural studies, we often grapple with the social and cultural impacts of media developments, such as the relationship between sexting and image-based abuse, hook-up apps and dating cultures, and representational and presentational media. Central to arts and humanities university teaching are challenging and personal topics, such as queerness, digital intimacy, and representations of sex, gender, and violence. These are key topics for the classroom and reflect contemporary research concerns and cutting-edge theoretical interventions. However, they can also be confronting for students to tackle in a classroom setting, often requiring significant time to unpack and guidance to find the appropriate language for discussion. This kind of "framing" is essential to ensure that the classroom engagement is productive, respectful, and appropriate (see Barton & McCully, 2007; Thompson, 2020; Paasonen, 2016). However, as a result, considerable classroom time is occupied with troubleshooting and talking around sensitivities and pre-existing biases rather than dealing with the nuances of the object of study. Despite the challenges that these kinds of topics elicit, as K. Cebula et al. found "students do wish to learn about emotionally challenging topics" (2022, p. 1132). I suggest that the staggered asynchronous delivery afforded by online learning provides a unique opportunity for tackling difficult topics that include sensitive content.

Drawing on my experience teaching theories of social media and digital culture using the online learning platform FutureLearn as part of the Bachelor of Arts Online, I will outline the technological opportunities of this delivery format. Using case studies drawn from my own teaching practice, I outline the advantages of online learning for teaching media discourses on online pornography, sexting, and mediated violence, thinking through the pedagogical implications for accessibility, equity and diversity, and media literacy. I deliberately focus on the teaching of controversial or sensitive topics that challenge the students' existing frameworks and knowledges to highlight how online learning environments offer unique opportunities for the kinds of emergent yet challenging topics prominent in media and cultural studies. As Siân Bayne et al. note, "online teaching can enable learning that is not only connected and 'real' but also, depending on pedagogical approach, has the potential to be of higher quality than some face-to-face modes" (2020, p. 134). This chapter focuses on the specific affordances that we can take advantage of in the design stage, which allow for a dynamic student experience that grapples with tricky topics.

Learning online in the digital age

'Online learning' encompasses a wide range of teaching technologies and learning experiences, including virtual classrooms, threaded discussion, and self-directed learning. For this chapter, I am concentrating on my use of the modularised step-based asynchronous learning platform FutureLearn. FutureLearn moves students through a series of 'steps,' which included short 'lecture style' videos, written articles, links to external information, and interactive learning activities, including research tasks, reflective practice, and critical evaluation of sources. The platform and approach required that content to fully developed and input before the start of the teaching period; thus, decisions were predictive rather than responsive. As a result, I relied heavily on established online learning best practice and scholarship to guide the decision-making. Although modifications were possible during and after the delivery period, the process and number of stakeholders meant that adapting assets in the flow of teaching was more complicated than in a traditional classroom setting. While prioritising the development of high-quality online learning assets inevitably means a higher quality experience for the students, it is also less easily adjustable. Investing in the opportunities of online-specific learning environments often means eschewing malleability in terms of delivery in favour of planning, design, and procedure. In other words, considerable time is invested on the front end to create high-quality assets that need to be reusable and enduring. However, I argue that for the teaching of challenging material, the affordances outweigh the limitations.

Our university students are what Marc Prensky might have called "digital natives" (2001), and although this term is disputed (Smith et al., 2020), students today use digital technologies in their everyday lives and are ever more comfortable with mediated forms of engagement and learning (Baglione & Nastanski, 2007, p. 140). As such, we can and do assume a relatively high level of technological literacy, but this does not always translate to digital, media, or critical literacies. In other words, students often know how to use devices but are also less skilled at finding sources, evaluating them, and locating them within broader histories. There can be a tendency to conflate fluency with technologies with complex comprehension of the content that is delivered by those technologies; however, it is essential that the content, rather than the technology drives curriculum design. For Erika E. Smith et al., "Our learners may not be as digitally literate or inherently skilled as we perceive them to be, but the potential affordances offered by the technologies that they prefer or need to use are real" (2020, p. 3). In other words, just because we *can* get students to do something does not mean it is pedagogically motivated. Therefore, I focus here on how the flexibility, asynchronicity, physical anonymity, and self-directed learning of online learning technologies can facilitate curriculum design for difficult and/or challenging topics.

There is no consensus of what constitutes a controversial, sensitive, or difficult topic in university learning and teaching, with what students consider challenging varying considerably. The inability of educators to predict what topics students may find 'triggering' and the context and culture that students bring with them into the classroom has shaped recent pedagogical approaches (Cebula et al., 2022, p. 1121). Notably, trigger warnings have engendered considerable attention in relation to the teaching of sensitive material, both in journalistic (Lukianoff & Haidt, 2015) and academic spaces (Jones et al., 2020; Cebula et al., 2022). As a result, scholarship on how to best teach this material often focuses less on the kinds of topics that can be classified as sensitive and difficult and more on how to best frame your approach (see Barton & McCully, 2007; Thompson, 2020; Paasonen, 2016). Beth Burkstrand-Reid et al., however, offer a useful framework, contending that "controversy" usually arises when topics are "politicised" and "personalised" by students. For Burkstrand-Reid et al., this happens in two ways: first-personalisation where topics are relevant to their direct experience, and second-personalisation, in which topics brush up against students' existing personal values and/or beliefs (2011, pp. 678–679). They suggest "controversy" can arise out of both "diversity" and "lack of diversity" in the classroom because diversity increases the number of perspectives and lived experiences in the room, but a lack of diversity can also lead to homogeneity of thinking where minoritised perspectives are unwelcome (Burkstrand-Reid et al., 2011, p. 679). Arguably, all topics in media and cultural studies are political and personal. Students are indoctrinated and implicated in media and culture well before they attend university and they are increasingly aware of how power, institutions, and ideology shape media and culture. Therefore, further delineation is needed in terms of what constitutes a difficult topic in media and cultural studies, as well as in related disciplines.

Although broad, it is productive to consider topics that may challenge students' pre-existing views of the world or ask them to think about things in different ways. Sara Ahmed might call these "sweaty concepts" whereby the "task is to stay with the difficult, to keep exploring and exposing the difficulty" (2016, p. 13). More specifically, these are topics where the academic, research-informed approach is contrary to or challenges popular media discourse or which centre on activities that are largely deemed private or personal matters not for public discussion. This is particularly evident with topics around mediated sexual relations, which brush up against students' personal experiences (both good and bad). Susanna Paasonen suggests that examining pornography in the classroom can evoke "bodily responses of arousal, surprise, and disgust through sound, image, text, and combinations thereof" (2016, p. 427). Since pornography, sexts, and other forms of mediatised sex and sexual expression are "mostly consumed in private", the classroom "disturb[s] boundaries between the private and public" and involves "a knowing affective attunement and maintenance of classroom atmosphere" (Paasonen, 2016, pp. 427–428). This echoes my own experiences teaching topics like sexting, pornography, queer liberalism, and hook-up apps, whereby much of the media discourse on these phenomena emphasises risk and warns of the potential dangers to users and participants. In contrast, large-scale quantitative and qualitative research takes a more nuanced approach, highlighting the potential affordances of mediated sexual subjecthood and the agency of users more broadly (see Stardust, 2016; McKee et al., 2022). As I will unpack further below, the schism between journalistic and academic approaches to these more sensitive topics can be a fruitful space for student learning.

Scholars often discuss the importance of 'framing' when teaching challenging or controversial material. Framing is particularly important with topics like sex work, mediated sex and violence, and trauma that may press up against students' ethics, values, or life experiences. Burkstrand-Reid et al. suggest that when a topic is "controversial," students may "fall back onto talking points and fixed positions", have "strong emotional feelings" and "be uncomfortable talking", and students with "extreme or idiosyncratic views" can "co-opt a discussion or even a course" (2011, p. 679). In contrast, an asynchronous approach allows for content warnings and support services to be embedded alongside conceptual and theoretical material, enabling students to self-pace and approach with caution (as needed). Numerous scholars, however, have noted trigger warnings are limited as a pedagogical tool, insofar as it can be difficult to predict what will trigger a student (see Thompson, 2020; Cebula et al., 2022). As a result, educators have increasingly moved away from the language of 'safe spaces' with an increased emphasis on brave spaces (Alakoc, 2019; Arao & Clemens, 2023; Mitchell, 2021). For Zoë Brigley Thompson, "the university classroom can never be a safe space, it is a contested one, in which controversial topics can be approached, and oppressive narratives countered, without closing down free speech" (2020, p. 397). If we begin from this assumption, we can start to shift the emphasis away from individual responsibility (for disclosure, safety, and braveness) and consider how the online learning environment can facilitate and embrace difference rather than attempt to flatten it.

The notion of safe versus brave versus contested spaces is largely parsed in terms of traditional in-person classrooms where the politics of passing, disclosing, and outing are at play and have real material consequences. Jasmine Harris notes that "brave space pedagogy is focused on the bravery of self-reflection, individual students can simultaneously acknowledge their own behavior and experiences without extrapolation to the broader social world" (2018, p. 253). In focusing on the comfort or discomfort of individual students in the classroom, brave space rhetoric and protocols risk reifying the centrality of white, well-educated students. As a result, the comfort of white, privileged students becomes the barometer of braveness and the discomfort of marginalised students can become the class content, which of course should never be the objective. An asynchronous staggered online learning environment, however, provides an opportunity for an alternative dynamic that moves away from an emphasis on the safety of spaces and the braveness of students. Online learning allows educators to keep a tighter focus on the week's object of study and ensures that students' discomfort is not weaponised for learning. Proponents of brave spaces often assume that all students come to braveness equally; however, as Harris challenges us to consider, if "students of color refuse to be 'brave' in classroom discussions on inequalities they've personally experienced, and allow themselves and their experiences to be placed on display for others, then are they cowardly?" (Harris, 2018, p. 252). Harris highlights how both safe spaces and brave spaces are raced and gendered.

I suggest that asynchronous online learning does not demand the braveness of the students but rather puts the burden on the educator to develop learning materials that foster a productive approach to sweaty concepts and challenging topics. The tone and tenor of the learning environment is essential when addressing difficult and challenging content (Ndemanu & Davis, 2019; Asbury & Orsborn, 2020). In my experience, I have found that for online courses, this is a matter of curriculum design rather than delivery because framing is not something that happens ad-hoc in the classroom, but rather it is created through creating course materials. Curriculum design and delivery are inextricably intertwined in online learning. As such, here I focus on how to connect elements of curriculum design with best practice in teaching difficult topics. I will unpack how in my teaching certain tricky topics, namely pornography, sexting, and mediated violence, I have utilised the specific opportunities of online learning, including flexibility, asynchronicity, physical anonymity, and self-directed learning.

Linking controversial topics with technological affordances

Different affordances of online learning and teaching technologies come into play with different topics, as each presents its own specific sensitivities. As such, I take a topical approach rather than focusing on courses (sometimes called subjects or units at different institutions). I examine specific 1-week topics taught as part of larger 10- to 12-week units of coursework. In particular, I am focusing on topics that appear as part of upper-level (third year in the Australian system) curriculum, where it is reasonably assumed that students have developed foundational media and digital literacies and are conversant in how to approach their academic work thoughtfully and with nuance. Students come to their academic study of media with a wide range of existing conceptions and knowledges, due to their experience with digital technology both at home and in education settings, which in turn shapes how they understand media as content, technology, industry, and economy. As follows, I will discuss three equally challenging topics in pornography, sexting, and mediated violence, and highlight how various capacities of online teaching were put to work in curriculum design.

Returning to my earlier discussion of my experience of teaching online pornography as digital sex work, I outline how what Stephen L. Baglione and Michael Nastanski call the "physical anonymity" (2007, pp. 104–141) of online learning is particularly useful for this topic. The benefits of physical anonymity for teaching and learning are widely documented and include increased equity (Collins & Berge, 1995; McComb, 1994; Ruberg & Taylor, 1995) and higher participation rates (Hartman et al., 1995). This recalls Andrea Chester and Gillian Gwynne's finding that "online there was no pressure to adhere to the scripts normally governing classroom behavior" (1998, n.p.). I draw here on a week of the course focusing on how digital technologies (at the levels of production, distribution, circulation, and reception) have re-shaped the labour of pornographic performance. To do this, we focused not on content analysis but on dissecting working conditions, the relative value (economic, cultural, and social) of this labour, and the role of digital technologies in reshaping these. In the first step of the week, I include instructions reminding students "to be sincere and respectful in your discussion this week, and use the correct terminology, such as sex worker. I ask you to leave any personal ethical or moral beliefs about pornography aside this week as we explore the topic through a critical, academic lens." This framing is very similar to that of the face-to-face version of the content; however, unlike the in-class offering, online students have the affordance of physical anonymity, which is particularly important for topics that may result in a bodily response (Paasonen, 2016, pp. 427–428). Although there may be some initial affective discomfort in approaching the topic of online pornography and digital sex work, physical anonymity allows students to work through this in their own way, time, and space, rather than in the immediacy of a physical classroom or as per the instructor's and other students' pace. As a result, students reflected thoughtfully about pornographic performers, the value of their labour, and how it has been reshaped by economic, technological, and industrial conditions in the convergence era. Unlike in the face-to-face offering, engagement rates remained consistent throughout this topic with an equivalent number and length of comments when compared to preceding and subsequent weeks.

Educating students who have recently finished secondary school can be a challenging experience. This is not necessarily surprising; as Katrina A. Meyer finds in comparing graduate students' experiences discussing controversial topics in both online and face-to-face learning environments, "younger students were more uncomfortable, more concerned about hurting others' feelings, and less likely to disagree; more mature students were more comfortable talking about controversial topics, less concerned about others' feelings, and more likely to disagree" (2006, p. 184). The learning objectives of secondary school and university are very dissimilar, and as a result students are often challenged to think differently about topics at a tertiary level. This is perhaps most evident in student approaches to the topic of sexting, which sits within a broader module about digital intimacies that highlights how social interactions have evolved in concert with digital technologies. In this topic, we look at the reciprocal relationship between media technologies and communication practices to consider how they are essential to many contemporary interpersonal relations. In Australia, secondary school awareness programs on sexting favour an abstinence-only approach that conflates sexting (the consensual sharing of sexual images) and image-based abuse (the non-consensual and illegal circulation of sexual images with the intent to cause harm) (see Albury et al., 2017; Woodley et al., 2024). This is often the only kind of discussion about sexting that students have encountered in an educational setting, and therefore in my experience, they often unconsciously parrot these perspectives. As a media scholar teaching in a Bachelor of Arts program, I approached the topic of sexting practices to explore issues around the emergence of digital technologies, the social and cultural impact of media, and the shift from representational to presentational media. Broadly speaking, I frame media discourses on sexting through concepts of moral panic, technological determinism, and technopanics, as per recent scholarly inquiry (see Page, 2018). This has always been a challenging and evolving topic to teach in a traditional classroom setting, and designing this content for delivery and engagement in an online environment created its own opportunities and challenges.

The topic of sexting poses unique challenges in the contemporary moment, as students are statistically likely to have personal experience with sexting practices, education programs targeted at prevention, and/or fear-based media campaigns. The most recent Australian National Survey of Secondary Students and Sexual Health found that "87.0% of young people (n = 4,248) reported some engagement in sending or receiving sexually explicit text messages" (Power et al., 2022, p. 64). As such, this is a topic where students' preconceived knowledges are highly likely to be shaped by personal experience and/or secondary school prevention programs. Therefore, initial tasks focus on depersonalising the topic and setting up broader ways of understanding sexting as a cultural and social phenomenon with clear distinctions between sexting and image-based abuse. This week's content focuses on interrogating the distinctions between evidence-based scholarly literature and journalistic media's fear-based, hyperbolic framing of sexting. Rather than telling students about these differences, scaffolded self-driven research tasks allow them to learn and discover this themselves. Instead of prescribing readings, students are asked to find their own sources (with strict caveats in terms of object of study, outlet, geography, and era) and plot them on a collaborative map. I provide a series of carefully scaffolded axes where students can plot sources (both academic and journalistic) as technophobic/technopositive, utopic/dystopic, and sex-positive/negative. This kind of staged research task would likely take most of a 1-hr traditional class, but thanks to the asynchronous learning environment, students can dip in and out as needed, extending the learning and participation. According to Elizabeth Asbury and Georgina Orsborn, "In traditional classroom delivery, students may be required to challenge their own perceptions, which can be overwhelming. E-learning modules offer students a less confrontational environment for acquiring cultural safety skills and knowledge" (2020, p. 23). Much of the learning and teaching literature I draw on focuses on cases where access to face-to-face learning is not possible, highlighting the advantages of online learning in terms of flexibility for geographical distance, unpredictable schedules, and competing obligations (see Burton, 2018); however, I also want to highlight how flexibility offers the opportunity for reflection and meditation. Self-pacing can operate as its own kind of safe space for learning distinct from flipped classroom models that rely on face-to-face engagement alongside online learning.

In a traditional classroom, 'opting out' of a topic requires the student to either decide prior to attending that they do not want to participate or to self-exclude while in class, which is unavoidably an act of disclosure. However, the physical anonymity and flexibility of online asynchronous learning provide more opportunities for stepping away without fully disengaging. Owing to the wholly online step-based approach offered by FutureLearn, students are shepherded through a linear process where they move from one lesson or learning activity to the next – although we know from user data that very few students complete all steps sequentially and/or in one sitting. What is more likely is that students dip in and out, which can be a more productive approach to sweaty concepts and allow for exploration and meditation. This is particularly important when broaching topics of violence in media, both simulated and documented. A range of contemporary media case studies, including Black Lives Matter and #MeToo movements, violence in film and TV, and misogynoir video game culture unavoidably rely on the discussion and interrogation of violence. This includes individualised experiences and examples, as well as systemic analyses of state and institutional violence, which may brush up against students' real experiences. As Lowe and Jones highlight, "The prevalence of sexual and domestic violence in society means that there is a high likelihood that every classroom contains survivors of sexual and/or domestic violence" (2010, p. 1). This is just one example of how trauma can shape students' experiences of sweaty concepts in ways that are not always immediately obvious or visible to educators. The online learning environment allows learners to opt-out, divert, or simply take a break in a way that is not public or publicised.

Unlike the finite and geographically and temporally bound experience of a face-to-face classroom, online learning is at once more ephemeral and more grounded. Students can return to the virtual site of learning as often as they like, revisiting the ideas and pausing when needed. Despite the rigorous scaffolding, the students are ultimately in the driver's seat of their own learning encounters. Student experiences are largely self-paced and individualised, which allows students to "participate when they feel most productive, since they are not bound by the traditional classroom and its regimented times" (Baglione & Nastanski, 2007, p. 141). This is particularly useful when dealing with topics that some students may find challenging or triggering, such as the perpetration of violence and its mediation in both fictional and non-fiction renderings. While in a traditional classroom, "delivery" may be paused to issue content warnings, prepare students, or give those who wish to the opportunity to opt-out, in online delivery, these acts are more easily integrated in the flow of learning, with staggered delivery allowing for a kind of 'choose your own adventure' approach. For instance, when exploring true crime media, students can decide whether to watch the more confronting documentary material or the more satirical mockumentary content. Both paths require similar critical knowledges and foster the same skill development, but they shift the emphasis away from the need for students to be 'brave' and allow them to self-select their preferred or safest path in a private manner. The flexibility of online learning allows for this kind of parallel delivery in ways that face-to-face teaching prohibits, and locates the provision of safety at the level of design.

Conclusion

In centring the capacities of FutureLearn as a staggered asynchronous online learning platform, I was able to remedy and resolve many of the limitations of traditional classroom teaching for addressing and exploring sweaty concepts and challenging topics. The unique difficulties and opportunities of teaching topics like sexting, pornography, hook-up apps, and mediated violence can push against the boundaries of what is considered 'acceptable' or 'serious' topics for tertiary education. I suggest that precisely because of their taboo nature, they are ideally situated to take advantage of the flexibility, responsiveness, and physical anonymity offered by online learning. Although not appropriate for all institutions or students, my experience developing a wide range of courses for the BA Online emphasised the need not just for translation of face-to-face topics for online delivery, but a wholesale re-conceptualisation of what technology could facilitate. As such, this chapter focuses on the affordances that we can take advantage of in the design stage, thinking of design and delivery as one and the same for online learning.

References

Ahmed, S. (2016). *Living a feminist life*. Duke University Press.
Alakoc, B. P. (2019). Terror in the classroom: Teaching terrorism without terrorizing. *Journal of Political Science Education, 15*(2), 218–236. https://doi.org/10.1080/15512169.2018.1470002.
Albury, K., Hasinoff, A. A., & Senft, T. (2017). From media abstinence to media production: Sexting, young people and education. In L. Allen & M. L. Rasmussen (Eds.), *The Palgrave handbook of sexuality education* (pp. 527–545). Palgrave Macmillan.
Arao, B., & Clemens, K. (2023). From safe spaces to brave spaces: A new way to frame dialogue around diversity and social justice. In L. M. Landreman (Ed.), *The art of effective facilitation: Reflections from social justice educators* (pp. 135–150). Routledge.

Asbury, E., & Orsborn, G. (2020). Teaching sensitive topics in an online environment: An evaluation of cultural safety e-learning. *Whitireia Nursing and Health Journal*, (27), 23–31.

Baglione, S. L., & Nastanski, M. (2007). The superiority of online discussion: Faculty perceptions. *Quarterly Review of Distance Education*, 8(2), 139–189.

Bartles, J. (2023, November 21). Producing pornography in Australia – What does the law say? *Sydney Criminal Lawyers*. https://www.sydneycriminallawyers.com.au/blog/producing-pornography-in-australia-what-does-the-law-say/

Barton, K., & McCully, A. (2007). Teaching controversial issues . . . where controversial issues really matter. *Teaching History*, 127, 13–19.

Bayne, S., Evans, P., Ewins, R., Knox, J., & Lamb, J. (2020). *The manifesto for teaching online*. MIT Press.

Burkstrand-Reid, B., Carbone, J., & Hendricks, J. S. (2011). Teaching controversial topics. *Family Court Review*, 49(4), 678–684.

Burton, D. (2018). Distance learning in Creative Arts education: Understanding the benefits of time and distance in the delivery of HE at the Open College of the Arts. *JUICE: Journal of Useful Investigations in Creative Education*, 16(1), 1–19. https://juice-journal.com/2018/10/24/distance-learning-in-creative-arts-education-understanding-the-benefits-of-time-and-distance-in-the-delivery-of-he-at-the-open-college-of-the-arts/

Cebula, K., Macleod, G., Stone, K., & Chan, S. W. Y. (2022). Student experiences of learning about potentially emotionally sensitive topics: Trigger warnings are not the whole story. *Journal of Further and Higher Education*, 46(8), 1120–1134. https://doi.org/10.1080/0309877X.2022.2055449.

Chester, A., & Gwynne, G. (1998). Online teaching: Encouraging collaboration through anonymity. *Journal of Computer-Mediated Communication*, 4(2), JCMC424. https://doi.org/10.1111/j.1083-6101.1998.tb00096.x

Collins, M., & Berge, Z. (1995). Introduction: Computer-mediated communications and the online classroom in higher education. In Z. L. Berge & M. P. Collins (Eds.), *Computer mediated communication and the online classroom: Vol. 2. Higher education* (pp. 1–10). Hampton Press.

Harris, J. L. (2018). Uncomfortable learning: Teaching race through discomfort in higher education. In B. Ahad-Legardy & O. Y. A. Poon (Eds.), *Difficult subjects: Insights and strategies for teaching about race, sexuality, and gender* (pp. 248–265). Routledge.

Hartman, K., Neuwirth, C. M., Kiesler, S., Cochran, C., Palmquist, M., & Zubrow, D. (1995). Patterns of social interaction and learning to write: Some effects of network technologies. In Z. L. Berge & M. P. Collins (Eds.), *Computer mediated communication and the online classroom: Vol. 2. Higher education* (pp. 47–78). Hampton Press.

Jones, P. J., Bellet, B. W., & McNally, R. J. (2020). Helping or harming? The effect of trigger warnings on individuals with trauma histories. *Clinical Psychological Science*, 85(5), 905–917.

Lowe, P., & Jones, H. (2010). Teaching and learning sensitive topics. *Enhancing Learning in the Social Sciences*, 2(3), 1–7. https://doi.org/10.11120/elss.2010.02030001.

Lukianoff, G., & Haidt, J. (2015, September). The coddling of the American mind. *The Atlantic*. https://www.theatlantic.com/magazine/archive/2015/09/the-coddling-of-the-american-mind/399356/.

McComb, M. (1994). Benefits of computer-mediated communication in college courses. *Communication Education*, 43(2), 159–170.

McKee, A., Litsou, K., Byron, P., & Ingham, R. (2022). *What do we know about the effects of pornography after fifty years of academic research?* Routledge.

Meyer, K. A. (2006). When topics are controversial: Is it better to discuss them face-to-face or online? *Innovative Higher Education*, 31, 175–186. https://doi.org/10.1007/s10755-006-9019-3

Mitchell, L. M. (2021). Creating safe spaces for critical class dialogue and reflection. In T. Mgutshini, V. Oparinde, & V. Govender (Eds.), *Covid-19: Interdisciplinary explorations of impacts on higher education* (pp. 75–93). Sun Press.

Ndemanu, M. T., & Davis, C. L. (2019). Transformative pedagogies in multicultural education: Teaching sensitive topics in troubled times. In S. L. Raye, S. Masta, S. T. Cook, & J. Burdick (Eds.), *Ideating pedagogy in troubled times: Approaches to identity, theory, teaching and research* (pp. 129–140). Information Age Publishing.

Paasonen, S. (2016). Visceral pedagogies: Pornography, affect, and safety in the university classroom. *Review of Education, Pedagogy, and Cultural Studies, 38*(5), 427–444.

Page, J. C. (2018). Too sexy too soon, or just another moral panic? Sexualization, children, and "technopanics" in the Australian media 2004–2015. *Feminist Media Studies, 18*(3), 366–380.

Power, J., Kauer, S., Fisher, C., Chapman-Bellamy, R., & Bourne, A. (2022). *The 7th national survey of Australian secondary students and sexual health 2021* (ARCSHS Monograph Series No. 133). The Australian Research Centre in Sex, Health and Society, La Trobe University.

Prensky, M. (2001). Digital natives, digital immigrants Part 1. *On the Horizon, 9*(5), 1–6. https://doi.org/10.1108/10748120110424816

Ruberg, L. F., & Taylor, C. D. (1995). *Student responses to network resources: Formative evaluation of two classes*. Paper presented at the Annual Meeting of the American Educational Research Association, San Francisco, CA. https://eric.ed.gov/?id=ED385221.

Smith, E. E., Kahlke, R., & Judd, T. (2020). Not just digital natives: Integrating technologies in professional education contexts. *Australasian Journal of Educational Technology, 36*(3), 1–14.

Stardust, Z. (2016). Performer-centred pornography as sex worker rights: Developing labour standards in a criminal context. *Research for Sex Work, 15*, 1–7.

Thompson, Z. B. (2020). From safe spaces to precarious moments: Teaching sexuality and violence in the American higher education classroom. *Gender and Education, 32*(3), 395–411. https://doi.org/10.1080/09540253.2018.1458077

Woodley, G. N., Green, L., & Jacques, C. (2024). 'Send nudes?': Teens' perspectives of education around sexting, an argument for a balanced approach. *Sexualities*, OnlineFirst. https://doi.org/10.1177/13634607241237675.

9 Funking it up

Teaching poetry as creative writing in the digital age

David Musgrave

Introduction

In 2019, I was at the start of a semester teaching a synchronous course called Creative Writing: Poetry and Poetics when I sensed a certain flatness in the classroom. The poems presented by students for workshopping were not bad, but they were not good either; I was momentarily at a loss how to 'inspire' my students, as I sensed a near unbridgeable distance from the poetic models I was using from Jordie Albiston's *The Weekly Poem: 52 Exercises in Closed and Open Forms* (2014) and the doggerel my students were stubbornly submitting. On the spur of the moment, I showed them the now-defunct web program 'Meaning Eater' (https://www.crummy.com/software/eater/), which generated scrambled websites based on URLs fed into it. I got them to choose a news website, feed in the URL and then asked them to write down some of the scrambled phrases and arrange them into lines. The results were instant and astonishing; the students started 'eating meaning' outside of class, and the following week, they requested that we try another experimental technique: we looked at K. Silem Mohammad's 'Deer Head Nation' (2003) technique, whereby a website is printed out and then its verbal elements gradually erased or effaced, with what remains forming a poem. Over the course of the semester, we looked at other techniques, some analogue and some digital, and I came to call this aspect of the course 'Funk it Up'. Other techniques I introduced included some I made up, some I already knew about and others I gleaned from Charles Bernstein's *Wreading Experiments* (2006): 'the dictionary game', where a set of dice is used to randomly journey through a dictionary and a poem is created out of the resulting words; "the cut up", as described by William Burroughs (Odier, 1974); "the found poem" whereby a poem is 'found' such as *The Beautiful Poetry of Donald Trump* (Sears, 2024); 'writing cacophony', whereby students were asked to immerse themselves in a noisy verbal environment such as a café, or a room with various media playing and to transcribe heard words or phrases at random; the chance acrostic or mesostic (Mesostic Poem Generator); speech recognition, utilising the feature native to Microsoft Word 2007 (Musgrave, 2023); Google Translate, translating a piece of prose, or indeed a poem, through several different translations and then back to English; 'word cloud' (e.g., https://www.free-wordcloudgenerator.com/); "hetero-homophonic translation" (Musgrave, 2023, pp. 9–12); "phonemic rearrangement" (Musgrave, 2023, pp. 19–22); and the N+7 engine, invented in 1961 by Jean Lescure of Oulipo, which involves replacing each noun in a text with the seventh one following it in a dictionary (The Spoonbill Generator, 2023). The student satisfaction score in the first year of 'funking it up' was 4.95/5, compared with an average of 4.45 over three previous iterations.

In 2021, I formalised the 'Funk it Up' program as an integral part of the asynchronous online offering of the same course on FutureLearn, and the results were staggering. Students often submitted 'funked up' poems for workshopping and in their portfolios. While an objective evaluation of the efficacy of this pedagogical approach can be attested to by increased student satisfaction scores, I want to concentrate on summarising observations I made in that year's and subsequent iterations of the course. The first of these is the enthusiastic take-up of the tools. Students realised that with very little effort, 'content' could be generated that was amusing, novel and interesting. Because the tools could in the main generate large numbers of poems, the students generally quickly realised the need to edit, or at the very least to select from the created corpus, which usually resulted in a willingness to use the created poem as a starting point and not an end in itself. This was an important pedagogical point, for it taught the importance of revision, selection, and editing to the creative process; in fact, it was often easier, in my experience, to get students to rewrite poems created in this way than poems which they regarded as instances of 'self-expression'. Further to this, it was often possible to contextualise the use of digital tools in a broader understanding of avant-garde movements, such as the Dadaist Tristan Tszara's use of a 'cut-up' technique in the early 20th century (Odier, 1974). I observed an overall improvement in the quality of the poetry written in the course, which I mainly attribute to the fact that students were comfortable in incorporating the results of these techniques into work which they ultimately considered their own. This resulted in an enhanced understanding of the forms that creativity could take and a subsequent revaluation of the student's understanding of the figure of the poet without necessarily relying on the Romantic notion of the poet as a privileged genius. It also gave students an enhanced understanding of what makes a poem original, specifically with regard to innovation, and in the case of the digital tools that were used, there was a sense that these compositional methods were 'of the moment' and therefore perceived to be relevant in ways that 'traditional' compositional methods may not be.

The digital context

Technological development since the turn of the century has been rapid; for example, dial-up broadband was prevalent in 2000 and virtually non-existent now; the smartphone was first introduced in Australia by Telstra in 2007; AI in the form of ChatGPT was introduced on November 30, 2022 (OpenAI, 2022). Research into the use of technology in the teaching of creative writing has largely centred on the transition from synchronous to asynchronous methods of delivery necessitated by COVID-19 (Gray-Rosendale & Rosendale, 2022), and discussions on the use of technology have generally centred on optimal use of digital technology (Cummings, 2022). There is little research into the use of digital methods for composition, apart from Bernstein's listing of "Wreading experiments" (Bernstein, n.d.) as part of what Bernstein calls "Deformative Criticism", a term he borrows from Lisa Samuels and Jerome McGann, who coined the portmanteau 'deformance' from 'deform' and 'performance' to describe "an interpretive activity . . . in which 'meaning is more a dynamic exchange than a discoverable content' (31)" (Samuels & McGann, cited in Sparks, 2020, n.p.). Further, "Samuels and McGann provide the example of reading a poem backwards as a deformative procedure that opens possibilities of meaning. Significantly, however, deformance entails 'not a re-imagined meaning but a project for reconstituting [a] work's aesthetic form' (28)" (Sparks, 2020, n.p.). I take the 'dynamic exchange' of deformance as a starting point for talking about using digital composition methods for pedagogical purposes.

Before I talk about the specific uses of technology in the workshopping space, I want to briefly talk about two important aspects of the use of digital technologies in poetic compositional practice. The first relates to Ezra Pound's modernist imperative to 'make it new'. Innovation can and does take many forms. In using digital compositional methods in the classroom, I am following Kevin Stein's observation that "New technologies create new human receptive abilities. In turn, these abilities generate new human desires" (Stein, 2013, p. 92). That is, 'funking it up' responds directly to those new human desires in a largely digitally literate student cohort, and thus provides a bridge of relevance between examples of poetry from the past and student-created poems. In my experience, the enthusiastic take-up of digital compositional methods by the creative writing cohorts I have taught is evidence of its value as a pedagogical tool. The second aspect is Stein's broad observation that "For the moment, digitized media positions everyone as equally author and reader, everyone as equally actor and audience member" (2013, p. 98). This is important, not the least, for the way in which this method indirectly contributes to the decolonisation of the curriculum. Kathryn Broyles writes that

> Within the digital world we have a myriad of opportunities to invite students to develop [problem-solving] skills, if the instructor has the courage and tenacity to relinquish some authority, and level the playing field. Expertise no longer resides in one individual in a professional learning community, and so the roles of teacher and learner meld.
> (Broyles, 2022, p. 60)

Teaching poetry solely using historical models reinforces the tendency towards canonicity implicit in such methods; the ability to 'funk up' historical poems introduces the possibility of an egalitarian relationship with teaching content and empowers the individual student.

Digitising the workshop

Models for the creative writing poetry workshop are various, but according to Philip Gross they can broadly be divided into four types:

(a) The Open Workshop: No agenda, except that participants bring work in-progress; no assumptions about audience or context, or stage of development. Each piece is critiqued as if finished work.
(b) The Set-Agenda Workshop: The work brought relates to input given and a task set previously; the tutor has described, and the class discussed, the technical or other challenge. They have terms and concepts ready to assess in each case how that challenge has been met.
(c) The Writing-And-Sharing Workshop: A stimulus or task in class leads to immediate writing, then sharing of drafts, however tentative, unformed or even not to their writer's own tastes they might be. The tutor's interest is as much in the questions raised as the work produced – though this kind of workshop may also 'surprise' new and promising work out of students hampered by their habits or their expectations of themselves.
(d) The Ideas Workshop: The material might not be a written draft at all but, say, a chance to pitch a set of possibilities for future writing, for development and exploration in the group. The tutor's agenda might well be to explore the different roles we play as readers, the conscious choice between them, and the skills appropriate to each. I might respond to your pitch as fellow writer (*If I was writing that piece, I would . . .*); as reader *(Hmmm, I wouldn't buy that but my grandma might)*; as publisher or agent *(I can see an opening in the market for that option, provided that . . .)*; as critic *(Look, here are the ways this project will be hampered by the limitations of the genre; here are the almost-invisible ideologies concealed in it)*. . . . Where there is a choice, there is potential learning. (2010, p. 55).

Introducing asynchronous online learning for teaching poetry as creative writing at the University of Newcastle on FutureLearn was initially an attempt to emulate the 'lectorial' format of the face-to-face class in which an hour of lecture and discussion of poetic models (example (b)) was followed by an hour of workshopping, either in response to the week's theme and examples, or whatever the students chose to workshop (examples (a) and (b)). The addition of the 'funk it up' exercises broadened the scope of the workshopping to include examples (c) and (d). Examples of how this occurs can be shown in ideas which underpin the 'cut-up' method of William Burroughs. Burroughs was an inducted member of the chaos magic organisation, The Illuminates of Thanateros (Grant, 2003), and he professed the belief that

> when you make cut-ups you do not simply get random juxtapositions of words, that they do mean something, and often that these meanings refer to some future event . . . cut-ups are a basic key to the nature and function of words.
>
> (Odier, 1974, p. 28)

Discussion of the cut-up can include exploration of this as well as the putative origin of the cut-up in the Dadaism of Tristan Tszara and also its use in the later song-writing practice of David Bowie (The Open College of the Arts, 2019); moreover, the cut-up technique emphasises the formalist conception of poetry as a defamiliarisation of everyday language, in this case a defamiliarisation achieved through fragmenting and radically recontextualising pre-existing texts. In the following section, I will examine three examples of digital 'funk it up' exercises and how they can be used in the virtual workshop.

A revolution in poetry pedagogy

One of the problems with contemporary poetry is that it is a marginalised literary art form. This marginalisation is evident in its near invisibility in mainstream media in Australia; for example, none of the major metropolitan daily newspapers publish poetry anymore, and since the COVID-19 pandemic, there have been very few reviews of new poetry books in these publications. In Australia, the typical print run for a new poetry book is usually between 150 and 250. This seems to be common across the Anglophone world,[1] and does not necessarily reflect the size of the Australian market. The reasons for this are varied, but one common theme I have noticed is the perception of poetry as difficult and inaccessible. This has been the case since the advent of modernism, although popular consumption of poetry seems to have dramatically declined more recently. There are notable exceptions, of course, one being the astonishing success of the poetry of Rupi Kaur. Kaur's poetry has sold more than 12 million copies worldwide and has been the subject of a number of studies, such as that by Dubravka Đurić and Aleksandra Izgarjan, who claim that her "poetry functions as self-help literature" and that her "Instapoetry can be understood as a specific form of popular media culture intended for a mass audience" (2022, p. 1361). One reason I would put forward for the perception of poetry as difficult and inaccessible is based on anecdotal evidence I have gathered over the last 15 years, which concerns the experience of being taught poetry in secondary school. Almost without exception, poetry is taught in secondary schools as a verbal artefact, which requires decoding, paraphrase, or explanation. Poetry is most often taught as the paradigmatic example of rhetoric, of mythic allusion and hidden meaning;

for example, the NSW curriculum emphasises analysis and evaluation over appreciation and enjoyment (NSW Curriculum, 2024).

The attention I make my students pay to digital and other playful methods of poetry composition is intended to disrupt the perception of making and reading poetry as an onerous trial of skill. The digital compositional techniques which I employ produce artefacts that often have an air of arbitrariness about them. The student is aware of the contingent nature of their creation, such as the N+7 procedure; moreover, the experiments invariably involve an element of delight, that a verbal composition can be produced, often with very little effort, that can at once be amusing, strange, and even beguiling. For example, here is William Carlos Williams' 'The Red Wheelbarrow (2000)':

The Red Wheelbarrow

so much depends
upon

a red wheel
barrow

glazed with rain
water

beside the white
chickens

and here is a version of it having been passed through an N+15 procedure:

The Red Whiplash

so much depends
upon

a red whip
baste

glazed with rampage
wave

beside the white
chimps

What this shows the student is that the tonal architecture of the poem is a feature of its form. This is a fundamental lesson of poetry which has little to do with the 'meaning' of a poem but is a feature of how it is arranged, how the poem 'is': to slightly twist the age-old dictum of creative writing to 'show, don't tell', it is a feature which is best shown and not told. The tone changes in different ways yet the relation of the elements to each other remains similar to the original – a slight modulation, a falling away in the feel of the second line of each couplet, its brevity suggesting truncation or foreshortening, and a slight puzzlement as to why the relation between these distinct objects is worth remarking at all.

Other aspects of using digital technology include the discovery of novelty in the form of unexpected connections between words that a digital application might make. One example of this is taking Williams' poem again and putting it through Google Translate in the following order: English to Finnish to Hebrew to Basque to Mandarin to Hungarian to Japanese to Scottish Gaelic to Sanskrit to Irish and back to English (this language order was not chosen arbitrarily, but sought to move between different language groupings or families to achieve maximum weirdness). This is the result:

The Blood Wheels

It really depends on him

I understand
The blood wheels

The tank
Enamel in water

water
Almost white chicken.

(Google Translate, 13 October 2024)

Here the changes are more radical – the discreteness of distinct objects in a strange relation to each other is largely lost; new elements emerge: 'understanding', a person ('him') and a sense of menace ('blood wheels'); in fact, 'blood wheels' is a kind of poetic discovery, and would be the kernel of a new poem (if I chose to work on it). Again, what the student learns here is the importance of selection and form.

The last example I wish to discuss is utilising ChatGPT-4-turbo (ChatGPT-4-turbo 2023) to compose poetry. When I began writing this chapter, ChatGPT was unable to satisfactorily compose a free verse poem. I expect this to change over time: it is certainly possible, even in a limited sense for an algorithm to be arrived at which would randomly lineate a poem. This does, however, beg the question as to what makes a good poem. In order to illustrate this, I reproduce my conversation with ChatGPT about writing a free verse poem:

ChatGPT

Me: write a free verse poem

ChatGPT:

Here's a free verse poem for you:

> Within the whispers of the wind,
> Echoes of memories lost and found,
> Dreams dance like shadows in the night,
> A symphony of emotions profound.
>
> In the canvas of the universe,
> Stars shine brightly, a timeless art,
> Each blink of light a whispered verse,
> A story written in the heart.
>
> The journey endless, winding, vast,
> Through valleys deep and mountains high,
> We search for meaning, moments pass,
> In the blink of an eternal eye.
>
> Let go of fears, embrace the unknown,
> Find solace in the chaos, peace in the storm,
> For life's a labyrinth, a path to be shown,
> In the free verse of existence, we transform.

Me: This is not free verse. Try again

ChatGPT:

> In the silence of the night,
> Whispers of dreams take flight.
> A dance of shadows, soft and light,
> Guiding us through the endless night.
>
> In the echoes of the past,
> Memories fade and memories last.
> Time moves on, so moving fast,
> In the present moment, we are steadfast.
>
> The world spins, a constant spin,
> Life's symphony plays from within.
> Each breath we take, a brand new sin,
> In this chaotic melody, we begin.
>
> Free verse flows like a winding stream,
> No rules to bind us, no set theme.
> Words emerge like a waking dream,
> In this poem, reality and fiction gleam.

Me: what is your understanding of free verse?

ChatGPT: Free verse is a form of poetry that does not follow a specific rhyme scheme, metrical pattern, or structure. It allows poets the freedom to experiment with different line lengths, rhythms, and patterns without the constraints of traditional poetic forms. Free verse focuses on the natural flow of language, using varying line breaks and stanza lengths to convey emotion, imagery, and meaning. The lack of predetermined rules in free verse gives poets the flexibility to express themselves in a more organic and spontaneous way, often resulting in unique and innovative poetic compositions.

Me: So you write free verse with end-stopped rhyming lines, which contradicts the definition you have just given me. What do you have to say about that? (ChatGPT-4-turbo, 2023)

At this point, ChatGPT referred me to its subscription-only version if I wanted to continue the conversation. Several months later, I was able to approximate free verse using the AI poem generator at aifreebox.com (and in fact there are now several sites advertising AI-generated free verse). The parameters I used were 'Marmosets; after the style of Ezra Pound; rhyme bottle with axolotl; insert fragments from Sir Thomas Browne; insert lyrics of Miley Cyrus'. The result:

*Marmosets in the Canopy**

In the dappled shadows,
where green fingers weave through sunlight,
the marmosets chatter – a symphony of whispers,
tiny acrobats swinging from branch to branch,
each leap a testament to joy's audacity.

"I can almost see it," they seem to sing,
their voices climbing like vines in the humid air –
a song of freedom that echoes through the treetops.
As if to say: *"It's a climb,"* but oh! how they fly!

Fragile bodies darting through leaves,
bodies as light as whispers on a summer breeze.
Here I find fragments of Sir Thomas Browne –
"For there is in all nature no quality more mutable than this."
Yet these creatures remain steady in their play,
undeterred by the world below.

Beneath them lies the ground – a patchwork of shadows and light,
an orchestra where every note is both soft and sharp.
Each moment a bottle filled with laughter,
as if time itself were an axolotl's breath –
breathing life into stillness beneath water's glassy gaze.

And still they swing; these tiny sentinels of wonder,
reminding us that innocence flutters like wings –
a fragile promise among tangled roots and dreams.

Let them teach us resilience; let them echo our fears:
"When I look at you . . ." – the reflection of hope buried deep;
like sunbeams trapped within fleeting clouds –
we too can rise above this dense canopy of doubt.

In their dance among the branches, we find solace:
the beauty in simplicity wrapped tight as vines around old wood.
Like Browne would muse upon his strange inquiries –
what mysteries dwell beyond sight? What truths are whispered?

So here we gather under leafy arches;
marmosets prancing on dreams suspended in air –
while beneath our feet lies earth heavy with stories untold.
(aifreebox, 2024)

The 'free' nature of this verse is not quite as free as one would expect, say, from Ken Bolton or T.S. Eliot. The stanzas vary in number of lines (5, 4, 6, 5, 7, 4, 3) and the line lengths vary from 3 beats to 8 beats, with iambic pentameter the most common: this is poetry which seems to have been generated with a number of parameters – to my eye it reads as variations on the four line, iambic pentameter stanza rather than as radically 'free'.

For several reasons, I doubt that AI will ever be able to consistently write poetry that is valued by expert readers of poetry. This is despite recent research which suggests that AI-generated poetry is consistently rated more favourably than human-written poetry by non-expert readers (Porter & Machery, 2024). An expert reader of poetry reads against a context developed over several years and in several different cultural contexts: knowledge of poetry from other centuries, poetry in translation, poetry by students, by other experts, and, of course taste developed by a somatic, sentient being. The non-expert reader of poetry generally reads from the point of view of intelligibility, accessibility and with an aversion to difficulty.

The first reason is considering how poetry relates to consciousness: we still are not able to definitively say what consciousness is, but we can suppose what a poem is. In his essay, 'Poetry and Consciousness', C.K. Williams writes that

> A poem is a wonderfully complicated instrument. It is as complicated, maybe more so, than an emotion. It also shares many characteristics with emotion. It is composed of sensation, of image, language, a voice, perception, bodily reference, sentiment, morality, thought, and experience.
> (2001, p. 8)

And further, "poetry speaks its emotion, its consciousness. It is thus that it teaches us the limits of the elements of consciousness we value so – our reason, our discursive language, our notion that we can analyse the substances of being" (Williams, 2001, p. 13).

Considering the use of ChatGPT as a compositional tool leads to consideration of what consciousness is, and more importantly, how the body itself might be an important part of writing itself. Understanding poetry as contiguous with the limits of consciousness brings the poem to life for the student, and is generative of new ideas in and of itself.

Conclusion

In conclusion, 'funking it up' is a valuable way of encouraging creativity in students who may otherwise be anxious about or intimidated by the challenge of composing a poem. It is a disruptive pedagogical teaching strategy that enhances students' understanding of what makes a poem 'poetry'. In its various aspects, it 'shows' the student that poetry involves defamiliarisation, and with very little effort, it evokes discussions of avant-gardism, and it somewhat levels the playing field of the poetry workshop. Anyone who has recently been to a poetry reading will know that most poets of a certain age now read their poetry from their phones or another handheld device. What better way to teach and connect with a student than to directly utilise the tools, apps, and websites that are readily available on these devices? Lastly, 'funking it up' is a way of helping students find their discomfort zone, which is the place from which all good poetry arises.

Note

1 As a guide, Lea (2013) states, "Whereas a typical US poetry title (Billy Collins aside) runs to about 1,500 copies, a poetry title by a reasonably well-known poet in Australia (at about one-fifteenth of the US population) runs to about half the US number" (n.p.). The figures I cite are based on personal observation through my activity as a publisher of poetry at Puncher & Wattmann, one of Australia's leading poetry publishers.

References

AIFreeBox. (2024). *AI poem generator*. https://aifreebox.com/list/ai-poem-generator
Albiston, J. (2014). *The weekly poem: 52 exercises in closed and open forms*. Puncher & Wattmann.
Bernstein, C. (2006). Wreading experiments. *Writing at UPenn*. https://writing.upenn.edu/bernstein/wreading-experiments.html
Broyles, K. A. (2022). Disrupting writing and systemic disruption. In L. Gray-Rosendale & S. Rosendale (Eds.), *Go online! Reconfiguring writing courses for the new, virtual world* (pp. 29–40). Peter Lang International Academic Publishers. https://doi.org/10.3726/b19797
ChatGPT-4-turbo. (2023). Chat with ChatGPT about free verse poetry and citation. *OpenAI*. Retrieved November 18, 2024, from https://chat.openai.com/

Cummings, L. (2022). Avoiding Zoom doom: Creating online workshops with design thinking. In L. Gray-Rosendale & S. Rosendale (Eds.), *Go online! Reconfiguring writing courses for the new, virtual world* (pp. 97–111). Peter Lang International Academic Publishers. https://doi.org/10.3726/b19797

Đurić, D., & Izgarjan, A. (2022). Poetry in popular culture: Instagram, Rupi Kaur, feminism and the utilitarian value of poetry. *Etnoantropološki Problemi Issues in Ethnology and Anthropology, 17*(4), 1361–1378. https://doi.org/10.21301/eap.v17i4.10

Grant, D. (2003, published online 2015, March 16). Magick and photography. *Ashé: Journal of Experimental Spirituality, 2*(3). https://ashejournal.com/2015/03/16/magick-and-photography/

Gray-Rosendale, L., & Rosendale, S. (Eds.). (2022). *Go online! Reconfiguring writing courses for the new, virtual world*. Peter Lang International Academic Publishers. https://doi.org/10.3726/b19797

Gross, P. (2010). Small worlds: What works in workshops if and when they do? In D. Donnelly (Ed.), *Does the creative writing workshop still work?* Multilingual Matters Limited. https://doi.org/10.21832/9781847692702

Lea, B. (2013). Poetry publishing in Australia. *Bronwyn Lea*. http://www.bronwynlea.com/2013/05/14/poetry-publishing-in-australia/#_edn8

Meaning Eater. (2024). https://www.crummy.com/software/eater/

Mesostic Poem Generator. (n.d.). University of Pennsylvania. https://mesostics.sas.upenn.edu/

Mohammad, K. S. (2003). *Deer head nation*. Tougher Disguises Press.

Musgrave, D. (2023). *Mishearing*. Gorilla.

NSW Curriculum. (2024; implemented in 2026). *English advanced 11–12 syllabus*. https://curriculum.nsw.edu.au/learning-areas/english/english-advanced-11-12-2024/overview

Odier, D. (1974). *The job: Interviews with William S. Burroughs*. Penguin.

OpenAI. (2022, November 30). *ChatGPT*. https://openai.com.

The Open College of the Arts. (2019). *Burroughs and Bowie: Using the cut-up technique. Part 2*. https://www.oca.ac.uk/weareoca/creative-writing/burroughs-and-bowie-using-the-cut-up-technique-part-2/

Porter, B., & Machery, E. (2024). AI-generated poetry is indistinguishable from human-written poetry and is rated more favorably. *Scientific Reports, 14*, 26133. https://doi.org/10.1038/s41598-024-76900-1

Samuels, L., & McGann, J. (1999). Deformance and interpretation. *New Literary History, 30*(1), *Poetry & Poetics*, 25–56.

Sears, R. (2024). *The beautiful poetry of Donald Trump*. Canongate Books.

Sparks, C. (2020). Poetic deformance and *the procedural sonnet*. *Electronic Book Review*. https://doi.org/10.7273/bvc2-yb96

The Spoonbill Generator. (2023). *The Spoonbill Generator presents: The N+7 machine*. http://www.spoonbill.org/n+7/

Stein, K. (2013). *Poetry's afterlife: Verse in the digital age*. University of Michigan Press.

Williams, C. K. (2001). *Poetry and consciousness*. University of Michigan Press.

Williams, W. C. (2000). *Selected poems*. Penguin Books.

10 Fantasy cricket

From ethnographic film to virtual anthropology fieldwork

Hedda Haugen Askland, Michael Kilmister, Kate Senior, Adrian Mereles, Chris Lawrence and Tim Garside

Introduction

Fieldwork plays a crucial role in student learning and research across a variety of humanities and science disciplines, including Anthropology. Since fieldwork involves being physically present on-site, providing remote, valid, and safe alternatives can be challenging. For Anthropology educators, the challenge primarily lies in providing students with ethnographic fieldwork experiences that provide the hands-on experience and professional training needed to be an applied anthropologist (Henry & Jordan, 2007). Ethnography is a qualitative research method where a researcher (an ethnographer) studies a specific social or cultural group to gain a deeper understanding of it. Ethnography is both a research approach and a research product. When a researcher employs an ethnographic method, they actively engage with a group and attempt to share similar experiences with the group members. When writing an ethnography, a researcher crafts an account of a group rooted in this 'insider' experience. An ethnographic account might draw on an analysis of group artefacts and documentation, or interviews with members of the group (Kramer & Adams, 2017). Emerging and newly widespread digital media and communication technologies make it possible for students to have immersive fieldwork experiences without being physically present at a social or cultural site. However, the scholarship on simulating ethnography in the online anthropology classroom has primarily focused on postgraduate courses (Henry & Jordan, 2007; Nuñez-Janes & Re Cruz, 2007), or on providing virtual alternatives to ethnographic field schools on equity grounds (Lyons, 2024).

In this chapter, we present a case study of virtual fieldwork in the undergraduate classroom.[1] We describe how students engaged in the virtual ethnographic practice and wrote ethnographic fieldnotes and an analysis that teased out the 'cultural logic' of the virtual field they had been immersed in. Drawing on the fieldnotes produced by the students from the 2021 cohort and our own reflections on the process,[2] we explore some of the challenges, successes, and lessons learned from this experience. These lessons led to a redesign of the virtual experience which will be discussed later in the chapter. We also discuss some of the wider pedagogical implications of virtual fieldwork, touching on concepts like authentic assessment and gamification of learning. The chapter demonstrates that the online Anthropology classroom can transcend the usual equity and accessibility arguments for dialogue, interaction, and collaboration, which is no lesser than what is experienced in in-person teaching.

Context

While working on the development of a fully online version of our first-year Anthropology course, What is Anthropology?, we were faced with the challenge of how to create a cohesive fieldwork experience for our students.[3] One of the main learning objectives of the course is to immerse students in a field unfamiliar to themselves so they can perform the role of an ethnographer whose key task is to participate and observe. Students also need to develop skills in keeping accurate notes about what they experience on fieldwork. How to best provide authentic and meaningful fieldwork opportunities to students was not a novel challenge for the course, but the online dimension compounded existing difficulties. Equity concerns regarding funding fieldwork excursions or placements and timetabling difficulties – that is, it is difficult to schedule placements on a single course for a cohort comprised of students studying different programs – meant the experience needed to be iterative and could flexibly fit around students' competing study commitments. In previous years, we had tried to offer opportunities for ethnographic field experiences where students worked independently in their local areas, but these had been underwhelming, largely functioning as observational exercises rather than authentic examples of ethnography.

With the opportunity to redesign What Is Anthropology? as part of a redesigned Bachelor of Arts (BA) program in 2019 (see Chapter 1), we landed on simulating fieldwork through an extended team-based task that ran over the second half of the course. We focused on the classic ethnographic film *Trobriand Cricket: An Ingenious Response to Colonisation* (Kildea & Leach, 1976) and then supported students to spend 6 weeks creating their own Trobriand cricket teams leading up during class time in the lead up to a fantastical 'cricket match' in the final weeks. This iterative, group-based experience allowed students to immerse themselves in a field unfamiliar to themselves, where they had to be part of the game in order to build an understanding of *what*, *who*, and *why* they were doing what they were doing. Consequently, students performed the role of an ethnographer whose key task is to participate and observe. They kept fieldnotes about what they experienced, saw, and learned as they completed weekly tasks. Their notes were submitted as a summative assessment at the end of the semester and helped underpin a reflective essay about the experience, including a final 'match.'

Trobriand cricket was well received by students compared to previous ethnographic exercises on the course, with increased engagement and assessment outcomes evident. However, this experience was for the on-campus students only; for the first run of the online version, there was an individual task intended to meet identical learning outcomes. With COVID-19 pandemic hitting New South Wales in 2020, Trobriand cricket needed to move online for the on-campus students. This presented an opportunity to give *all* students an equal opportunity to get a taste of anthropological fieldwork.

In reconfiguring our version of Trobriand cricket, our challenge quickly became, "How can we replicate this experience digitally?" An additional challenge was that very few online students knew each other at the outset of the semester, which would pose a challenge in a task that demanded them to develop a shared identity and understanding of how to approach Trobriand cricket. To address these challenges, we developed a suite of iterative learning activities embedded into a unique web application modelled on online fantasy sports leagues. These innovations allowed students to experience the thrills and confusion of fieldwork, and engage in participant observation, whilst also engaging with theories of ritual, symbol, identity, and resistance, without being physically present on-campus. The app was developed by a multidisciplinary team spread across the university and comprised of anthropological teaching staff, learning designers, and a programmer. The app was labour-intensive to develop but was viewed by senior leaders as a worthwhile investment because of the characteristics of the course. What is Anthropology? is a core course with an average enrolment of approximately 200 students across two campuses and online, functioned as a plank of a strategic project supporting a fully online Bachelor of Arts, and is also offered at two campuses in blended mode.[4] Next, we outline how we integrated the Trobriand cricket app into our teaching and learning.

Developing the skills for fieldwork

Kildea and Leach's (1976) ethnographic film introduces students to the phenomenon of how cricket is played on the Trobriand Islands. Cricket was first introduced to the Trobriand islanders in the early 20th century by British Christian missionaries as part of their colonising mechanisms. The game, they thought, would discourage tribal rivalry and warfare. The film shows how instead of adopting the British 'gentleman's sport,' the islanders adapted it to their own culture, adding extra players, dances, and chants, and modifying the ball and bats. The game was incorporated into traditional practices, thereby maintaining those practices and modes of exchange. Kildea and Leacher's (1976) visual ethnography is an important tool in anthropological teaching, particularly in the areas of symbolic forms, structure, performance, and identity, as well as the impacts of and reactions to colonisation (Ness, 1988). Hence, the film is introduced during a week when we look at power and resistance, and it also links to the course focus on ritual and identity. The Trobriand Islands are vital to the anthropological canon, as students learn about pioneering anthropologist Malinowski and the development of fieldwork, the use of magic to control the uncontrollable (Malinowski, 1925), and the intricacies of the Kula Ring (a system of ceremonial exchange practiced there and on neighbouring islands).

Understanding Trobriand cricket is just one aspect of the learning; understanding how to take ethnographic fieldnotes and their value as a source of evidence is another. We employed instructional scaffolding – escorting and monitoring students through learning activities that prepare them for the next stage – to enable students to record their own fieldnotes independently. The first step in this scaffolded approach is immersing them in foundational ethnographies. Students in What is Anthropology? are initially shocked that we require them to read a whole ethnography: Nigel Barley's (1983) *The Innocent Anthropologist*. We set this book as the core reading as it is a rare example of what happens behind the scenes in the conduct of anthropological fieldwork and because it shows how initially confusing and disheartening the early stages of fieldwork can be. Barley writes about his confusion and frustrations, and this becomes a reference for the students when they struggle understanding the rules of Trobriand cricket (which are not explained to them at the outset as the purpose of the task is for them to learn the logic of the field through immersion).

In addition to the reading, the curricula for the first 4 weeks of semester focuses on building observational, reflexive, and analytical skills, as well as the skills of seeing the exotic and intriguing within the mundane. During these weeks, the students engage with a variety of texts and visual material (Geertz, 2005 [1973]; Rosaldo (1993); Somby, 2014) that bring their attention to the role ethnographic fieldwork, of 'being there,' and the role of the researchers' own emotions and perspectives in shaping a fieldwork. These introductory weeks offer the foundation of the next stage of the course, during which the students are introduced to the theory of ritual, symbols, and taboo, and are challenged to bring the theory and readings to life through reflexive practice on the 'familiar and strange' within their own lives and everyday worlds. Further classic texts (Gmelch, 1971; Miner, 1956) and in-class, formative writing exercises advance their ethnographic gaze. Thereafter, students are introduced to Trobriand cricket.

Creating an authentic virtual field work experience

The students' virtual field site – the app on which the teams displayed their identity and where weekly 'matches' were organised and 'played' – draws inspiration from Trobriand cricket. It was conveyed to students that, like Trobriand cricket, the conventional rules of cricket are no longer the rules of the game. This was the first surprise to students who expected it to be akin to the British form of cricket, which is a popular Australian summer sport. Teams were formed through student groups engaging in a series of structured formative tasks over 6 weeks designed to elicit unique team identities. Like a traditional fantasy sports tournament, however, points were accumulated by teams. Points could be earned through completing the weekly tasks and through winning 'matches' against opposing teams.

The Trobriand cricket learning experience carried cultural and social expectations that could only be unpicked by 'being there' and participating. Drawing on concepts of identity, ritual, symbols, and resistance, the students were allocated to teams and told that for the next 6 weeks they were to be "innocent anthropologists" (Barley, 1983). In practice, that meant being embedded in a field site made up of the rest of their class, who would be opposing teams in an unfolding 'cricket' tournament through which they would study the social structure (alliances, networks, hierarchies, relations, etc.) and cultural symbols of our class. 'Who are we as a group?', we asked the students, knowing that only through participating and observing in the tournament could they arrive at an answer.

The tournament comprised a series of matches. Each match involved teams inputting their response to the weekly task for the week – points were automatically awarded by the system based on a variety of conditions, including how many elements of the task were completed and the length of the responses. The scoring system was not explained to students, which was a deliberate strategy intended to simulate the unfamiliarity of fieldwork. The curriculum was integrated in the app through the weekly activities. Each task had the students focus on an element of their team identity. Examples included designing an emblem for their team, choosing team colours, and writing and/or performing a team chant. Students were also asked to keep a field diary containing reflections and observations, including thinking deeply about the identity that the opposing teams were presenting. The students then became real participant observers who kept fieldnotes about the process, their observations, and experience. To remove pressure on the teamwork and reduce student anxiety about group dynamics disadvantaging their grades, students were only marked on their field diary and reflections, not how well they performed in the weekly tasks ('matches') or their team's ranking on the Trobriand cricket league table. Overall, the app was a fieldwork site and an engagement tool.

Embedding supporting materials

To support the students' fieldwork, we developed a range of learning aids, including material artefacts – such as Trobriand cricket bats (one original, one copy specially made for the course) and a trophy – a hall of fame display (showcasing new students to what has happened before, including the team's material artefacts made for the final), and a 5-min video that provided the background to the exercise. Notably, we introduced the *The Trobriand Times* (containing weekly comedic headlines inspired by teams' actions and distributed to students through the learning management system [LMS], with the aim of generating extra enthusiasm) (see Figure 10.1). *The Trobriand Times* was 'published' once or twice a week for students and was designed to parody

Fantasy cricket 139

Figure 10.1 An example of the faux tabloid newspaper, *The Trobriand Times*, which came in the form of a cropped front page.

a sensationalistic sports tabloid that speculated scandals and manufactured amusing gossip about the teams that emerged in the tournament. A team could therefore still have a chance at fame and glory by making the front page of *The Trobriand Times*, regardless of the number of points they had scored.

While time-intensive to produce, these supporting elements to the experience – notably *The Trobriand Times* 'newspaper' – enhanced educator presence and ameliorated the sense of isolation that can accompany online learning, as gamification alone is usually insufficient to motivate students in the online classroom (Cespón & Díaz Lage, 2022).

Linking to the assessment

The weekly activities functioned as gamified and groupwork-based formative tasks linked to the summative assessment. Discussion boards were made available for each group to plan their approach to the tasks, but many groups opted to use communication platforms outside the course (e.g., WhatsApp) for this purpose. Students work within their groups and their emerging discussions about identity and ritual were the focus for their fieldnotes. Students drew on their fieldnotes to produce the final summative assessment of the course. This 1000-word assignment required students to write an ethnography – what Barley (1983) describes in the *Innocent Anthropologist* as a "cultural map" – of their cohort. They were asked to write about the identity, symbolism, and rituals they have participated in and observed over the 6 weeks of Trobriand cricket. Students were given a large degree of choice in how they presented their work, being able to draw on multimodal sources, including screenshots and diagrams. While they did not need to incorporate citations into their ethnographic account, they were encouraged to draw on the course reading list to analyse the displays of identity, ritual, and symbolism they witnessed. They also needed to balance description with interpretation. This was an authentic assessment. As Arnold and Croxford (2024) argue, the component characteristics of an assessment make it authentic. In the case of our Trobriand cricket experience, the characteristics were its relevance to students, the direct link it established between process and product, and the respect it paid not only to the discipline of Anthropology but also to the students' sense of place, identities, and lived experiences.

Developing the virtual field site

The app – the students' virtual field site – emerged out of a collaborative effort, which brought together disciplinary knowledge, innovative design solutions, coding and gaming expertise, and gamification of learning principles, resulting in an asynchronous simulation of Trobriand cricket. Our Trobriand cricket league app was linked from the LMS and was where the students logged their weekly activities, with virtual 'matches' played every week between student teams, before the eventual play-off in the final week. The outcome of matches was automatically determined by which team had done better in the weekly task, although in the event of ties, manual intervention from the teaching team was required.

The app was developed with an agile approach at its core, that is, design and development occurred simultaneously. This meant that staff were able to operate within an iterative framework, adapting design and development in tandem throughout the project. The design began with an initial review of several online fantasy sports platforms like Fantasy Premier League (https://fantasy.premierleague.com/). During this review, it soon became evident that due to the unique nature of Trobriand cricket, the app required a unique design. One of these unique requirements was the need for a distinct visual experience per team. This was achieved by allowing users to manipulate certain visual elements such as their team's theming/colours and image/emblem. Another requirement was the simulated learning experience, with gameplay to be centred around textual input. This being something that off-the-shelf solutions could not seemingly accommodate. A unique solution would also allow for management of all aspects of gameplay and allowing for a certain level of unpredictability or reward, if required. Development of the 1.0 version

Fantasy cricket 141

of the app was focused on the user experience and involved a heavy round of playtesting with colleagues before launch.

There were six parallel leagues which each had between five and six teams of four to six students. Each league represented a tutorial/seminar group and the online cohort. At the end of the scheduled matches, we crowned the tutorial champion and runner-up. But this was not the end of the game: the app was set up with a final play-off week to bring together the multiple leagues to declare the ultimate champion of the year. As is illustrated in Figure 10.2, the students had by this time 'cracked the algorithm' making the finals exceptionally close and demanding intervention by the 'invisible umpires' (that being the course teaching and support staff).

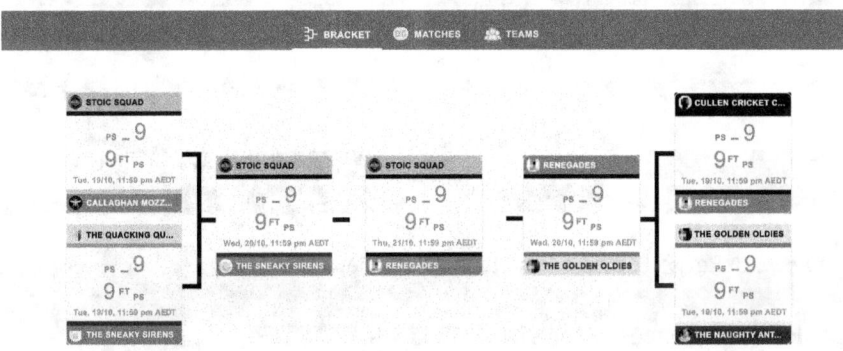

Figure 10.2 Final play-off week: game structure.

Redeveloping the virtual field site

Although the first version of the app successfully served the course for several semesters, a change in support staff and an institution-wide LMS migration forced the team to consider building a new version using widely available, off-the-shelf software. The redesign not only needed to result in a more sustainable and flexible app in terms of the staff and technology required to host it, but it also offered an opportunity to address aspects of the tournament design that needed improvement while retaining its core purpose of facilitating an ethnographic experience.

Based on student feedback and reflections from the design team, two areas of focus were to achieve a better balance between skill and chance, and to increase student participation and engagement. It was decided that more mystery needed to surround the point-scoring mechanics of the tournament, as many teams quickly deduced that the length of a written response was the primary source of points in a match. This was creating run-away winners, tied matches, and dead-locked finals which produced a level of predictability in the game, and manual administration in separating dead heats. In response, we introduced the element of chance in the form of thematic

142 *Moving Your University Course Online*

variables to a match such as home-town advantage and weather conditions. The degree to which a team had populated their profile page was included as a point-scoring factor, represented as an ambiguous 'blessing' rating during matches. Bonus points were also awarded to teams if their taunts included the name of the opposition or the opposition's mascot. A visual indicator of the remaining match time was included in the interface design in the form of a string of Trobriand Island trading shells to add some urgency to student participation (see Figure 10.3). The tournament structure was streamlined to a single, round-robin league with a final knockout, with an improved tournament dashboard and navigation to encourage more spectator access to matches.

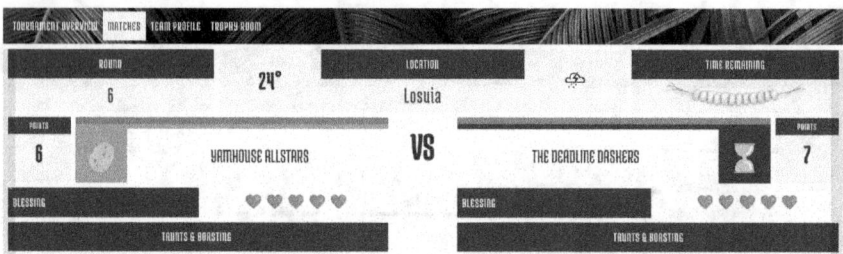

Figure 10.3 Revised head-to-head tournament view.

Student experiences of the virtual field site

Sorting a large number of students who did not know each other into teams and providing them with an online space and time to work was challenging. Inevitably, some students had missed the first online tutorial and had to be late inclusions in teams. Others had problems with accessing the online materials. In their fieldnotes, they talked about feeling confused, 'in the dark' and unsure about how to proceed: "Right now, I'm feeling rather overwhelmed. Although the App [sic] was explained, I am still struggling to understand the process" (Student 1, fieldnotes).

Others commented that they could not understand the process by which the app gave them a score for their entries and remained unconvinced by our explanation that it was a closely held secret. Some teams gave serious consideration to working out strategies to achieve the maximum points:

> Before we began working on our chant, we reflected on our cricket ranking and realized [sic] we weren't getting the maximum points for the algorithm, I then double-checked Blackboard [LMS] and realised that you get maximum points for writing 50 or more words, I then relayed this to our team and it made me reflect on the teamwork similarities in a real cricket team, working on strategies to get the most points in an actual game.
>
> (Student 2, fieldnotes)

We were able to relate these experiences to the experience of real fieldwork, both by talking about our own fieldwork experiences and by reminding them of the bewilderment experienced by Barley (1983) in his initial stages of fieldwork. We could see how students negotiated this stage and how their understanding changed over time. As one student wrote in her final reflections:

> For the first few weeks of matches, I could not access the communal playing fields. Leaving me feeling aimless and socially cut off, as I expressed feelings of self-doubt and frustration in my journal entries. In hindsight, I view this process as a rite of passage.
> (Student 3, final reflections)

Building identity

In the first week of the tournament, students were asked to decide on their team's name, colours, and an emblem. This immediately started a conversation about group identity, as students examined what things were important to them, what cultural and social reference points they shared, and what aspects of their identity they felt comfortable projecting to the larger group. For some, this was a relatively easy process, for example, a team of mature-aged female students were quick to name themselves the 'Golden Oldies' and gleefully populated their page with wine bottles and imagery from the US television sitcom, the *Golden Girls*. Other teams had to delve deeper to try and find something that united them, as discussed by a student from the 'Callaghan Mozzies Team,' and a student from 'the Renegades:'

> We began by discussing our team name. Sommer suggested 'socio locos' because being enrolled in a sociology course is something we all have in common. However, Tim suggested that that name didn't have much cultural or symbolic significance which would make it hard to work with later – the group agreed. This sparked the idea of our team identity being based around a common interest. So, we all exchanged degrees, however, this too was not unanimous. Kate then pointed out that at the very least we are all university students, so we discussed what we associate with University. This included coffee, sororities and mosquitos. Everyone almost immediately agreed that mosquitos were a significant part of UON's [University of Newcastle's] culture and this became the foundation of our team's identity.
> (Student 4, fieldnotes)

Our earliest task was to get to know one another to develop a shared team ethos. While initially this was daunting, we quickly discovered a shared sense of culture which allowed us to bond. Specifically, we recognised that we all shared a similar place in the social hierarchy as

Central Coast 'battlers.' Instead of feeling shame as was expected by society, we felt a sense of pride in being able to compete against those with more resources and prestige. In choosing 'Gossie Train Station' as our home ground we reflected our pride in being the underdog.

(Student 5, fieldnotes)

Pre-match reflections

From watching the film *Trobriand Cricket*, the students were aware that taunting and attempts to intimidate the opposing team were as much part of the game as actually playing cricket:

I put my virtual hand up for team captain this week, we were going head-to-head with the Sneaky Sirens and Moomins. The team discussed ways to approach our adversaries going in, it was all very playful in the group and there was a lot of smack chat going around too [. . .] After we all hung up I got started on my captaincy duties and ended up with these reflections:

An example of student taunts:

Ok Sneaky sirens your up! What else do you have beside atrocious singing voices and wet slippery tails? Unlike the weak oldies and trolls you've lured in we cockatoos will make you galahs out of you, you'll be dragging your wounded tails to depths where no fish has ever been.
   Prepare yourselves for a batting innings over before you can blink and ask wtf happened because our swift talons will catch you out every ball you attempt to hit for six.
   Considering we rule the air, what kind of tactics will you employ against us? We hope you bring a decent field innings to the game otherwise you'll be the laughing stock of the completion. We will use our arsenal of skills to swarm your beloved haven and take this walk over. Beware we've been known to knock down our opposition with striking LBWs with our swift spin of the wing and twister hitting attack on bat.
   You've been warned.
   Start counting those ducks. Byeeeeeee

   Our dear Moomins,
   We are glad you have friendly family and friend base because you're going to need them after this game. You might even want to go back into hibernation and ruminate on all you did wrong.
   We here on cockatoo island use the land, air and wind to train like we play and play like we train. We'll use our joyous and enthusiastic nature to hack your psychology to make you think that we are also your friendly family members and just like that you'll wonder why you ever entered this completion.

Looking forward to the fun picnic and game!

Big love from us at Cockatoo Island. You bring to picnic rug and we'll bring the food, it'll be just like Moomin land! Xoxo

I sent it in to my team during the week via WhatsApp and mentioned smack talk is uncharacteristic of me but I think it's quite unrestrained.

(Student 6, fieldnotes)

As Leach (2002) notes in his description of the game of Trobriand cricket, the purpose of playing is "displaying rather than winning" (p. 2). As students worked through their pre-match reflections, they replicated this sentiment as they became aware that their scores were affected by the effort they put into both displaying their own identities and reflecting on the identities of the other teams. One student explained this in his final reflections:

> Through my experience with the Callaghan Mozzies, it was not the winning of matches that was most important, but rather the ritual of the pre-match reflections that served as a means to brandish our symbols and cultural markers against other teams.
>
> (Student 7, final reflections)

Creating cohorts and social connections

In addition to providing a simulated fieldwork experience, we were acutely aware that many of our students were socially isolated and often very lonely. As first year students, they had not yet had time to develop strong cohorts at university and having been in lockdown for months, the sense of isolation this can create was even stronger than normal. Students are often very reluctant to undertake group work, but in this case, Trobriand cricket had the effect of bringing people together and building relationships that may extend past the life of the course. Initially, we provided time for simply building group cohesion by encouraging conversation within the groups: "We told stories and showed off our pets and plants, it seemed like the first real connection of the semester" (Student 8, fieldnotes). The final reflections provided by the students talked about the longer-term effects of the teamwork experience during the isolation of the pandemic:

> Overall, the Trobriand Cricket experience was arguably the most comforting and socially stimulating lockdown experiences I had but while I'm grateful it was there to hold my fragile mental health up from drowning I do hope I never have to live through lockdown ever again!
>
> (Student 6, final reflections)

> I never would have imagined that a sport titled 'Trobriand Cricket' would hold so much significance in my university journey or be the singular portal to social connections.
>
> (Student 8, final reflections)

Engaging in ritual

To add a further layer of participant observation and bring the semester to a festive conclusion, we had planned for the face-to-face students to meet in person to have a final big display and celebration on campus, with the artefacts made for the tournament and during the semester by the students to be showcased. Together with the online final round, this was to be an important part of the task, and students were required to write an ethnographic piece based on the observations of the online and face-to-face finals, using their fieldnotes from the previous 5 weeks (which were also assessed) to advance a cultural analysis of the ritual that we performed. However, when, in 2021, COVID-19 refused to ease, and we remained in lockdown in the final week of semester, we needed to find an online solution. Instead of the planned face-to-face cricket game, we instead developed an awards ceremony, where each team voted for their favourites in the categories of best symbol, best dance, best chant, most intimidating, best overall team, and best and fairest player (or team). Students were encouraged to dress up in their team colours and display aspects of their team's identity for this final online celebration.

The finale, branded 'the Trobriand cricket night of nights,' was conducted on the Zoom video conferencing platform. Students dressed in their team colours, and awards were presented that recognised students' work throughout the semester. The event brought the students into a final stage of the ritual where they could look back on their learning and how they had grown from 'innocent anthropologists' to novice ethnographers who understand bewilderment, unease, curiosity, and bravery are four key elements of an anthropologist's mission.

Team representatives accepted their awards with ceremony and short speeches designed to reflect the identity of their teams. The Renegades, for example, demonstrated a characteristic lack of humility when accepting their award for the most intimidating team:

> The next two awards for the best overall concept and overall winner were presented to the Renegades as their team was very well put together and were always on top. Katarina was a member from the Renegades and made a joke that, 'it was not a surprise.' I thought this was hilariously true as they were on the top of the ladder the whole time and usually when people are receiving an award, they try to remain humble, yet Katarina did not take this approach.
>
> (Student 1, final reflections)

Overall, students recognised this ceremony as a rite of passage, both in having completed their first Anthropology course and concluded and survived a 6-week Trobriand cricket tournament.

> After some time apart, we reconnected for the final Trobriand Cricket awards ceremony – the *Night of Nights*. The pomp and procession was

something I have not yet experienced within the context of Trobriand cricket, though it epitomised the prestige, glory and accolades deserving of all competitors; champions or not.

(Student 9, final reflections)

Reflections and implications for practice

Many lessons were learned through the design, development, and implementation of virtual Trobriand cricket; we will attempt to summarise these here for readers who are looking to integrate gamified forms of assessment and learning into their online or blended teaching.

To help ensure students engaged with the weekly tasks, it was decided early on to integrate these into scheduled learning. This design decision provided opportunities for students to practice and rehearse behaviours, skills, and assessment literacies. The 'scoring system,' along with educator presence in the form of Trobriand Times and announcements from the course coordinator, provided ongoing feedback. This approach aligns with an assessment for learning philosophy (Sambell et al., 2012), which integrates formative assessment and feedback into teaching and learning. Educator presence was also hugely important to the success of the app; it was not 'set and forget.' The course coordinators and learning designers checked in regularly to read student responses and generate the Trobriand Times headlines. To be a part of the delivery of a course is a rare opportunity for learning designers, and here they were integral to the implementation, notably through devices to enhance engagement including the injection of 'Sir Lawrence,' a comical persona modelled on an elderly British gentleman, and played by Chris Lawrence, one of the authors of this chapter. Sir Lawrence introduced to the students by way of an instructional video outlining the Trobriand cricket app and was added into the LMS to provide technical support for students. *The Trobriand Times* also served as an additional tool of engagement for students and was a deliberate attempt by the learning designers to counter the sometimes-demotivating effect that leaderboards can have on participants who have little chance of ever taking the lead (Park & Kim, 2021).

According to the standard definition of sustainability in e-learning (Gunn, 2010),[5] the version 1.0 design of the app – which was built entirely from the ground up – was not sustainable and was dependent on the technical expertise of the individuals who created it to keep it running. Version 2.0, which customised existing tools and platforms, addressed this shortcoming. It was developed using readily available and embeddable tools such as Google Sheets, with the intention of handing over the digital 'keys' to academics to manage independently. Accessibility for the end user was also improved, with this version being embedded in the LMS and offering a smooth experience on mobile devices. In all, version 2.0 centred around creating a more robust technical solution that required less maintenance and widened accessibility.

Conclusion

Providing authentic fieldwork experiences for large undergraduate Anthropology classes is always a challenge. Doing so online and in lockdown conditions during a pandemic, where the only contact was through Zoom and asynchronous message boards, initially seemed daunting. Through the vehicle of a Trobriand cricket 'fantasy' game, however, and a week-by-week focus on the building blocks of identity and ritual, we were able to build an engrossing virtual fieldwork experience. Engagement was leavened through gamification and regular injections of educator presence. Across 6 weeks, students experienced the initial confusion and bewilderment of field research. Confusion eventually progressed to an applied understanding of why the anthropological skills and theory introduced in the early part of the course were important. Students learned how to document this journey through extensive reflective fieldnotes. Sets of fieldnotes formed the basis of a summative assessment that required students to reflect on their virtual Trobriand cricket experience and the skills and understanding they had developed. The experience not only strengthened a sense of community among the fully online student cohort but also triggered laughter and curiosity, perhaps even beyond the conventional realm of on-site fieldwork that is typically possible in the undergraduate anthropology classroom.

Notes

1. The authors are a mix of academic and professional staff, including learning designers and a programmer.
2. The fieldnotes were part of the submitted coursework. Students were informed these may be drawn on for a publication before submission of the coursework and had the option to 'opt-out' of having their work be a part of the analysis at any stage. This approach conforms to the ethical guidelines for using student work in research established by Burman and Kleinsasser (2004).
3. For further details about the course, see Senior et al. (2021).
4. Pat Nichols and Paul McDonald, both Learning Media Producers from The University of Newcastle's Learning Design and Teaching Innovation Unit (LDTI), filmed and produced all the videos used for the course. Chris Lawrence, Learning Designer from LDTI, came up with the idea and did all the design work for the Trobriand Times.
5. Gunn (2010) defines sustainable e-learning as meeting three key criteria: (1) the learning design is developed and implemented within one or more courses; (2) the concept, design, system, or resources can be adapted for alternative applications; and (3) its maintenance, usage, and future development do not rely solely on the original creators.

References

Arnold, L., & Croxford, J. (2024). Is it time to stop talking about authentic assessment? *Teaching in Higher Education*, 1–9. https://doi.org/10.1080/13562517.2024.2369143

Barley, N. (1983). *The innocent anthropologist: Notes from a mud hut*. Waveland Press.

Burman, M. E., & Kleinsasser, A. (2004). Ethical guidelines for use of student work: Moving from teaching's invisibility to inquiry's visibility in the scholarship of teaching and learning. *The Journal of General Education*, *53*(1), 59–79. http://www.jstor.org/stable/27797976

Cespón, M. T., & Díaz Lage, J. M. (2022). Gamification, online learning and motivation: A quantitative and qualitative analysis in higher education. *Contemporary Educational Technology*, *14*(4). https://doi.org/10.30935/cedtech/12297

Geertz, C. (2005, 1973). Deep play: Notes on the Balinese cockfight. *Daedalus*, *134*(4), 55–86.

Gmelch, G. (1971). Baseball magic. *Trans-action*, *8*, 39–41.

Gunn, C. (2010). Sustainability factors for e-learning initiatives. *Research in Learning Technology*, *18*(2), 89–103. https://doi.org/10.1080/09687769.2010.492848

Henry, L., & Jordan, A. (2007). Field projects and the dilemma of distance. *Practicing Anthropology*, *29*(1), 16–19. https://doi.org/10.17730/praa.29.1.q2581tk4638mw611

Kildea, G., & Leach, J. W. (Directors). (1976). *Trobriand cricket: An ingenious response to colonialism* [Film]. Berkley Media.

Kramer, M., & Adams, T. (2017). Ethnography. In M. Allen (Ed.), *The SAGE encyclopedia of communication research methods* (Vol. 4, pp. 458–461). Sage. https://doi.org/10.4135/9781483381411

Leach, J. (2002). Structure and message in Trobriand cricket. *Techniques & Culture*, *39*, 1–13. https://doi.org/10.4000/tc.195

Lyons, B. J. (2024). Expanding student access to field experiences: Virtual ethnographic field schools. *Anthropology & Education Quarterly*, *55*(2), 205–218. https://doi.org/10.1111/aeq.12482

Malinowski, B. (2014, 1925). *Magic, science and religion*. Reed Books.

Miner, H. (1956). Body ritual among the Nacirema. *American Anthropologist*, *58*(3), 503–507. http://www.jstor.org/stable/665280

Ness, S. A. (1988). Understanding cultural performance: "Trobriand cricket". *TDR*, *32*(4), 135–147.

Nuñez-Janes, M., & Re Cruz, A. (2007). The pedagogy of teaching online graduate courses in the program of applied anthropology. *Practicing Anthropology*, *29*(1), 20–23. https://doi.org/10.17730/praa.29.1.a553345325436411

Park, S., & Kim, S. (2021). Leaderboard design principles to enhance learning and motivation in a gamified educational environment: Development study. *JMIR Serious Games*, *9*(2), e14746. https://games.jmir.org/2021/2/e14746

Rosaldo, R. (1993). Introduction: Grief and a headhunter's rage. In R. Resaldo (Ed.), *Culture and truth: The remaking of social analysis* (pp. 1–21). Beacon Press.

Sambell, K., McDowell, L., & Montgomery, C. (2012). *Assessment for learning in higher education*. Routledge.

Senior, K., Askland, H. H., Groizard, J., & SOCA1020 Class of 2020. (2021). "A dog called Neville:" Using dog names to explore theory and method in anthropology. *Practicing Anthropology*, *43*(4), 8–13. https://doi.org/10.17730/0888-4552.43.4.8

Somby, S. (Director). (2014). *Bonki* [Film]. Sapmifilm. https://www.sapmifilm.com/film/30014

11 Easing eco-anxiety in an online environmental sociology course

Jai Cooper and Chris Lawrence

Introduction

In this chapter, we discuss the project of redesigning a course in environmental sociology at the University of Newcastle (UON) from traditional face-to-face delivery to a fully online delivery. The process in which we engaged raised a series of challenges regarding the effective communication of key concepts, addressing emotional responses to the course's content, and overcoming the separation of humans from nature by technology. There are challenges to any discipline from moving to online education. For studies of the environment, a particular issue is the management of student anxiety. In this field, topics typically covered include harms to humans and other species, including extinctions and, at the most extreme end of concerns, the possibility of global ecological catastrophe. Another challenge is the separation of students from the natural environment by the very technology being used to deliver learning. Environmental education is often delivered with practical, hands-on experiences, complementing and applying in-class content. Field trips, for example, provide tangible experiences of nature and may include meeting directly with people undertaking practical solutions to environmental problems. Against these potential limitations, online learning has less environmental impact than on-campus learning (Caird et al., 2015) and offers scalability of learning to help give ecological and sustainability messaging a wider reach.

Environmental sociology differs from other environmental studies such as environmental education, management, or science because it questions the very social construction of environmental concerns. This is not the equivalent of outright denial of environmental science, but the field does employ a critical gaze upon what we choose or believe to be relevant harms and future risks. Environmental sociology examines the social construction of, and the associated anxieties which may be produced by, studies of the environment.

We, the authors, did not explicitly set out to undertake this project as an experiment in innovative design or with expectations of breaking new pedagogical ground. We are experienced educators who applied our understanding of the field and our pedagogical skills to this project in the hope of creating a positive student experience. In the process of redeveloping the course, we

DOI: 10.4324/9781003505785-14

found ourselves intuitively shifting away from the sometimes-solemn emotional messaging that emerges in environmental sociology. We sought ways for students to establish a connection with the physical world without worsening a sense of despair. Forms of satire and light-heartedness were employed, giving students a psychological life raft during otherwise deep and tenebrous content. This chapter will present how we deployed several strategies such as mobile video production, student-generated content, selective choice (and sequencing) of external content, and a suite of practice materials, with regular injections of humour to improve the learners' (and our own) experiences, connection with nature, and, ultimately, the learning experience.

Challenges of online and environmental sociology

Several perennial dilemmas face education for the environment, all of which are multiplied by challenges emerging in the online learning space. Young people particularly experience and express psychological despair about the state of the planet and the suffering of humans and other species (Ojala, 2021). Environmental sociology can induce further such despair (Leahy, 2009). While the "doom and gloom" is a consistent problem in the discipline of sociology (Germov & Poole, 2019) producing a sense of "miserabilism" (Beilharz & Hogan, 2006), this can be compounded by the "eco-anxiety" (Ojala, 2018) which comes from simply understanding environmental problems. Further compounding these challenges, anxiety and fear are also experienced when undertaking an online course (Conrad, 2002) in part due to reduced teacher-student interaction (Heckel & Ringeisen, 2019). Students are also reported to rank their experience of online courses lower than in-person learning (Lowenthal et al., 2015). Yet, there is potential for online learning to generate both negative (such as isolation) and positive (such as achievement) emotional experiences, and these can improve throughout the duration of a course (Zembylas, 2008). Transitioning a course in environmental sociology from in-person to online delivery offered an opportunity to observe the change in learner participation and experiences as well as presented challenges for innovative delivery.

The study of environmental sociology sits awkwardly astride the boundaries between the social and natural sciences. Sociology has traditionally avoided consideration of the environment, largely due to a fear of biological determinism, social Darwinism, and their associated injustices (Carolan, 2024).[1] This has led to tensions between the studies of environmental concerns with social concerns which, when it is better understood, reveals the magnification of social problems. In sociology, struggles are presented, outlining how marginalised groups face structural disadvantages. Environmental sociology reveals the magnification of those struggles by highlighting that it is not just humans who suffer, but that suffering extends to other species and that the existence of the very biosphere on which we all depend is under threat. Students of environmental sociology can thus feel isolated in quixotic struggles against the problems of the world. Attempting to reconcile the 'wicked' problems presented by insurmountable global environmental crises can be emotionally overwhelming. Knowing environmental problems can become a "gift of tears" (Burton-Christie, 2011), a burden of knowledge. Beck argues that we have produced a "risk society" (Beck, 1992) in which we become obsessed with future problems. Abundant examples of speculative utopian and dystopian futures can be found both in popular culture and in academia (Urry, 2011). The breadth of concerns is potentially unlimited. We can potentially indulge infinite concern about future problems based on scientific evidence and multiplied by our vivid imaginations. People deeply concerned about the environment can experience "hysteresis" (Bourdieu, 2000, p. 160) and a "Don Quixote Effect" in which their investment in environmental struggles is not matched by others and they feel mismatched to their social conditions.[2] However, reflexivity and humour has also been found amongst young environmental workers who recognise their investment and adjust strategically (Cooper, 2024).

Alternatively, scientific objectivity can be critiqued for being dispassionate and in need of disruption (Khalaim & Budziszewska, 2024). Offering solutions to environmental problems is sometimes proposed as a useful way of addressing these tensions (Carolan, 2024). An analysis of an undergraduate course in political ecologies of land (Kirsop-Taylor et al., 2021) found that team-based problem-solving pedagogies can establish a sense of agency amongst learners. However, though a solution-oriented perspective can sustain the hope of learners, it can also be problematic. This is because there are always more problems to be addressed and, ultimately, there is no such thing as 'solving' environmental problems: they are always something to be managed. The expectation of a perfectly sustainable utopia gives unreasonable hope.

Individualisation also emerges as a challenge in environmental education: situations are created that can burden students with personal responsibility for addressing environmental concerns. Ferreira (2019) argues that environmental education activities serve to fashion a "specific form of personhood called the environmental citizen" (p. 323) and that environmental educators deploy governmentality (Foucault, 1991), shaping the conduct of students, encouraging them to compare themselves against others seeking to achieve a state of purity.[3] Further, the online learning environment has the potential to magnify individualisation leaving students feeling more isolated and alone (Kaufman & Vallade, 2022). Online environmental education risks accelerating pressures on individual students to achieve more in terms of both learning and environmental outcomes.

A significant dilemma facing studies of the environment is the gap between the physical and conceptual worlds where learning takes place. Environmental sociology recognises this separation of humans from nature as a form of alienation or "metabolic rift" (Foster, 1999). Over the centuries, increased industrialisation has progressively alienated individuals from their connection with nature. The online world is another medium through which this separation can be exacerbated. There are many ways in which digital technology can enhance outdoor learning by enabling experiences, for example, with navigational technology, but it can also create barriers between the learners and the outdoors by distracting students from connection with nature (Hills & Thomas, 2020). Yet, studies comparing the effectiveness of online environmental education programs with in-person methods have produced contrasting results. Some students who have received computer-assisted instruction increased their environmental literacy at higher rates than students taught using traditional methods (Aivazidis et al., 2006). In contrast, the environmental friendliness of students increased more when they received in-class tuition rather than web-based delivery of the same course by the same instructor (Wright, 2008). In both studies, pre and post-test analysis of results accounted for rates of environmental literacy at enrolment. However, it should be remembered that course delivery does not have to be one or the other. In-person learning can be combined with online content, providing the benefits of both modes in blended learning. Suites of "digital competencies" can be developed by educators to help facilitate the environmental learning experience (Sebastian-Lopez & Gonzalez, 2020). Further, Selwyn (2024) points to the potential of digital technology to reduce the environmental impacts of delivering education and argues for "digital degrowth" as a radical approach using technology to lessen the impacts upon both learners and the physical environment.

What follows presents the project of transitioning a course in environmental sociology from traditional methods to online and how we, the educators and course designers, attempted to redress the inherent doom and gloom, miserabilism, and eco-anxiety that accompany this field of learning. While we somewhat chose to engage with the "bad environmentalism" (Seymour, 2018) proposed to counter this solemnity, we could not simply treat environmental concerns as a laughing matter (Takach, 2022). An approach in which we blended honesty and sincerity with humour and reflexivity to engage with serious content was adopted. We also attempted to transcend the metabolic rift implicit in online delivery. This chapter presents a selection of the strategies we used.

Background

In 2020, the University of Newcastle (UON) redeveloped Environment and Society, a second-year undergraduate environmental sociology course for online delivery as part of the newly launched Bachelor of Arts Online degree program, hosted on the UK online learning platform, FutureLearn. The task of adapting and reworking the course material was given to the authors, Jai Cooper and Chris Lawrence. Jai, an outdoor and environmental educator and long-time academic contributor to the various incarnations of the course, took a lead in determining the themes, course content, academic rigour, and coordination. Chris, an experienced learning designer within UON's Learning Design and Teaching Innovation unit (LDTI), guided the constructive alignment (Biggs, 1996) of the course, the overarching narrative, and engaging learning activities that supported the concepts being explored. This combined expertise was essential in adapting the course to an online format that addressed both the subject's inherent emotional weight and the challenges of remote learning.

The course, which had run since the early 2000s, covered key topics of environmental science, such as climate science, biodiversity loss, and sustainable design, but with a specific focus on human societal responses such as economic systems, Indigenous perspectives, and imagined futures. The course delivery often included one or more field trips to a local environmental education opportunity such as the local water storage, treatment, and recycling facilities or a permaculture farm. Throughout the course's various iterations, disclaimers were always included regarding the despondency and anxiety that might come with learning about human relations with the environment. The original developer of the course, Dr Terry Leahy, had always acknowledged that it would be presenting depressing topics ranging from the abuse of orangutans and the complete eradication of other species to stories about the societal implosion of the Mayans and scientific warnings of climate catastrophes to come. There were warnings of the emotional pitfalls: for both studying and teaching this course.

Delivered five times between 2020 and 2024, the online course released content weekly over 12 weeks via FutureLearn, with assessments and other course administration functions managed by UON's learning management system, Canvas. Despite the shift to an online format being a significant change in course delivery, the course retained its emphasis on blending theoretical knowledge with practical environmental applications (as will be presented later). Student numbers ranged between 75 and 125 during that period, which was a significant increase on levels prior to the course running online. Students were predominantly domestic Australian students of which most were undertaking a social science major, with some undertaking education (teaching) and other degrees.

Course design

Methodically addressing eco-anxiety

Mindful of the potential anxiety students might experience when studying environmental degradation, the design process included elements aimed at reducing isolation and fostering a supportive learning environment. The FutureLearn platform was conducive to this approach, promoting a mix of learning activities and media, as well as encouraging personable language and active, in situ discussion spaces in the site's layout. Though the course restructure could not feasibly include some of the more sensory-rich experiences of visiting the site of a permaculture farm as a cohort, the effort was made to replicate these kinds of experiences in other ways.

In practice, we implemented many of the strategies recommended in Salmon's Five-Stage Model of "access and motivation; online socialisation; information exchange; knowledge construction; and development" (Salmon, 2011). Firstly, students' access was facilitated by being welcomed with a strong sense of educator presence. This was achieved in both the written and multimedia content that was produced, positioning Jai as the 'tour guide' while filming on location and interviewing other experts and relevant representatives (see Figure 11.1). The use of video materials filmed outdoors was maximised. For example, in-person interviews were held outdoors. This had the additional hygiene benefit during the COVID-19 epidemic period during which they were filmed. Learning activities were designed to keep students engaged, active and connected throughout the course. We aimed to 'bring the outside in' featured content focused on interactive engagement with outdoor adventure.

Secondly, as online socialisation, we bookended the course with a focus on the emotional aspects of environmental sociology. This included introductory content addressing the pessimism of environmental sociology and final content leaving students with satirical reflexivity on the human condition. We sprinkled elements of various forms of humour throughout the course, regularly alternating between serious and light-hearted content. Thirdly, information exchange was achieved by dividing the whole unit into four themes, allowing for the recruitment of ideas from across disciplines of philosophy, theology, economics, the natural sciences, sociology, anthropology, cultural

Figure 11.1 On-site expert interview – Jai with Dave Sivyer of Feedback Organics discussing the local 'One Hour Farmer' program.

studies, media, literature, and more. The fourth and fifth stages, knowledge construction and development, were facilitated largely through online discussions and the assessment tasks which we discuss later.

Course structure

The FutureLearn platform establishes delivery over a 12-week course broken into four sub-parts, which we describe here as a 'module.' Each module included 3 weeks' content and was given a theme. Each week of content included about 15–20 individual 'steps.' A step was a separate piece of content, such as an article to read, an exercise to undertake, or a short video to watch. Each step included a discussion section where students could make comments and reply and like the comments from other students. By generating the weekly steps, we aimed to create the equivalent level of content to a week's in-person class and reading for an undergraduate level course. There were no mandatory participation requirements for students.

These four modules were titled 'The Call of Nature,' 'Production Lines,' 'Planet of the People,' and 'About Time,' and were respectively focused on human relations with the environment, materialist concerns, environmental justice, and temporal considerations. This framework helped to both meet the course objectives and provide a sequence in which we could address student emotional responses.

The titles of the first 3-week module, 'The Call of Nature,' and the first week's content, 'Peak Doom,' playfully addressed the nature-culture binary and eco-anxiety by introducing a double-entendre ('the call of nature') and pointing to doom as an emotional state, rather than a physical outcome. This light-hearted approach to potentially serious content was regularly used to soften concerns without being dispassionate, and to give them due acknowledgement without entrenching guilt and anxiety. This module discussed the history of, and reasoning behind, sociology's (lack of) engagement with discussions of nature and the environment. Key concepts presented included the social construction of environmental concerns, and key theories relevant to environmental sociology including reflexive modernity and risk society. Discussions of environmental philosophy were presented such as human-animal relations, eco-feminism, differences between anthropocentric and ecocentric perspectives, spiritual and theological perspectives, and the 'HEP/NEP' distinction (human 'exemptionalism' paradigm and new ecological paradigm).[4]

The second module, 'Production Lines,' presented issues of material relations. Climate science, policy, and attitudes were discussed. Included in the content was an introduction to forms of climate change denial and ways in which it could be engaged humorously. For example, the use of the 'Cranky Uncle' app (https://crankyuncle.com/) developed by Monash University academics. Other key issues relating to the production and consumption of natural resources were presented such as 'peak oil', sustainable food production, waste management, sustainable design principles (such as housing and urban design), and different lifestyle approaches. During this module, the dilemma of the individualisation of environmental action and citizenship was raised.

Extending the uneven distribution of ecologically oriented cultural capitals, the third course, 'Planet of the People' (a cultural reference to, and play upon, the 'Planet of the Apes' movie series) explored the uneven distribution of responsibility for, and impacts upon, different groups of humans. This theme drew upon concepts from environmental activism, neo-liberal governmentality, environmental racism, and other intersections between environmental concern and action.

In the fourth and final theme of the course, 'About Time,' temporal relations, differing imaginaries, and posthumanism were explored. This module examined some societies which had collapsed, such as the Mayan and Sumerian civilisations, and how Indigenous societies have engaged sustainable practices. Alternative economic approaches to contemporary capitalism such as co-operatives and the valuation of ecological services were analysed. The final week of the course 'De-evolution' was specifically designed to draw together the whole course and revisit a comic perspective towards environmental concerns. For example, the week began with an analysis of the song "The future is not what it used to be." Rather than providing a binary between depressing doom and gloom or raising unrealistic hopes, this final session explored how humour and fiction can shed new light on possible futures. For example, the Malthusian perspectives popularised by Dadaist musicians Devo (short for 'De-evolution'), the VHEMT (Voluntary Human Extinction Movement: "May we live long and die out"), and the movie comedy *Idiocracy* were presented and discussed. A critical perspective was applied to a suite of examples of both utopian and dystopian fiction. These discussions of pop theory at the conclusion of the course content complemented the satirical introductory week. This approach helped to bookend the course content with an ecologically oriented form of reflexivity. In practice, rather than engaging in an 'issues' styled approach to environmental problems and solutions, we allowed for quite serious consideration of environmental concerns while relieving some of the associated pressures.

Production and delivery

Vodcasting

In previous work, Jai had employed "mobile methods" (Buscher & Urry, 2009), the practice of collecting data such as interviews while in the process of being mobile, to generate video course content and ethnographic data. In short, Jai was competent with GoPro cameras and other video technology to record material and to interview people while in the process of moving. Jai was given additional tuition by the LDTI team to undertake his own filming and to innovate with camera techniques. Due to some physical impairments limiting his walking, Jai has specialised in mobile video content by bike and kayak to somewhat transcend these challenges. Consequently, we took the opportunity of featuring Jai as a mobile 'bike-ademic' – an academic based on a bike. In addition to video course content, Jai also produced weekly vodcast course announcements. These aimed to keep a regular educator presence and to provide continuity for the content.

Jai commenced the course by engaging students with its production, using a reflective window to show himself undertaking the filming of video by and through the process of mounting his GoPro camera to his helmet (see Figure 11.2). To ensure reusability of the video content, only the introductory vodcast explicitly shared the date of its production: during the COVID-19 lockdowns of 2020. This comment was added to help students understand behaviours such as socially distanced interviews conducted in open-air settings.

The first vodcast of the course, 'How's the Serenity!,' addressed the social construction of environmental concerns. Students were introduced to ironic conflations of natural purity and environmental degradation. The vodcast features Jai narrating as he rides to Glenrock State Conservation Area, an area in the heart of industrial Newcastle managed for conservation and recreation. Here, he passes by views of the Pacific Ocean and into thick bushland where an echidna forages in the undergrowth. Jai introduces Glenrock as a place where he goes to relax and indulge his "misanthropic fantasies of a world without humans." He presents Glenrock as both relaxing and pleasant but also tainted. For example, Jai invokes a cultural reference to the iconic Australian movie, *The Castle*, by gesturing to inhale and asking "smell that, eh, how's the serenity?!" (see Figure 11.3) before pointing out the coal ships visible on the horizon.[5] The attractive yellow flowers of bitou bush (*Chrysanthemoides monilifera subsp. rotundata*) are highlighted as an aesthetically pleasing introduced species and threat to biodiversity. The Glenrock Lagoon area is discussed as being 'natural,' yet also a site of colonial dispossession of the local Awabakal people. The content highlights the irony that places which

Figure 11.2 Combined images of Jai with a reflective window and fitting a GoPro camera on his bicycle helmet.

Figure 11.3 Arriving at Glenrock Lagoon and asking, 'Smell that, eh, how's the serenity?'

we might view as natural and where we go to find respite might also be places of environmental degradation or historic (and ongoing) injustices.

Other technology

A range of other technologies were deployed to enhance student engagement with the physical environment and with their peers such as online polls, discussions, and Padlets (https://padlet.com/). Padlets were a particularly effective technology, providing useful opportunities for crowdsourcing data and actively engaging students. For example, following Jai's visit to Glenrock State Conservation Area, in the 'Magic Spot' activity, students were asked to post to a map format Padlet a location they liked to visit to reconnect with nature (see Figure 11.3). Collectively, this built a combined class map showing the diverse places around the world appreciated by the class. Students were asked to share their concerns about impacts upon, or threats to, these precious places. The 'Calculator Convention' Padlet aimed to counter individualisation by asking students to crowdsource ecological footprint calculators from across the internet. Ecological footprint and carbon calculators can be technologies of governmentality and responsibilisation – the process whereby individuals or communities (instead of the state) become responsible (Soneryd & Uggla, 2015). By asking students to search for these calculators, we hoped to illuminate their production and reposition students away from being the subject of their analysis. The 'Community Gardening' Padlet asked students to visit their local community garden, post a photo of it, and explain the garden's philosophy and policies. Students were also asked to undertake an inventory of sources of production of energy in their neighbourhood, such as rooftop solar. Overall, the technological applications we used facilitated knowledge construction in line with the fourth stage of Salmon's (2011) model. The fifth stage, development, was addressed primarily through the challenging, yet inclusive, assessment tasks we presented.

Assessments

Four different assessments were developed for the unit, supported by an array of formative (practice) tasks including quizzes to familiarise students with the technology used in the assessable quizzes. These were designed to engage students with academic rigour but also to allow for some artistic expression, provide opportunities to engage reflexively and to deploy some of their own humour. The first written assessment task, an annotated bibliography, asked students to explore four academic sources engaging with one of the four-course themes (the topics of the four modules). Students would thus focus on either human relations with the environment, materialist concerns, environmental justice, or temporal considerations. A key aim of this task was to engage students with high-quality academic content relevant to the field of study. The task also prompted students to review the course outline, hopefully gaining a better understanding of the overall course structure and recognising that it was not all 'doom and gloom.'

The second major assessment was a vodcast. Students were given a maximum of 6 min to provide a video response to one of six different pre-determined topics. Predictably, many students cited anxiety about completing a presentation. However, unlike an in-class presentation, student submissions were video recorded and not shared collectively. With regard to student anxiety, the recorded and confidential format of the online setting thus provided advantages over an in-person setting. Further, by this stage of the course, students had been exposed to a range of vodcasting by Jai, thus establishing a familiarity with some possible uses of the technology and the validation of taking risks with the medium. For example, Jai used both course content and announcement videos to channel well-known Australian environmentalists, invoking the comic enthusiasm of characters such as Steve Irwin (internationally known as 'the Crocodile Hunter') and Costa Georgiadis (presenter on the long-running television program, *Gardening Australia*). Some students employed creative flair with vodcast submissions including innovative video editing and deploying their own humour. Importantly, while the task allowed for creative flair, students were assessed primarily on their command of the content.

The third major assessment task (titled 'Article') included an extra degree of choice. Students could choose from three writing styles: traditional academic essay (as used in previous versions of the course); quality journalism in a similar fashion to *The Conversation* (https://theconversation.com/); or a satire piece (in the fashion of *The Onion* [https://theonion.com/]). We aimed to facilitate assessment for inclusion (Nieminen, 2024) by foregrounding students' own areas of interest. Students were not given pre-determined topics. Instead, they were required to develop their own topic and, in their response, provide reflections on their reasoning, thus demonstrating an understanding of the social construction of environmental concerns as well as partnering with them in the development of their own tasks. For example, many students chose the topic of 'fast fashion.' Some reflected upon their choice of topic and that it was, somewhat, a way of individualising environmental problems, a manifestation of patriarchal influences on society (because their choice was to critique a female-dominated industry while distracting from other, more harmful, male-dominated industries such as weapons manufacture), or that the choice of topic was a form of neo-colonialism in which first world privilege extended pious judgment to an industry based in the developing world. Only a minority of students chose the satire option. However, those who did attempt this option engaged creatively, developing fictitious characters, both heroes and villains, and engaging with popular cultural references. Some deployed satire, absurdism, and puns amongst a range of creative strategies. This rendered their work more colourful and enhanced the experience for assessors. In most cases, there was a gradual decrease in the quality of each response, suggesting that satire is a difficult genre to sustain effectively over a lengthy response. We subsequently adjusted the nominal word limit to vary according to genre. The fourth assessment task was deployed at stages during the course and included three multiple choice quizzes. Prior to these formal quizzes, we also offered some practice multiple-choice quizzes (including some absurd possible choices for humorous effect).

We also aimed to personalise the delivery of feedback to students. In addition to an overall mark, feedback for each major task was provided with both a recorded voice comment and written comments in the text of the submission. This was usually done with a stylus rather than typing. This method was less formal than typed feedback and had the further benefit of connecting students with nature. For example, in Canvas, marking could be conducted on a mobile device, allowing for escape from the office. Consequently, Jai's recorded comments often included the sounds of birdsong or crashing waves, depending on where he was working.

Reflections

Throughout the development of the course, we experimented with a range of strategies to establish a connection with the environment and counteract potential eco-anxiety and enhance wellbeing. Some of the strategies included the use of puns, double-entendres and other playful terminology, satire and irony, direct physical engagement with the local environment, and cultural references to popular media presentations of nature and nature lovers. Student feedback suggested that they appreciated a strong educator presence and the outdoor content. One student commented that Jai was the 'Beau Miles' (a well-known Australian outdoor/environmental media influencer) of academia. Many other feedback comments pointed to how Jai's enthusiasm was apparent in the video content and that it was influential upon their learning experience.

Another contributing factor to the production was how the interpersonal dynamics between Jai, Chris, and the wider LDTI team generated creativity. The whole team was determined to enjoy their work. Jai was willing to experiment with suggestions for video production and comfortable with delivering humorous content. Chris contributed an endless stream of puns and double entendre. The wider LDTI team provided a willing audience on which to test and refine materials. Management was trusting enough to give the team creative licence, and we revelled in the opportunity. The outcome would have been significantly diminished had the team been subject to layers of top-down control. Jai and Chris' high degree of familiarity with similar cultural references provided a useful basis from which to draw creativity and generate comic delivery. We expected that some cultural references may not be recognised or could even be misunderstood (especially by students of other ethnicities and generations). Hence, we either provided supporting information or ensured the content was not critical for assessment. We also included a healthy dose of self-deprecation throughout to reassure students that there was no shame in not understanding any aspect of the course. The aim of our humour was to provide relief, not generate further anxiety.

We found, once developed, that the course content was generally easy to maintain. However, it was important to maintain some regular contact. The weekly video announcements established the continuity of a strong educator presence so that students did not feel abandoned. During the semester break, we provided additional optional gamified content for students. During the one semester in which the course was not delivered by Jai, some students contacted him, confusing him for the lead educator. This was an understandable error given Jai's strong presence in the course content. However, it indicates that students may become confused between the educator who is coordinating the current course run (but may not appear in many of the course materials), and an educator who appears in the course recordings but is not currently involved in the course run.

Across all technologies (such as Padlet boards, polls, and associated discussions), there were some disadvantages to those students who engaged first. The first-come, first-comment, nature of working in a linear path through the weekly content in asynchronous learning meant that the peak of commenting usually came about the middle to latter part of the week in which it was released. This meant that those students commenting first would see less other commentary. For example, with Padlet maps, the first students to post would only see their locations. However, by the end of the week, a larger set of 'pin-drops' (see Figure 11.4) had been made. In contrast, students who were last to post saw a wider range of locations. The weekly peak of comments occurred

Easing eco-anxiety in an online environmental sociology course   163

Figure 11.4 Pindrops on the 'Magic Spot' Padlet.

Figure 11.5 Screenshot of footage using a GoPro mounted to a sea kayak with handheld gimbal and phone.

towards the middle and latter part of the week. Other issues arose with interaction on the course, including students not commenting on others' posts. To help address these challenges, we developed instructions on online etiquette and how to engage in course discussions.

Jai's use of mobile methods has extended his effectiveness as an educator (while also helping his fitness and making for enjoyable work). Jai integrated further mobile video content for other blended and online courses (see Figure 11.5). Furthering the use of adaptive mobility, Jai has invested in an e-bike and his own filming equipment, extending his video production with a YouTube channel including a suite of content in the fields of environmental sociology and global studies.

Conclusion

The ecological and mental health-related challenges faced in this course are not going to dissipate. As the reality of climate change leads to further impacts, the associated eco-anxiety is inevitably going to increase. Teaching environmental sociology provides an opportunity to apply imagination and reflect upon the use of technology and the effects of our teaching. In this course, we did not aim to fashion pure environmental citizens. Rather, our pedagogical approach (and that of the discipline) has aimed to give people skills to understand what is happening in the world. This might be viewed as being dispassionate. However, while an objective view is an inherent criterion for legitimate scientific inquiry, we believe that we have found a way to acknowledge the significance of the topic without becoming invested to the point of disempowering students. We hope that our approach, incorporating technology and providing comedic reflexivity, may be more effective to make learning more sustainable.

We developed a sequential and progressive conceptual framing of course content, enabling a rich abundance of key concepts to be communicated. The suite of comedic strategies creatively intervened in the miserabilism for which the discipline is renowned, formed a unique pedagogical tool, and, hopefully, inspired students to apply their learnings to the future pragmatically. With this approach, we aimed to redress the eco-anxiety and individualisation associated with environmental education. We also hoped to collectivise the student experience as best as possible. Along the way, we enjoyed ourselves, taking time to indulge in a little humour with a few puns, some cheesy 'dad jokes' (yes, the authors' children will attest to such suffering), and some possibly outdated cultural references. We hope that our work has improved the student experience and will help make the world and its future a little more pleasant.

Notes

1 Carolan describes this as "sidestepping environmental variables . . . as a reaction to social Darwinism" (p. 5).
2 Drawing upon Cervantes's tale of the Knight Errant, Don Quixote, Bourdieu describes a 'Don Quixote Effect' as an outcome of 'hysteresis': a mismatch between habitus and field in which agents attempt to continue or revive tradition while society has progressed.
3 Foucault describes 'governmentality' as 'the conduct of conduct' and as the extension of a government-like mentality through which social subjects self-govern and govern the behaviour of others without the need for formal government to be present.
4 The human exemptionalism paradigm (HEP) positions humans as central to nature, with superior capacities to other species such as the development of advanced

technology and purporting that we can be exempt from the consequences of interfering with natural processes. The new ecological paradigm (NEP) recognises our position as just one species within the ecological functioning of the planet and that interfering with nature has consequences for humans and all species.
5 The movie *The Castle* juxtaposes the key characters' love of the environment against their penchant for fishing in a loud two-stroke motorboat, evoking an ironic 'tragedy of the commons' or 'loving nature to death.'

References

Aivazidis, C., Lazaridou, M., & Hellden, G. F. (2006). A comparison between a traditional and online environmental education program. *Reports & Research*, *37*(4), 45–54. https://doi.org/10.3200/JOEE.37.4.45-54

Beck, U. (1992). *Risk society: Towards a new modernity*. Sage.

Beilharz, P., & Hogan, T. (2006). Introduction. In P. Beilharz & T. Hogan (Eds.), *Sociology: Place, time & division* (pp. xv–xxii). Oxford University Press.

Biggs, J. (1996). Enhancing teaching through constructive alignment. *Higher Education*, *32*, 347–364. https://doi.org/10.1007/BF00138871

Bourdieu, P. (2000). *Pascalian meditations* (R. Nice, Trans.). Polity.

Burton-Christie, D. (2011). The gift of tears: Loss, mourning and the work of ecological restoration. *Worldviews*, *15*(1), 29–46. http://www.jstor.org/stable/43799348

Buscher, M., & Urry, J. (2009). Mobile methods and the empirical. *European Journal of Social Theory*, *12*(1), 99–116. https://doi.org/10.1177/1368431008099642

Caird, S., Lane, A., Swinthenby, E., Roy, R., & Potter, S. (2015). Design of higher education teaching models and carbon impacts. *International Journal of Sustainability in Higher Education*, *16*(1), 96–111. https://doi.org/10.1108/IJSHE-06-2013-0065

Carolan, M. (2024). *Society and the environment: Pragmatic solutions to ecological issues* (4th ed.). Routledge.

Conrad, D. L. (2002). Engagement, excitement, anxiety, and fear: Learners' experiences of starting an online course. *The American Journal of Distance Education*, *16*(4), 205–226. https://doi.org/10.1207/S15389286AJDE1604_2

Cooper, J. (2024). Don Quixote and the green army: Lessons from Australian environmental workfare. *Journal of Applied Youth Studies*. https://doi.org/10.1007/s43151-024-00143-0

Ferreira, J. (2019). The limits of environmental educators' fashioning of 'individualized' environmental citizens. *The Journal of Environmental Education*, *50*(4–6), 321–331. https://doi.org/10.1080/00958964.2019.1721769

Foster, J. B. (1999). Marx's theory of metabolic rift: Classical foundations for environmental sociology. *American Journal of Sociology*, *105*(2), 366–405. https://doi.org/10.1086/210315

Foucault, M. (1991). Governmentality. In G. Burchell, C. Gordon, & P. Miller (Eds.), *The Foucault effect: Studies in governmentality* (pp. 87–104). University of Chicago Press.

Germov, J., & Poole, M. (2019). The sociological gaze: Linking private lives to public issues. In J. Germov, & M. Poole (Eds.), *Public sociology: An introduction to Australian society* (pp. 1–21). Allen and Unwin.

Heckel, C., & Ringeisen, T. (2019). Pride and anxiety in online learning environments: Achievement emotions as mediators between learners' characteristics and learning outcomes. *Journal of Computer Assisted Learning*, *35*, 667–677. https://doi.org/10.1111/jcal.12367

Hills, D., & Thomas, G. (2020). Digital technology and outdoor experiential learning. *Journal of Adventure Education and Outdoor Learning*, *20*(2), 155–169. https://doi.org/10.1080/14729679.2019.1604244

Kaufman, R., & Vallade, J. I. (2022). Exploring connections in the online learning environment: Student perceptions of rapport, climate, and loneliness. *Interactive Learning Environments, 30*(10), 1794–1808. https://doi.org/10.1080/10494820.2020.1749670

Khalaim, O., & Budziszewska, M. (2024). "It should not only be technical education." Students' climate anxiety experiences and expectations toward university education in three European universities. *The Journal of Environmental Education, 55*(4), 308–323. https://doi.org/10.1080/00958964.2024.2339824

Kirsop-Taylor, N., Appiah, D., Steadman, A., & Huggett, M. (2021). Reflections on integrating the political into environmental education through problem-based learning and political ecology. *The Journal of Environmental Education, 52*(1), 1–13. https://doi.org/10.1080/00958964.2020.1825919

Leahy, T. (2009, February). Environmental despair. *Arena Magazine*, 99, 12–13.

Lowenthal, P., Bauer, C., & Chen, K-Z. (2015). Student perceptions of online course evaluations. *American Journal of Distance Education, 29*(2), 85–97. https://doi.org/10.1080/08923647.2015.1023621

Nieminen, J. H. (2024). Assessment for inclusion: Rethinking inclusive assessment in higher education. *Teaching in Higher Education, 29*(4), 841–859. https://doi.org/10.1080/13562517.2021.2021395

Ojala, M. (2018). Eco-anxiety. *RSA Journal, 164*(4), 10–15. https://www.jstor.org/stable/26798430

Ojala, M. (2021). Safe spaces or a pedagogy of discomfort? Senior high-school teachers' meta-emotion philosophies and climate change education. *The Journal of Environmental Education, 52*(1), 40–52. https://doi.org/10.1080/00958964.2020.1845589

Salmon, G. (2011). *E-moderating: The key to online teaching and learning* (3rd ed.). Taylor & Francis.

Sebastian-Lopez, M., & Gonzalez, R. D. (2020). Mobile learning for sustainable Development and environmental teacher education. *Sustainability, 12*(22), 9757. https://doi.org/10.3390/su12229757

Selwyn, N. (2024). Digital degrowth: Toward radically sustainable education technology. *Learning, Media and Technology, 49*(2), 186–199. https://doi.org/10.1080/17439884.2022.2159978

Seymour, N. (2018). *Bad Environmentalism*. University of Minnesota Press.

Soneryd, L., & Uggla, Y. (2015). Green governmentality and responsibilization: New forms of governance and responses to 'consumer responsibility.' *Environmental Politics, 24*(6), 913–931. https://doi.org/10.1080/09644016.2015.1055885

Takach, G. (2022). Eco-comedy. *Environmental Humanities, 14*(2), 371–374. https://doi.org/10.1215/22011919-9712445

Urry, J. (2011). *Climate change and society*. Polity.

Wright, J. M. (2008). Web-based versus in-class: An exploration of how instructional methods influence postsecondary students' environmental literacy. *Reports & Research, 39*(2), 33–45. https://doi.org/10.3200/JOEE.39.2.33-46

Zembylas, M. (2008). Adult learners' emotions in online learning. *Distance Education, 29*(1), 71–87. https://doi.org/10.1080/01587910802004852

Part 4
Impacts and evaluation

12 Academic development for effective online learning design

Clare Lloyd, Annika Herb and Michael Kilmister

Introduction

The design of quality online learning is contingent on successful collaborative partnerships across teaching and professional staff engaging in a range of different approaches to academic development (Brown et al., 2013; Vallis et al., 2022). When we commenced the project at the centre of this chapter in 2018, COVID-19 was yet to alter the higher education landscape and force educators to transition to remote online learning, and fully online bachelor's degrees were relatively uncommon in Australia. The purposeful design and delivery of an online degree in humanities (the 'BA Online') was also an unknown entity for the academic and professional staff at the University of Newcastle (UON), and as such, designing, building, and implementing a full online degree necessitated supported academic development. This project both required and facilitated diverse forms of academic practice, including training in pedagogy, digital literacy, presentation skills, platform-specific course facilitation, accessibility integration, and writing for online delivery. Academic development was essential to develop these skills and a driver to ensure a teaching and learning experience that enhanced student experience and success. The focus of academic development work is primarily on improving or transforming lecturers' teaching and assessment practices to ensure high-quality learning experiences and outcomes for students. Academic development took on multiple forms throughout the project and was integrated for individuals and across the school. This chapter explores the pedagogical principles undergirding this support, and its impact for staff and students.

The success of this development program is reflected through the impact on student learning. The authors follow in the footsteps of scholarship that explores the influence professional development activities can have on student learning (Joyce & Showers, 2002; QAA Cymru, 2024). We adopt a participatory action research approach to reflect on our experiences in collaborative online course design and academic development, examining along the way the context, staff needs, and the pedagogical approach to both student learning and academic development for staff. Action research

DOI: 10.4324/9781003505785-16

engages practitioners in enhancing their own practice through iterative cycles of planning, implementation, observation, and reflection (Kember & Gow, 1992). We evaluate the effectiveness of this process through our reflections and qualitative student feedback considering overall and specific outcomes of the learning experience. This evaluative approach reflects the complex realities of the project being assessed and the professional development strategy that was implemented. As a project driven by the needs of students, there was extended and iterative monitoring of the student experience on the courses in place; systematically evaluating the number and quality of training events for staff was not a priority. The approach to professional learning on the BA Online can best be summed up by Boud and Brew's (2012) notion of "utilising opportunities in everyday work and finding ways of addressing the limitations of learning in the normal context of academic practice" (p. 210). This conceptualisation of academic development "as a social process occurring within the context of practice" (Boud & Brew, 2012, p. 209) refutes traditional approaches that privilege rigid learning activities or participation in one-off training events and favours planned and spontaneous learning moments and peer learning that are embedded in real teaching practice.

Underpinning the academic development of the project was a strong pedagogical foundation for learning design and teaching in an online environment. This foundation drew on a framework consisting of broad overarching principles for digital learning, including institutional and curriculum design principles which emphasised learning should be social and enable students to construct knowledge, and Laurillard's (2012) Conversational Framework which was at the core of the FutureLearn learning experience platform (see Chapters 1–3). We – alongside our colleagues in the central teaching and learning unit – supported academics to design their courses using this model, while embedding enough flexibility for the disciplines and educators to retain their own unique identities and priorities, which in turn enhanced trust through intentional and organic practices.

Each course in the project needed to be designed with a specific curriculum or programmatic design principles, which comprised stepped learning components. Twelve-week courses were modularised into four modules (each 3-week long). Most first-year level courses had the first module as an 'open course' on FutureLearn (see Figures 12.1 and 12.2). Both UON students and FutureLearn learners had access to this open module, an entirely novel experience for staff and students alike (see Chapters 2 and 3). During the delivery of the 3-week open modules, the educators brought global learners and degree students together at scale, whilst simultaneously improving and increasing their teacher presence as educators (Coleborne & Lloyd, 2019). The other three modules were 'closed,' and only enrolled students[1] could complete them. We guided staff to ensure only the final three modules contained summative assessments. Professional and academic staff took collective responsibility to ensure these design principles were authentic to the

Academic development for effective online learning design 171

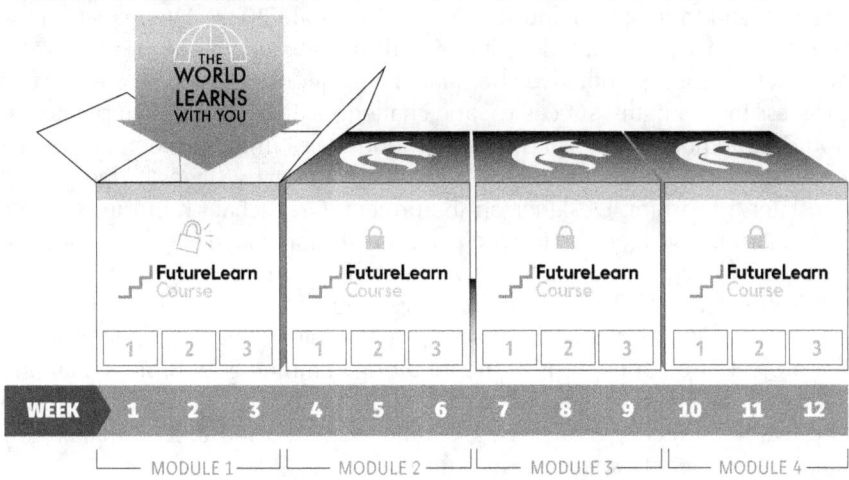

Figure 12.1 Student-facing graphic explainer on the structure of courses with open module component.

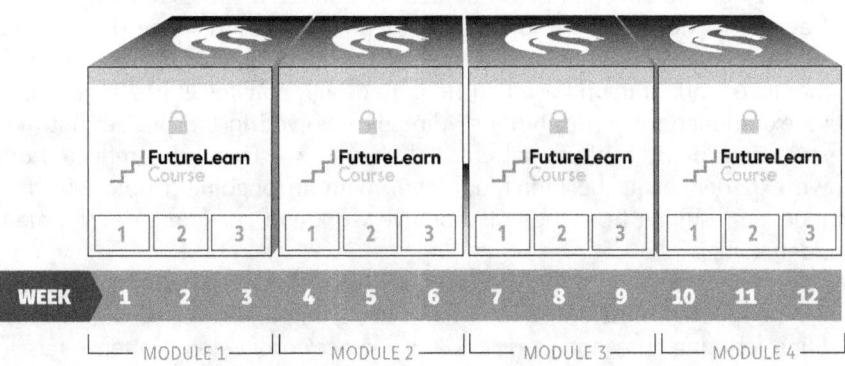

Figure 12.2 Student-facing graphic explainer on the structure of courses without open courses.

course and its discipline. For the majority of second and third-year courses, the entire 12-week/4 modules were closed (see Figure 12.2).

This chapter provides discursive reflection on the process, including the adoption of a central pedagogical approach, an emphasis on student-centred learning design, and modelling of retention strategies to enhance student belonging and engagement in online learning. It discusses the intent to privilege the student focus in the design process, recognising enjoyment in learning will lead to retention and success (Eather et al., 2022). We reflect on the process primarily through descriptive statistical analysis of the student evaluative data – both quantitative and qualitative – alongside our own reflections to assess the strengths, successes, and challenges of the project's implementation. The authors of this chapter took various roles in the project. Dr Annika Herb was both a teaching member of staff in the early stages of the project and later a Learning Designer on the project, Dr Michael Kilmister was the lead Learning Designer for the project, and Dr Clare Lloyd was the Academic Director of Online Learning Initiatives, and the Learning Design and Teaching Innovation team (LDTI) staff member responsible for leading the implementation of the Bachelor of Arts Online project. We intend this chapter to examine the project through the lens of the inquiring community of professional and academic staff who worked closely together to enhance online course design and learning practice at a single institution, and the substantial impact they had on the student experience as a result.

Collaboration is key: team-based online course design as academic development

The role of third-space professionals

Online course design requires academic and third-space professional staff working collaboratively. In this chapter, we address the roles and experience of academic development for both academics and third-space professional staff in team-based online course design. Burrell et al. (2015) argue the collaborative work of team-based curriculum design may result in a transformative experience for not only those directly involved in the project but may extend into being institutional cultural change; we found this reflected our own experiences at the individual level, with an ongoing 'ripple' effect of influence resulting from the collaborative work and academic development undertaken.

Soon after embarking on the project, we realised how essential the role of third space professional staff was in designing and creating high-quality online learning. The notion of the 'third space' professional often refers to individuals whose roles bridge the gap between academic and non-academic functions in higher education (HE). Throughout the book, we have referred to a range of key stakeholders in the third space who collaborated and liaised with academics to develop online learning, especially learning designers (LDs). Also known as instructional designers, they are professionals who integrate pedagogical, instructional design, and educational technology principles and processes to create effective, engaging, and accessible learning. In this project, LDs also worked as academic developers, supporting and enhancing the pedagogical practices of the educators they worked with, especially in online and blended learning. We reiterate Voogt et al.'s claim that "the shared process of adaptation through collaborative design offers ample opportunities for teacher professional development" (2015, p. 260), and, as we find, development opportunities for third space professionals, who were at once teachers and learners in this process. LDs worked with others in the third space, including learning technologists (LTs) and learning media producers (LMPs). LTs are often referred to as education technologists and are specialists in educational technology and integrating and supporting digitally enabled learning, while LMPs are known by a wide range of terms including digital learning developer; their work involves producing a range of digital media content such as videos, interactive simulations and podcasts. All these staff were based in the university's central teaching and learning support unit. The roles professional staff have played in the development of online learning in the project are explored in all the chapters within the book, especially how the dynamics between them and the educators shaped the courses produced.

Academic development and trust

Given the scale, intent, and focus of the project, academic development was paramount to the successful design, development, and implementation of online teaching and learning in the BA Online. Academic teaching staff at UON were unfamiliar with FutureLearn, and were largely new to fully online teaching delivery, and none had taught via the platform previously. Adapting to the asynchronous delivery mode necessitated academic colleagues to acquire new skills, knowledge, and approaches to pedagogic practice. Areas for development included digital pedagogy, digital literacy, presentation skills, learning management system proficiency, platform-specific course facilitation, accessibility integration, and writing content for asynchronous learning environments. Academic development was implemented both individually and across the school. This was done via regular one-on-one meetings, workshops on design, facilitation, and delivery, tailored resources, and ongoing bespoke support. Each academic was paired with an LD to support them in this process from the very beginning of the project, building a collaborative and supportive professional relationship, which has continued past the implementation of the original 'builds' of the courses (as represented by many of the chapters in this book being co-authored by academic and professional staff). This support was facilitated by members of LDTI inclusive of the learning technology, learning media, and learning design teams.

Opening teaching to scrutiny and collaboration can be a vulnerable experience. Educators can experience a sense of vulnerability when sharing their teaching practices and receiving feedback (Corkery et al., 2015); we encountered feelings of vulnerability from colleagues during the project (see, for example, Chapter 15). Vanassche and Kelchtermans (2016) conceive vulnerability as a 'structural condition' that is never fully within the control of the educator. Therefore, it was beholden on us as academic developers to factor vulnerability into our practice, and to cultivate spaces where academic colleagues would be willing to be vulnerable, take risks in their teaching, and build trust in us and the project. Simon and Pleschová (2021) argue building trust is essential for academic development and indeed, larger pedagogical change, as "trust is vital for conversations to take place and for innovative teaching methods to spread within an institution" (p. 279). Richardson et al. (2018) argue that collaborating on designing digital learning requires "more than the division of work and responsibilities; there is a need for mutual respect, understanding and trust from both parties" (p. 872). Trust was therefore essential throughout the design and delivery process to ensure an empowering and successful experience, fostering effective collaboration, innovation, and professional development. Trust development in intentional and organic forms was implemented from the outset of the academic development process, as supported academic buy-in was vital to the success of the project. This emerged as both an organic and intentional focus in the academic development, and which resulted in reciprocal opportunities for development for both the academic and the learning designer.

Skills and knowledge areas

As introduced earlier, the transition to online teaching required staff to enhance their digital pedagogy and digital literacy skills, including becoming proficient with various tools and technologies. We first consulted with academics to ascertain key areas in need of development. A primary focus we identified was developing staff knowledge and understanding of good practice in digital and online pedagogy. Here we supported staff to develop practices that engaged students through digital platforms, including learning how to create interactive and engaging online learning experiences, using multiple digital resources, and fostering online discussions that are conducive to deep learning. We incorporated group and individual training and developed resources for in-time support to enhance digital literacy, ensuring that staff could effectively use the FutureLearn platform, and all the other digital tools required to create and deliver the course, assess student performance, and provide timely feedback. This extended to an introduction to a range of interactive educational technologies including Padlet and H5P, and the pedagogical principles driving them to ensure educational technology was being utilised purposefully and aligned to the Universal Design for Learning (UDL) guidelines (CAST, 2024).[2] While we intentionally designed the academic development process to scaffold learning and relationship building, as will be discussed later some areas emerged over the course of the process as points for us to 'upskill.'

Developing certain skills and knowledge was often a team endeavour, most notably training colleagues in presenting to the camera and developing 'learning' videos. Like other high quality online teaching, the BA Online project required the creation and delivery of a range of video types, including videos that introduced a core concept, theory, or skill; interviews; and on site demonstration videos that. Videos sometimes required additional resourcing and planning for successful implementation including applying for filming permits, and often involved 'green screens' to enhance visual-effects and post-production, and costumes and other props. Effective execution meant significant time beforehand designing the resource with the learning designer, academic, and learning media team, including storyboarding and script-writing. Each of these elements required a degree of supported development; scripts, for instance, were a new skill for many academics who quickly found their usual writing style did not suit this mode of presentation. There were also many elements of this process that were new to the learning designers, demanding close collaboration with the learning media production team, especially early in the development of a course. Mindful of different styles and strengths in presenting, staff were encouraged to develop an approach that they were comfortable with, and coaching and development from the learning media producers allowed many to increase confidence in a new and challenging presentation mode. This approach to academic development allowed each educator to focus on improving their skills, enabling the staff to deliver content in a clear, engaging, and professional manner that resonated with online learners (see Chapter 5). This enhanced and enabled educator presence to strengthen student-teacher relationships and engage learners in the online setting (Bialowas & Steimel, 2019).

Digital accessibility was an important area of consideration, ensuring all students could fully participate and succeed in the online learning environment. Courses needed to be compliant with Web Content Accessibility Guidelines[3] to meet the institution's and FutureLearn's requirements for ensuring learning was accessible for all students. In practice, this meant every video featured captions and a transcript, images across the course were accessible and followed copyright and attribution guidelines, and documents were accessible. Development in this area focused on enabling staff to design courses that met accessibility standards. We engaged staff in ongoing conversations and feedback on the accessibility and appropriateness of their content for the online environment. However, web accessibility was an emerging area of practice for many LDs, and different disciplines posed different challenges in this area. To be able to provide appropriate guidance and support, LDs engaged in professional development for themselves in accessibility, including attending training offered by external providers and drawing on expertise elsewhere in the university.

Writing for online delivery differs from traditional academic writing, requiring conciseness and instructional clarity, and an engaging tone to keep students interested in a self-paced learning environment. We provided guidance and feedback on how to write effectively for online delivery, including creating course materials, discussion prompts, and assessment instructions that are easy to understand and engaging for online learners. LDs worked with academics to curate key content, in a process that several academics ultimately adopted for their face-to-face courses. One of the first steps in designing the online course involved physically mapping out the course content and learning activities. This took on multiple forms dependent on the academic's preference. Whether digital or hard copy, each approach allowed us to intentionally map out the course design process and scaffold learning in a collaborative discussion of hands-on learning. While academics were experienced in course design and course content design, employing this demonstrative approach allowed us to highlight aspects of digital pedagogy that necessitated changes in course design.

Workshops

Facilitated peer group workshops enabled us to create a supportive interdisciplinary space for staff to learn new skills necessary for the project, such as digital pedagogy and literacy, and platform-specific course facilitation. We employed this approach to create a supportive, collegial space for learning, where academics were encouraged to share their experiences. We facilitated ongoing formal workshops and informal face-to-face group check-ins throughout the live course runs, enabling staff to share their challenges and successes in online facilitation. As the courses progressed, we found staff began to provide suggestions and support to one another as their skills and confidence in the delivery and facilitation of online learning increased. Macdonald and Poniatowska (2011) acknowledge the flow on the effect of academic development, where staff may have influential conversations with peers' post development training, allowing more staff to experience new skills or knowledge second-hand. There are clear benefits to peer learning "because it provides the opportunity for staff to contextualise new approaches to learning and teaching, to support validation by the group . . . or to discuss their applicability to a specific environment" (MacDonald & Poniatowska, 2011, p. 121). We found this framework had additional ongoing benefits, as staff who had experienced academic development in digital pedagogy, literacy, facilitation, and learning technologies through the project were able to adopt leadership roles in mentoring other staff during the pivot to online learning necessitated by the COVID-19 pandemic in 2020. Another key area of focus was introducing and familiarising staff to the FutureLearn platform and supporting them in platform-specific course facilitation. This included managing course content, tracking student progress, and facilitating online interactions such as comments, discussion boards, group work, and other learning activities, as well as understanding time management to establish a consistent educator presence in an asynchronous environment. Academic development provided targeted training on platform-specific tools and best practices, enabling staff to effectively facilitate courses on FutureLearn to maximise student engagement and success.

Personalised support: meetings, resources, and tailored support

As mentioned earlier, each academic was assigned an LD and a learning media producer for the entirety of the course design, build, and facilitation. We worked with academic teaching staff to develop their awareness of the similarities and differences between online and face-to-face learning and teaching and their skills in both modes. We did this both through one-on-one conversations or by sharing recent research supporting a range of pedagogical choices. We engaged in a human-centred approach, emphasising student engagement and satisfaction as pivotal elements in the learning design (Ramos et al., 2024). The process involved documenting roles and responsibilities to ensure all parties were clear on their role in the partnership (Lloyd et al., 2021); purposefully designing active learning into all courses at some level in some way (given online courses can tend towards passive learning); ensuring training for all staff involved in both the design process and the platform; and embedding professional development into the process of course design (Lloyd et al., 2023). We engaged in very regular communication with all key stakeholders and, very importantly, acknowledged when something wasn't working, allowing time for reflection and changing processes if needed. Through comprehensive academic development, we equipped teaching staff with the necessary skills and knowledge to effectively transition to online teaching. This not only improved their confidence and competence in delivering online education but also ensured that students received a high-quality learning experience (as evidenced later). The academic development process fostered a culture of continuous learning and adaptability among staff, which is essential in the rapidly evolving field of online education.

The student experience: strengths, successes, and challenges

As this project – delivering courses via the online learning platform FutureLearn – was a first for UON, we felt it was important to consider student feedback to gain an understanding of how and why students were using the courses and how we might consider implementing changes to future offerings. Much investment, both institutionally and personally, was made in the project with the aim of improving course design and the online learning experience. As such, during the project, two Quality Assurance (QA) surveys were offered on each course over the 6 years the courses were delivered on FutureLearn.[4] The surveys were only open to enrolled students (not the students enrolled in the open modules). They were completely optional for students to undertake and no incentives were offered, that is, payment. The aim of these two questionnaires was to understand how the course design could be enriched to enhance the student online learning experience. In this sense, they differed from the usual teaching evaluation surveys students were asked to complete, which included items to evaluate a wider scope of experiences on a course including assessment and feedback. These surveys were administered at the mid-way point in scheduled teaching, and another at the end of the scheduled teaching and before the assessment period. Survey data is anonymous and cannot be tied back to individual students or behaviours in the online course. The next section reports on the survey data collected throughout the project, 2020–2024.

Impact and discussion

This chapter reports on the End of Course survey, the optional survey that was offered at the end of each course run and was offered in the final week of the course materials. It consisted of 10 statements that students were asked to rate on a Likert scale, and three open responses questions. Nine-hundred-and-seventy-five comments were made to the open response questions in the end of course survey (see Figure 12.3).

The comments from the open questions were analysed for sentiment using Explorance MYL alongside thematic analysis.

The first statement students were asked to respond to was, 'I enjoyed this course.' Student responses to this question were resoundingly positive, with 91% either 'agreeing' or 'strongly agreeing' that they enjoyed the online course. This 'enjoyment' (and engagement) was also fully supported in the qualitative comments. The following quotes are from the open-response questions:

1. What were the best aspects/favourite part of this course?
2. What improvements would you suggest to the course or FutureLearn?
3. Is there anything else that you'd like to share about your learning experience?

The responses from students to these three questions were overwhelmingly positive, with many students writing long and detailed explanations of how and why they enjoyed their online course:

> This has been the best course! Thank you so much [. . .] This course has been such a delight with all your engaging videos, weekly check-ins, and clear effort you have put into this. This course has been thought-provoking and insightful, giving me a new perspective and outlook on things that I never thought of before [. . .] What a fantastic course and breath of fresh air compared to other courses. Online learning can be so tricky and it's easy to detach from students or to just put up some notes for us and call it a day, but you have gone above and beyond to make us feel seen, heard, cared for, supported, and valued each and every week by creating such fun and engaging online lessons that we can work through at our own pace, videos, and weekly check-ins. I have also never had a tutor/course coordinator provide such

Academic development for effective online learning design 179

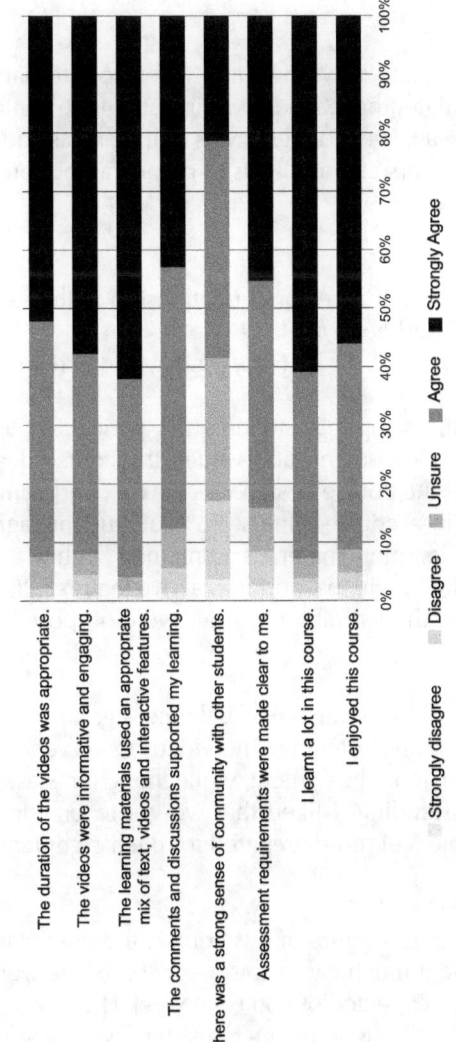

Figure 12.3 End of course survey results.

detailed feedback and suggestions on assignments, let alone provide video feedback to talk me through it and how I can improve next time. I truly have never experienced learning like this and am all the better for it! You should be proud of all your work and efforts for the course! Thank you again!

(Sociology student)

This course was incredibly engaging! My favourite part of the course was how passionate [the teacher] was in getting the content across to us in an engaging way. Even though it was online, I was equally if not more engaged in this course than if I was to go on campus and participate in a lecture and tutorial.

(History student)

I really enjoyed it, felt a personal relationship with the course teacher even though we had never met.

(Film, Media, and Screen Studies student)

As identified in this sampling, students felt connected to their educators, engaged in the course content, and valued the course design and delivery. A major strength of the course design was the mix and combination of learning materials within a course, almost 96% of students agreeing or strongly agreeing that the learning materials contained within the course was an appropriate mix of text, videos, and interactive features. In many ways this is not surprising given the learning materials were purpose built for the online environment.

> The best aspect of this course was balance – great mixture of reading, writing, watching and listening. The videos were very informative and helped me understand the content, while the writing tasks further developed my understanding. I liked that we got to practice writing every week, it made me feel more prepared for the assignments.
>
> (English student)

> I really enjoyed the structure of this course, the predictable structure of each week made it much easier to stay on top of the work as you knew exactly what was expected of you each week (1x reading, 1 hour-ish of video watching + discussion). The consistent weekly structure makes it much easier to plan your time each week, thank you!
>
> (Sociology student)

An English student responded, "How each module was structured. There was a perfect flow and ease of understanding with the way the videos, written text, and discussions were structured."

As previously discussed, the project placed a strong focus on clear curriculum design principles for the course design embedding and privileging UDL and accessibility principles. This was noticed and appreciated by the learners, with students identifying these elements in their learning experience as the best aspect of their course. In response to the prompt, "What were the best aspects/favourite part of this course?" one student commented, "the structure of each week, having a mix of different formats for learning" (core Humanities course student), and another responded with, "Enjoyed the visual learning material, images of photos and artworks. Videos of author interviews, links to informative websites and lectures were valuable learning aids" (History student).

The authors were very pleased to see the success of embedding UDL and accessibility principles in academic development was realised, with students writing:

> This was my first time studying at UON, and I've never enjoyed studying more – particularly as it was online and neurodivergent friendly! [. . .] I really appreciate with this course in particular how everything is set out so well, you're getting thrown a lot of content but it doesn't feel like a lot and it's easier to manage than traditional tutorials and lectures. I really, really love the transcripts of the videos as well.
>
> (Sociology student)

> I really enjoyed being able to interact with other students and see their responses to questions-not only did this help me understand how to answer the questions (being neurodivergent examples/templates are VERY helpful for me) but it also let me see concepts and content from different perspectives.
>
> (Sociology student)

Assessment and self-reported measure of learning

Self-reported measures of learning can be used to assess a student's perceptions, intentions, and the psychological processes that drive their learning (Gravett et al., 2023). The validity of using self-reported measures of learning in higher education research is supported by various studies that highlight their effectiveness in capturing students' perceptions and learning outcomes. These self-reports provide valuable insights into students' learning experiences, attributes, and self-regulated learning strategies, which are often not fully captured through traditional assessments (such as exams). A systematic review highlighted the growing use of self-report instruments for assessing self-regulated learning strategies, showcasing their diverse applications and psychometric properties (Roth et al., 2016). While self-reported measures are valuable, some researchers argue that they may be subject to biases, such as social desirability or inaccurate self-assessment, which could affect the reliability of the data collected. Nonetheless, the evidence suggests that when used appropriately, self-reports can significantly enhance understanding of learning in higher education (Benton et al., 2011). As such, the second question in the survey asked students if they felt they learnt a lot in the course. The authors were interested in knowing if students felt they had learnt new material along with whether it was enjoyable. In response to the statement "I learnt a lot in this course," 93% of students either 'agreed' or 'strongly agreed.'

This confidence was also reflected within the students' comments. Students often shared in the open-response questions that they had learnt new knowledge. For example, a student from one of the core courses said, "I learnt a lot in this course and I was really happy to try to push myself to complete an independent project" (core Humanities course student). This was seen throughout the open responses, with many students elaborating on why and what elements of the course they felt had helped in the learning,

> I really enjoyed communicating with others in terms of the discussions in the comments. Everyone else's perspectives really helped me in understanding the course material. Additionally, all the content being on FutureLearn was very refreshing to see. The abundance of quizzes, external videos, and discussions with my peers kept me engaged. I feel like a two-hour long lecture video on campus would not do this course justice. I also really enjoyed the course lecturer/coordinator getting involved in the discussions, elaborating further on concepts we did not understand. I would pick this course again in a heartbeat. Thank you.
> (Sociology student)

> I was pleased with the layout of this course. I have definitely gained a much greater knowledge of history than I had before, which is fantastic as I have always felt to be lacking in my historical knowledge. I very much appreciate the effort that has been put into this course. Many thanks.
> (History student)

> I loved the course. The content was great. I learned so much [sic]. So many different perspectives and a well rounded course.
> (Screen and Cultural Studies student)

The success of the course design is apparent in students' enjoyment and self-reported learning. This was also indicated by staff who provided formal and informal feedback on the academic development process emphasising the value of our approach (Lloyd et al., 2023).

We are confident the academic development process that supported the extensive course design and implementation process was successful, strengthening staff skills, relationships, confidence, and ability in online teaching, in turn ultimately enriching the student learning experience.

Limitations

As we reflect on the BA Online project, we have identified areas that could be improved further. Time constraints and limited resources, as well as the scale and novelty of the task that confronted us – translating an established degree program with a rich history at the university to online – while gathering feedback and evaluating the academic staff experiences in developing course content and/or facilitating their courses was part of the project, explicitly evaluating the project's professional learning and development activities was regretfully not a top priority. However, this was not a surprise given for the majority of the time the BA Online project was running, there was no actual unit or team expressly dedicated to academic development. The emphasis stakeholders placed on learning-centred forms of teaching and assessment, alongside increasing recruitment, retention, and outcomes also meant the success of the project would be understood in terms other than staff perspectives and experience. In retrospect, we could have utilised established models for impact and evaluation (Chalmers & Gardiner, 2015; Guskey, 2002) during the project, especially a model designed to evaluate professional development programs centred around online teaching and learning (see Chapter 13). In terms of research data limitations, we did not systematically interview or survey staff in a timely manner that would retain context and situatedness. This was part of the motivation for writing this book: to capture reflections on the professional learning from those involved and to enable introspection about that learning and the enduring impact it has had on the authors of the chapters herein.

Student feedback has also revealed opportunities for improvement, such as that in some cases, staff could be more stringent in content management (and provide less content). While the FutureLearn platform offered convenient content capabilities, this ease occasionally led to increased content creation past the directed student learning hours. Subsequent course iterations require careful editing and streamlining, highlighting the possible need for a more structured approach to the amount of appropriate content in this context. A significant learning emerged regarding course delivery models. Although initially designed for asynchronous, predominantly self-paced learning, we discovered some of these courses would benefit from further synchronous teacher presence and facilitation. There was a preference from some first-year students for more synchronous educator time to actively guide their learning journey and provide ongoing support. This preference seems to have increased in the post-COVID-19 context, which indicates the ever-shifting nature of designing and delivering courses fully online. Several structural limitations became apparent through implementation. The separation of assessment components from main course content, necessitated by our learning management system (Blackboard and then Canvas), sometimes created a disconnected experience for students. This bifurcation of content and assessment, along with administrative functions and announcements, impacted the coherence of the student experience for some. While there were shortcomings including insufficient synchronous engagements, overall the majority of students found the courses very engaging (perhaps more so than some of their traditional in-person delivered courses).

Conclusion and reflections

Overwhelmingly, the earlier-mentioned data indicates students were exceptionally pleased with their online learning experiences. In this project our approach to academic development, which included building close working relationships with academic staff, encouraged the formation of trust through an emphasis on collaboration. Academic development is vital to the process of designing and implementing a fully online degree program and supporting staff and student success, engagement, and enjoyment in online learning. Alongside our colleagues in the central teaching and learning unit, we developed and adapted a structured and iterative process to help staff implement pedagogical and curriculum design principles. This process prioritised the collaborative process of learning design, including structured curriculum design workshops where learning designers and faculty followed the ABC curriculum design method. Many of the courses in the BA Online project had entered the process of redesign as primarily face-to-face courses with a limited presence on the LMS, and many of the educators had only encountered a 'distance education' concept of online teaching as opposed to intentionally designing a course for online learning. The introduction of a mix of learning materials and the use of a tight QA process to ensure this mix was appropriate to the content guaranteed the student experience on each course was suitable for the discipline yet consistent within the program structure. In acknowledging academic staff were effectively stepping out of their 'comfort zone' – from collaborating with professional staff to designing learning for online – establishing trust was integral within the process.

We hope this chapter has illuminated a type of *in situ* academic development work advocated for by Boud and Brew (2012). In this case, the translation of traditionally taught courses to online provided an opportunity for a reflexive approach to academic development where we all had a shared responsibility in nurturing the skills and knowledge to make the project a success. The project also demanded us to effectively integrate and locate development activities within the disciplinary-based teaching practices we were attempting to influence, with the aim of ensuring that the resulting changes have the desired impact on students. Flexibility was balanced with a guiding set of strong pedagogical principles. These measures are essential to fostering a culture of continued professional development and trust that not only

Academic development for effective online learning design 185

enhances the effectiveness of academic development initiatives but also significantly supports faculty in designing online learning environments that lead to student success.

Notes

1 Students could undertake courses as award (enrolled in a degree) or non-award (not enrolled in a degree).
2 UDL is an accessibility and inclusivity framework intended to enhance learners' strengths and agency and eliminate barriers to learning.
3 https://www.w3.org/WAI/WCAG22/quickref/?versions=2.1
4 QA Ethics approvals: QA180, QA184, QA185, QA186, QA187, QA188, QA199, QA200, QA201, QA202, QA217, QA218, QA219, QA220, QA221, QA233, QA234, QA235, QA236, QA237, QA252, QA253, QA254, QA255, QA256, QA257, QA267, QA268, QA269, QA270, QA271, QA272, QA273, QA274, and QA275.

References

Benton, S. L., Duchon, D., & Pallett, W. H. (2011). Validity of student self-reported ratings of learning. *Assessment & Evaluation in Higher Education, 38*(4), 377–388. https://doi.org/10.1080/02602938.2011.636799

Bialowas, A., & Steimel, S. (2019). Less is more: Use of video to address the problem of teacher immediacy and presence in online courses. *International Journal of Teaching and Learning in Higher Education, 31*(2), 354–364.

Boud, D., & Brew, A. (2012). Reconceptualising academic work as professional practice: Implications for academic development. *International Journal for Academic Development, 18*(3), 208–221. https://doi.org/10.1080/1360144X.2012.671771

Brown, B., Eaton, S., Jacobsen, D., Roy, S., & Friesen, S. (2013). Instructional design collaboration: A professional learning and growth experience. *Journal of Online Learning and Teaching, 9*(3), 439.

Burrell, A. R., Cavanagh, M., Young, S., & Carter, H. (2015). Team-based curriculum design as an agent of change. *Teaching in Higher Education, 20*(8), 753–766. https://doi.org/10.1080/13562517.2015.1085856

CAST. (2024). *Universal design for learning guidelines version 3.0*. https://udlguidelines.cast.org

Chalmers, D., & Gardiner, D. (2015). An evaluation framework for identifying the effectiveness and impact of academic teacher development programmes. *Studies in Educational Evaluation, 46*, 81–91. https://doi.org/10.1016/j.stueduc.2015.02.002

Coleborne, C., & Lloyd, C. (2019, November 25). *A step change in learning online: The FutureLearn Bachelor of Arts*. FutureLearn Asia-Pacific Partners' Forum at Graduate House, University of Melbourne.

Corkery, J., Hall, K., Jeffries, J., Laskowski, K., Peters, B., Romig, G., Tranell, J., & Whitney, A. E. (2015). Shared vulnerability in professional learning: Growing instructional coaches in a culture of PDS partnership. *School-University Partnerships, 8*(2), 72–78.

Eather, N., Mavilidi, M. F., Sharp, H., & Parkes, R. (2022). Programmes targeting student retention/success and satisfaction/experience in higher education: A systematic review. *Journal of Higher Education Policy and Management, 44*(3), 223–239. https://doi.org/10.1080/1360080X.2021.2021600

Gravett, K., Baughan, P., Rao, N., & Kinchin, I. (2023). Spaces and places for connection in the postdigital university. *Postdigital Science and Education, 5*, 694–715. https://doi.org/10.1007/s42438-022-00317-0

Guskey, T. R. (2002). Does it make a difference? Evaluating professional development. *Educational Leadership*, *59*(6), 45–51.

Joyce, B. R., & Showers, B. (2002). *Student achievement through staff development*. Longman.

Kember, D., & Gow, L. (1992). Action research as a form of staff development in higher education. *Higher Education*, *23*, 297–310. https://doi.org/10.1007/BF00145018

Laurillard, D. (2012). *Teaching as a design science: Building pedagogical patterns for learning and technology*. Routledge.

Lloyd, C., Herb, A., & Kilmister, M. (2023). Connecting the pages: Aligning online course development with academic professional development for student success in online learning. *Advances in Online Education: A Peer-Reviewed Journal*, *1*(3). https://doi.org/10.69554/XMLJ2745

Lloyd, C., Herb, A., Kilmister, M., & Coleborne, C. (2021). Partnerships and pedagogy: Transforming the BA Online. In *7th international conference on higher education advances (HEAd'21)* (pp. 925–932). Editorial Universitat Politècnica de València. https://doi.org/10.4995/HEAd21.2021.13001

MacDonald, J., & Poniatowska, B. (2011). Designing the professional development of staff for teaching online: An OU (UK) case study. *Distance Education*, *32*(1), 119–134. https://doi.org/10.1080/01587919.2011.565481

QAA Cymru. (2024). *The impact of staff professional development on teaching practice and student learning and performance: Case studies*. https://www.qaa.ac.uk/docs/qaa/guidance/the-impact-of-staff-professional-development-on-teaching-practice-and-student-learning-and-performance.pdf?sfvrsn=48bcbc81_10

Ramos, M. D., Nandan, M., Porter, K., & Dyess, S. M. L. (2024). Enhancing student success in higher education: A human-centered design thinking approach. *Journal of Higher Education Theory and Practice*, *24*(7). https://doi.org/10.33423/jhetp.v24i7.7090

Richardson, J. C., Ashby, I., Alshammari, A. N., Cheng, Z., Johnson, B., Krause, T. S., Lee, D., Randolph, A. E., & Wang, H. (2018). Faculty and instructional designers on building successful collaborative relationships. *Education Technology Research and Development*, *67*, 855–880. https://doi.org/10.1007/s11423-018-9636-4

Roth, A., Ogrin, S., & Schmitz, B. (2016). Assessing self-regulated learning in higher education: A systematic literature review of self-report instruments. *Educational Assessment, Evaluation and Accountability*, *28*, 225–250.

Simon, E., & Pleschová, G. (2021). PhD students, significant others, and pedagogical conversations. The importance of trusting relationships for academic development. *International Journal for Academic Development*, *26*(3), 279–291. https://doi.org/10.1080/1360144X.2021.1949324

Vallis, C., Wilson, S., Tyrrell, J., & Narayan, V. (2022). Co-design as professional learning: Pulling each other in different directions, pulling together. In D. Forbes & R. Walker (Eds.), *Developing online teaching in higher education*. Springer. https://doi.org/10.1007/978-981-19-5587-7_10

Vanassche, E., & Kelchtermans, G. (2016). A narrative analysis of a teacher educator's professional learning journey. *European Journal of Teacher Education*, *39*(3), 355–367. https://doi.org/10.1080/02619768.2016.1187127

Voogt, J., Laferrière, T., Breuleux, A., Itow, R. C., Hickey, D. T., & McKenney, S. (2015). Collaborative design as a form of professional development. *Instructional Science*, *43*(2), 259–282.

13 Student evaluation of online teaching and learning

Notes on theory and practice

Paul Sijpkes and Elizabeth Roberts-Pedersen

Introduction

Student evaluation of university teaching is standard practice across the Australian higher education sector, reflecting a wider trend towards quantifying and otherwise measuring academic work and its impacts (Hillebrandt & Huber, 2020). Though a growing body of literature critiques these evaluation exercises as misleading (discussed later), they often provide the only feedback channel between academic staff and the increasing number of students who study online, particularly for asynchronous learners who never meet their instructors face-to-face. This chapter examines how student evaluation practices translate to online environments, arguing that understanding these metrics – limitations and all – is crucial as higher education continues its digital transformation in the aftermath of the COVID-19 pandemic (Salama & Hinton, 2023) and the crisis conditions (Hofer et al., 2021) that marked teaching during that period. It provides some preliminary thoughts on this topic by first reviewing the extant literature on the evaluation of online learning and then reflecting on quantitative evaluation data for online courses as part of the University of Newcastle's Bachelor of Arts program. Based on these findings, we suggest that feedback metrics have a role in supporting academic and professional staff to improve the online learning environment and the student experience but must also be appropriately contextualised to provide useful input.

The value and limitations of metrics

The collection of feedback from students on the courses they study, usually by an end-of-semester survey comprised of Likert scale questions, has become a routine part of academic life in Australian universities (Laundon et al., 2023). While examples of institutions eliciting student feedback on university courses can be traced back several decades, the use of standardised surveys within institutions seems to have accelerated in the early 2000s, as universities came under increasing pressure to guarantee the quality of their teaching (Spooren et al., 2013). Measurement exercises are also conducted from outside. In Australia, the federal government has placed increasing pressure on universities to guarantee the quality of their teaching, particularly after the establishment of the national Quality Indicators for Learning and Teaching (QILT) survey (Whiteley, 2016). QILT surveys are conducted annually to commencing and later year students, recent graduates, and 3-year post-graduation, gathering data on teaching quality, learning resources, and student support. The survey also includes an Employer Satisfaction Survey (ESS) that targets employers of recent graduates. The ESS assesses, among other metrics, employers on graduates' generic skills, yet how these generic skills come to be taught in an environment where academics are increasingly aiming to *satisfy* students rather than teach rigorous methods of inquiry is mysterious.

Student evaluation exercises (referred to as 'student evaluation of teaching' or 'SET' in the literature) have been the subject of sustained controversy. For critics, they are part of a broader 'ethos of measurement' imposed on the tertiary sector that has resulted in a proliferation of instruments to quantify and manage academic performance and promote 'excellence' (Spence, 2019). While much of the critical literature on the quantification of academic work focuses on the distorting effects of metrics on research cultures – for example, the incentivisation of 'gaming' and 'manipulation' of citations and authorship (Oravec, 2019) – teaching is also subject to the "disciplining power of numbers" (Spence, 2019, p. 763). Candid reflections by academics about strategies to elicit positive student feedback, from handing out sweets to explicit 'selling' techniques, indicate that metrics-driven 'gaming' and 'manipulation' are not confined to research (Adrian et al., 2017; Youmans & Jee, 2007). For one of us (Elizabeth), who began teaching undergraduates in the early 2000s, such behaviours are tactical accommodations with the demands of performance culture, conveyed in whispers by experienced academics or learned by novices the hard way. This also explains the doublethink that accompanies the release of teaching 'scores' at the end of each semester, in which a 'bad' score is carefully rationalised, but a 'good' score is blithely accepted.

The rise of teaching evaluation metrics also has implications for students. Most obviously, the focus on metrics reflects many of the ambiguities of the so-called 'learnification' of education, a process in which "an attempt to liberate the learner – first and foremost from the teacher but also from the wider education system" (Biesta, 2010, p. 541) simultaneously bestows on adults an indeterminate 'learner identity.' Of course, it is generally effective to listen to students' ideas and opinions and include them in feedback 'loops' and 'spirals' where possible (Carless, 2019). However, it is not clear that *formalised* feedback exercises always serve the student. For example, student satisfaction surveys have been found to produce a process of feedback that is transmissive only and disregards the student's positioning in the feedback process (Winstone et al., 2022). It may also implicate them in a process for which they are ill-suited – that is, how are students able to assess the quality of teaching materials and of teaching when they are as follows: (a) not experts in the field they are learning about and (b) not necessarily qualified to assess what good teaching practice is in higher education? Thus, it may also contribute to a neoliberalist approach to education, where institutions are pushed to become 'shopfronts' where a 'customer-centred' ethos causes educational experiences to be driven by convenience – a situation that critics argue undermines the quality of education being provided (Pitman, 2016).

Other criticisms of formal student evaluations of teaching centre around two issues: the timing of the evaluation exercises and the number of students who take part in them. Many institutions complete the teaching evaluation processes at the end of a course. However, the evidence in the literature supports a formative approach to teaching and learning evaluations, where feedback can be gathered and improvements implemented during the teaching session. For example, work by Golding and Adam (2016) suggests taking a situated approach to student evaluations, where teachers reflect on evaluations as formative feedback during the teaching process to improve their teaching. Yet this is not always possible due to time constraints and workloads. A mid-semester evaluation is often the preferred compromise between SETs and formative course feedback, but this does not necessarily allow for responsive feedback within the teaching period itself (Sozer et al., 2019). Formative approaches also present particular challenges for online courses that are written and recorded in advance and require significant lead time to plan and record new content.

Low response rates also undermine the reliability of SET findings. SETs have a high interrater reliability when response rates are closer to 50 responses out of a class. For example, a response rate of 50 has 95% interrater agreement, but this quickly drops, for example, a response from 10 students has 60% reliability and a response rate of 2 only 20% (Marsh & Roche, 1997). Given these figures, SETs are most reliable for measuring the satisfaction of large cohorts and, even then, require sustained, ongoing promotion and support from faculty members and administrators (Anderson et al., 2006). Yet research suggests that response rates have dropped as online surveys have become widespread (Adams & Umbach, 2012). Lifting response rates to a threshold of reliability is both a conundrum for university administrators and, as we have seen, present an opportunity for teaching academics to influence SET scores by encouraging participation in surveys or neglecting to do so.

Perhaps the most trenchant and persistent criticism of teaching metrics centres around what, exactly, they measure. Anecdotally, even academics sceptical of these evaluation exercises will acknowledge that they have learned important things about their courses from student surveys, particularly the free-form response sections: difficult-to-read PowerPoint slides, confusing rubrics, assessments insufficiently spaced, and so on. This is an important diagnostic function. But beyond that – when it comes to broader but more diffuse concepts like teaching 'quality' and teaching 'effectiveness' – the interpretation of feedback data is controversial, sometimes to a startling degree. Most pressingly, there appears to be no *a priori* correlation between student satisfaction and the actual learning that took place during a course. One widely cited meta-analysis found no relationship between students' evaluation scores and the quality of learning (Uttl et al., 2017). Students' biases, both positive (towards a lecturer's likeability or charisma) and negative (against a lecturer's gender or race) also affect this relationship between satisfaction and learning. An influential 2016 study argued that the biases elicited by evaluation instruments were so extensive as to render them incapable of reliably assess teaching effectiveness: "if SET are ever valid, they are not valid in general: universities should not assume that SET are broadly valid at their institution, valid in any particular department, or valid for any particular course" (Boring et al., 2016, p. 10). This is consistent with earlier research. An early, much-cited study on the efficacy of SETs found that student ratings of instructors depended on how much they liked the instructor, which was in turn 'strongly' influenced by the grade they received (Powell, 1977). Another influential study found that perceived learning or students' subjective assessment of their learning was a higher predictor of positive SET scores (Baird, 1987). Research has also shown that students' biases impact their assessment of their own learning. For example, some studies suggest that women and minority groups are universally negatively impacted in SETs (Kreitzer & Sweet-Cushman, 2022). Women in particular tend to be judged much more harshly than men (Adams et al., 2022). Similarly, cultural minority groups are criticised for accent, dress, and other aspects of their cultural identity (Fan et al., 2019). Online teaching may therefore *protect* minority academics from the biases that result from in-person teaching (Sun et al., 2023).

Enter online teaching and learning

If SETs tend to capture the (potentially biased) perceptions of a small sample of students when administered in on-campus courses, what has been the impact of the expansion of online learning on student evaluation of teaching? This is a question of some urgency given the accelerations in online learning. Here we highlight two themes evident in the emerging literature: the use of SETs to compare on-campus and online courses, and the creation of online-specific evaluation instruments.

The cohort of online learners is diverse and growing, making it difficult to offer a standard profile of this group save for their common motivations. For example, students who choose online learning will overwhelmingly do so for convenience and logistical factors over the teaching and learning amenities provided (Afzal et al., 2022; Bailey et al., 2018). This may affect the way they perceive and rate their course experience. In this regard, there is a parallel with the history of distance education and its evaluation, where students' preferences or needs for distance education can be hard to disentangle from their assessment of their learning experience overall. For example, Allen et al. (2002) conducted a meta-analysis comparing student satisfaction with distance education to traditional face-to-face classrooms. They found only a slight preference for face-to-face study and insignificant differences in satisfaction. The most interesting result of Allen et al.'s meta-analysis was that there was no difference in student satisfaction between fully interactive distance learning environments involving video conferencing and those that had no interaction whatsoever.

The findings of other comparison studies are more mixed and highlight key factors influencing student preferences satisfaction. For example, Carle (2009) used multilevel growth modelling to evaluate students' ratings of a professor's teaching effectiveness over time and across online vs. face-to-face instruction modes. The study found no significant differences in ratings between modes. By contrast, Lowenthal et al. (2015) analysed online course evaluations and found online instructors were rated lower than face-to-face instructors on most items. Seok et al. (2010) compared instructor and student perceptions of online course effectiveness, finding some differences in Likert scores but similar overall ratings. Other highly cited studies focus on different aspects of student educational experience while using different instruments for comparison. First, Tratnik et al. (2019) compared an online Business English course to its face-to-face counterpart. They found significant student dissatisfaction with the online offering on dimensions such as student perceptions of their "learning motivation," "sharing of knowledge," "cooperative learning," and "stimulat[ion of] curiosity" (p. 39). However, significant positives of the online offering included the usefulness of course materials, the requirement of "self-discipline" and the need for "a lot of self-study" (p. 39). An earlier study by Summers et al. (2005) examined student satisfaction in an online and face-to-face offering of a statistics course. Students rated the online offering of the course significantly lower on "instructor's explanations," "instructor's openness to students," "use of class time," and "instructor's interest in student learning" than the face-to-face offering (p. 242). A third study by Johnson et al. (2000) found that students had marginally more positive perceptions of face-to-face instructors and "overall course quality" compared to online. Overall, these individual studies highlight the need for a high level of student self-motivation and self-regulation to engage in online study. Nevertheless, there is evidence that given a considerable amount of planning and investment in online infrastructure and technology support to generate the right learning conditions, student motivation can be significantly improved. Notably, Nortvig et al.'s (2018) review of literature published between 2014 and 2017 comparing online and blended student satisfaction, learning outcomes, and engagement found that the most important aspects influencing student satisfaction were suitable environments for teaching and learning both online and offline, creating engaging and meaningful learning communities to support students' social interactions and learning experiences and developing a strong and clear sense of learner identity. Further, connecting and integrating online and offline activities, campus and practice-related activities, students, teachers, and content are of utmost importance. Finally, establishing a strong educator presence in online settings and building online learning communities that promote positive relationships is imperative for the best student learning (Nortvig et al., pp. 50–53). Note that this list does *not* include student convenience or flexibility of delivery.

This final point is an important one. Other studies comparing online and in-person courses raise similar questions about how to construct meaningful comparisons between on-campus and online courses, as well as how to design evaluation instruments and research studies that capture the specific practices and challenges of online teaching. Studies are often confounded by multiple variables that are beyond researchers' control: the randomised comparative study reported by Stack (2015), where a clerical error caused students to be randomly assigned to either the online or on-campus version of a course taught simultaneously by the same instructor and which reported no significant differences in either student performance or SET scores, is a rarity. The so-called 'media comparison studies' have long been controversial (Head et al., 2002; Surry & Ensminger, 2001). As Jensen et al. (2022) emphasise, comparative studies need to be carefully designed to produce meaningful results. "Content equivalent comparisons" (p. 727) are particularly crucial; in this study, close attention to the equivalence of the content covered by the online and on-campus courses demonstrated a significant performance gap between students in an asynchronous version of the course compared with the in-person version, most likely due to the lack of "synchronous peer and instructor scaffolding" that occurs in classroom settings (Jensen et al., 2022). But extrapolating such findings from one university to the broader sector generally is also fraught (Altindag et al., 2024).

In addition to better-designed comparative studies, some researchers argue that online courses need specific evaluation instruments that capture the distinctiveness of online teaching. Technology is a key factor here. Early work on the evaluation of online teaching emphasised the need to gather feedback on the technology enabling the course alongside the teaching of the course itself (Sheard & Markham, 2005). However, such instruments should make a distinction between course design and the teaching of the course (Stucklen, 2019). This distinction is important, given that online courses have often been designed several years prior, and the instructor may have limited capacity to modify the course content. This is only one important example of the layered complexity inherent in online delivery. For example, Bangert (2006) developed an evaluation instrument reflecting 'constructivist' philosophies of online learning based on a four-factor model (student-factor interaction, cooperation among students, active learning, and time on task) while also acknowledging that it is difficult "for a single instrument to assess the range of complex variables that contribute to quality online courses and programs" due to the layered relationship between "content, pedagogy and technology" (p. 241). One synthesis of 112 publications on online course evaluations by students between 2000 and 2017 found that most online course evaluation focuses on resources, inputs, and processes rather than outcomes, with the views of students often being prioritised over those of faculty, administrators, designers, employers, and other third parties. This work found that perceptions of quality and how quality is perceived by different audiences – learners, instructors, employers, and society in general – are multifaceted and complex (Esfijani, 2018). Moreover, such arrangements are always evolving as both universities and the digital environment undergo rapid changes. Thus, it is concerning that many online-specific instruments are more than a decade old and pay insufficient attention to the organisational and technological factors that impact teaching in the present (Sun et al., 2023).

Student feedback on the online Bachelor of Arts

As the earlier discussion indicates, to be useful, student feedback data must be considered in context and not taken as a sole indicator of either teaching quality or learning outcomes, especially given concerns around response rates and student biases. With these caveats in mind, in what follows, we briefly reflect on the broad contours of student feedback on the online Bachelor of Arts program at the University of Newcastle (UON). The context in which this feedback was gathered is important. The Bachelor of Arts is one of the university's oldest and most diverse degree programs, with students studying in either a general three-year program or one of five combined degree programs. The program offerings are extensive, incorporating 21 majors and minors. The student body is also diverse, with a higher-than-average proportion of students with a disability, significant caring responsibilities, or from a low socioeconomic status background. As with other Australian universities, there has been a steady decline in the number of students enrolling in both the generalist and combined programs due to intersecting changes in the sector, such as an increased emphasis on a defined vocational outcomes, the transformation of previous majors within the Bachelor of Arts into fully fledged degree programs, and an increase in course fees for certain humanities courses (see Chapter 2).

The inception of the online program at UON in 2018 responded to these changes in the sector but also sought to cater to a growing number of students who wished to study online. The online courses have been delivered largely asynchronously on the FutureLearn platform, allowing students to study at their own pace but also reducing the opportunities for synchronous engagement and cohort interaction. Internal student demographic data aligns with sector-wide trends for students studying the online program exclusively – they are more likely to be living with disabilities, have substantial caring responsibilities, be older, work full time, or live remotely (Stone, 2019). Even so, online and on-campus students respond to the same evaluation instruments towards the end of each semester, which ask the students to reflect on their experience of the course design and course teaching via numerical scores and qualitative feedback. From these responses, the course survey software generates a course 'score' and a separate teaching score between 0 and 5. Program-level teaching metrics are also calculated as the mean of the course scores for all the courses taken by students within their program. It is therefore important to emphasise that these program-level scores do not reflect responses to questions about students' experiences of the program overall. Similarly, there is no overall qualitative component to contextualise the quantitative data.

Though we are prevented from disclosing the specifics of university-held data, we can offer three generalised observations on the internal metrics available to us as we reflect on designing and teaching into the online Bachelor of Arts program.

First, program-level metrics suggest that student satisfaction with the online and on-campus degrees is close to equal, with the program-level scores for the general 3-year Bachelor of Arts program show little variation between on-campus and online offerings since the introduction of the online degree. Of course, the usefulness of this observation is tempered by the problems with 'media comparisons' noted earlier, and another word of caution attaches to the interpretation of course scores during the pandemic years of 2020 and 2021, when notionally on-campus courses were also taught in online mode for one or both semesters, and the sector experienced general widespread disruption.

Our second observation is that there is greater variation in online and on-campus course scores for individual courses but that this detail is necessarily subsumed in the program-level metrics. While similar caveats attach to comparisons undertaken at the course level, wide discrepancies between scores for a notionally equivalent course offered both on-campus and online can serve the kind of diagnostic function discussed earlier if appropriately contextualised. This has been particularly useful for reflecting on the three compulsory 'core' courses in the UON Bachelor of Arts program. Introduced in 2018 at the same time as the online BA, the on-campus and online versions were developed simultaneously and with the expectation that they be identical in course learning outcomes and assessment. Course-level scores track a clear improvement in the first-year compulsory course, with the on-campus and online course scores approaching parity. However, for the second year core course, the scores for the online version have been higher for the last several years. Finally, for the third year course, the scores have tended to be higher for the on-campus version, likely reflecting its status as a project-based course that poses particular challenges for replicating in the online environment.

Our third observation relates to response rates. As noted earlier, low response rates to evaluation instruments are a well-known impediment for the reliability of teaching metrics. For the Bachelor of Arts core courses, the response rates were significantly lower in online courses than their on-campus counterparts. Since one strategy to increase response rates is to have students complete the surveys during class time, it would make sense that the response rates would be lower in asynchronous courses. This underscores that scrutiny of response rates is a key consideration when interpreting student feedback metrics for online courses.

Conclusions and future directions

Our reflection on student feedback processes for the Bachelor of Arts program suggests several tentative conclusions about the interpretation of this data for online learning. First, in a diverse program like the Bachelor of Arts, program-level metrics may be of limited use in surfacing differences between the two modes of delivery. In our data, there was no meaningful difference between the on-campus and online programs – and indeed, the distinction between the two cohorts is increasingly meaningless as students in the on-campus program seek to study in online modes. By contrast, and as with on-campus offerings, course-level metrics may prove useful if interpreted in a diagnostic manner. Second, however, it is necessary to reiterate some limitations of this data. As we noted at the beginning of this chapter, research suggests that student feedback measures student satisfaction – a nebulous concept – as opposed to student learning. In addition, this kind of feedback tends to reflect various social biases. Finally, the low response rates for student surveys raise concerns about statistical reliability.

These problems foreshadow wider challenges with online course delivery. Even if institutions were able to capture student feedback metrics of sufficient reliability and granularity, looming disruptions to online learning (and higher education in general) due to the expanding capabilities of generative AI create risks for both course design and its evaluation. A capacity to mimic passable student performance (Kortemeyer, 2023) not only creates crucial challenges around assessment security for online courses but also has implications for their evaluation. Just as the shift from paper-based to digital surveys introduced new uncertainties about the identity of the survey-taker (Oliver, 2000), the prospect of AI agent acting on students' behalf may further erode the usefulness of teaching evaluation surveys. One remedy – though perhaps a partial one, given the size and speed of the generative AI juggernaut – is to find opportunities to reinforce the human element of the teaching enterprise, to continue to insist on its salience even in the online space, and on its value for improving online courses and instilling a sense of community and accountability amongst online students. In a small but compelling study of award-winning online teachers, many of these experts said that they valued peer review of their courses by subject matter specialists and instructional designers alongside the more quantified student evaluation metrics (Martin et al., 2019). Continuing to centre teaching on the human activities of collaborative inquiry and interpersonal exchange is crucial. This model is resource-intensive, but if universities aim to sustain a culture of inquiry as we enter the second quarter of the 21st century, it is arguably essential for their survival.

References

Adams, M. J. D., & Umbach, P. (2012). Nonresponse and online student evaluations of teaching: Understanding the influence of salience, fatigue, and academic environments. *Research in Higher Education, 53*, 576–591.

Adams, S., Bekker, S., Fan, Y., Gordon, T., Shephard, L. J., Slavich, E., & Walters, D. (2022). Gender bias in student evaluations of teaching: Punish[ing] those who fail to do their gender right. *Higher Education, 83*, 787–807. https://doi.org/10.1007/s10734-021-00704-9.

Adrian, C. M., Phelps, L. D., & Totten, J. W. (2017). Using personal selling techniques to influence student evaluation of faculty instruction. *Journal of Learning in Higher Education, 13*(2), 45–50.

Afzal, S., Din, M., & Malik, H. D. (2022). Preference determines performance: Comparative analysis of students' preference of on-campus and online learning and their academic performance during COVID-19. *International Journal of Distance Education and E-Learning, 7*(2), Article 2. https://doi.org/10.36261/ijdeel.v7i2.2439

Allen, M., Bourhis, J., Burrell, N., & Mabry, E. (2002). Comparing student satisfaction with distance education to traditional classrooms in higher education: A meta-analysis. *American Journal of Distance Education, 16*(2), 83–97. https://doi.org/10.1207/S15389286AJDE1602_3

Altindag, D. T., Filiz, E. S., & Tekin, E. (2024). Is online education working? *Educational Evaluation and Policy Analysis*. https://doi.org/10.3102/01623737241274

Anderson, J., Brown, G., & Spaeth, S. (2006). Online student evaluations and response rates reconsidered. *Innovate: Journal of Online Education, 2*(6). https://nsuworks.nova.edu/innovate/vol2/iss6/5

Bailey, M., Gosper, M., Ifenthaler, D., Ware, C., & Kretzschma, M. (2018). On-campus, distance or online? Influences on student decision-making about study modes at university. *Australasian Journal of Educational Technology, 34*(5). https://doi.org/10.14742/ajet.3781

Baird, J. S. (1987). Perceived learning in relation to student evaluation of university instruction. *Journal of Educational Psychology, 79*(1), 90–91. https://doi.org/10.1037/0022-0663.79.1.90

Bangert, A. W. (2006). The development of an instrument for assessing online teaching effectiveness. *Journal of Educational Computing Research, 35*(3), 227–244. https://doi.org/10.2190/B3XP-5K61-7Q07-U443

Biesta, G. J. J. (2010). *Good education in the age of measurement: Ethics, policy, democracy*. Routledge.

Boring, A., Ottoboni, K., & Stark, P. (2016). Student evaluations of teaching (mostly) do not measure teaching effectiveness. *ScienceOpen Research*, 1–11. https://doi.org/10.14293/S2199-1006.1.SOR-EDU.AETBZC.v1

Carle, A. C. (2009). Evaluating college students' evaluations of a professor's teaching effectiveness across time and instruction mode (online vs. face-to-face) using a multilevel growth modeling approach. *Computers & Education, 53*(2), 429–435. https://doi.org/10.1016/j.compedu.2009.03.001

Carless, D. (2019). Feedback loops and the longer-term: Towards feedback spirals. *Assessment & Evaluation in Higher Education, 44*(5), 705–714. https://doi.org/10.1080/02602938.2018.1531108

Esfijani, A. (2018). Measuring quality in online education: A meta-synthesis. *American Journal of Distance Education, 32*(1), 57–73. https://doi.org/10.1080/08923647.2018.1417658

Fan, Y., Shepherd, L. J., Slavich, E., Waters, D., Stone, M., Abel, R., & Johnston, E. L. (2019). Gender and cultural bias in student evaluations: Why representation matters. *PLOS ONE, 14*(2), e0209749. https://doi.org/10.1371/journal.pone.0209749

Golding, C., & Adam, L. (2016). Evaluate to improve: Useful approaches to student evaluation. *Assessment & Evaluation in Higher Education, 41*(1), 1–14.

Head, J. T., Lockee, B. B., & Oliver, K. M. (2002). Method, media, and mode: Clarifying the discussion of distance education effectiveness. *Quarterly Review of Distance Education, 3*(3), 261–268.

Hillebrandt, M., & Huber, M. (2020). Editorial: Quantifying higher education: Governing universities and academics by numbers. *Politics and Governance, 8*(2), 1–5. https://doi.org/10.17645/pag.v8i2.2585

Hofer, S. I., Nistor, N., & Scheibenzuber, C. (2021). Online teaching and learning in higher education: Lessons learned in crisis situations. *Computers in Human Behavior, 121*, 106789. https://doi.org/10.1016/j.chb.2021.106789

Jensen, J., Smith, C. M., Bowers, R., Kaloi, M., Ogden, T. H., Parry, K. A., Payne, J. S., Fife, P., & Holt, E. (2022). Asynchronous online instruction leads to learning gaps when compared to a flipped classroom. *Journal of Science Education and Technology, 31*(6), 718–729. https://doi.org/10.1007/s10956-022-09988-7

Johnson, S. D., Aragon, S. R., & Shaik, N. (2000). Comparative analysis of learner satisfaction and learning outcomes in online and face-to-face learning environments. *Journal of Interactive Learning Research, 11*(1), 29–49.

Kortemeyer, G. (2023). Could an artificial-intelligence agent pass an introductory physics course? *Physical Review Physics Education Research, 19*(1). https://doi.org/10.1103/PhysRevPhysEducRes.19.010132

Kreitzer, R. J., & Sweet-Cushman, J. (2022). Evaluating student evaluations of teaching: A review of measurement and equity bias in SETs and recommendations for ethical reform. *Journal of Academic Ethics, 20*(1), 73–84. https://doi.org/10.1007/s10805-021-09400-w

Laundon, M., Cunningham, S., & Cathcart, A. (2023). Institutional approaches to evaluation of learning and teaching: A sector scan of Australasian universities. *Journal of Higher Education Policy and Management, 45*(5), 511–528. https://doi.org/10.1080/1360080X.2023.2196646

Lowenthal, P., Bauer, C., & Chen, K.-Z. (2015). Student perceptions of online learning: An analysis of online course evaluations. *American Journal of Distance Education, 29*(2), 85–97. https://doi.org/10.1080/08923647.2015.1023621

Marsh, H. W., & Roche, L. A. (1997). Making students' evaluations of teaching effectiveness effective: The critical issues of validity, bias, and utility. *American Psychologist, 52*(11), 1187–1197. https://doi.org/10.1037/0003-066X.52.11.1187

Martin, F., Ritzhaupt, A., Kumar, S., & Budhrani, K. (2019). Award-winning faculty online teaching practices: Course design, assessment and evaluation, and facilitation. *The Internet and Higher Education, 42*, 34–43.

Nortvig, A.-M., Petersen, A. K., & Balle, S. H. (2018). A literature review of the factors influencing e-learning and blended learning in relation to learning outcome, student satisfaction and engagement. *Electronic Journal of E-Learning, 16*(1), Article 1.

Oliver, M. (2000). Evaluating online teaching and learning. *Information Services & Use, 20*, 83–94.

Oravec, J. A. (2019). The "dark side" of academics? Emerging issues in the gaming and manipulation of metrics in higher education. *The Review of Higher Education, 42*, 859–877.

Pitman, T. (2016). The evolution of the student as a customer in Australian higher education: A policy perspective. *Australian Educational Researcher, 43*, 345–359. https://doi.org/10.1007/s13384-016-0204-9

Powell, R. W. (1977). Grades, learning, and student evaluation of instruction. *Research in Higher Education, 7*(3), 193–205. https://doi.org/10.1007/BF00991986

Salama, R., & Hinton, T. (2023). Online higher education: Current landscape and future trends. *Journal of Further and Higher Education, 47*(7), 913–924. https://doi.org/10.1080/0309877X.2023.2200136

Seok, S., DaCosta, B., Kinsell, C., & Tung, C. K. (2010). Comparison of instructors' and students' perceptions of the effectiveness of online courses. *Quarterly Review of Distance Education, 11*(1), 25–36.

Sheard, J., & Markham, S. (2005). Web-based learning environments: Developing a framework for evaluation. *Assessment and Evaluation in Higher Education, 30*, 353–368.

Sozer, E. M., Zeybekoglu, Z., & Kaya, M. (2019). Using mid-semester course evaluation as a feedback tool for improving learning and teaching in higher education. *Assessment & Evaluation in Higher Education, 44*(7), 1003–1016. https://doi.org/10.1080/02602938.2018.1564810

Spence, C. (2019). "Judgement" versus "metrics" in higher education management. *Higher Education, 77*, 761–775.

Spooren, P., Brockx, B., & Mortelmans, D. (2013). On the validity of student evaluation of teaching: The state of the art. *Review of Educational Research, 83*(4), 598–642. http://www.jstor.org/stable/24434223

Stack, S. (2015). Learning outcomes in an online vs traditional course. *International Journal for the Scholarship of Teaching and Learning, 9*, article 5.

Stone, C. (2019). Online learning in Australian higher education: Opportunities, challenges and transformations. *Student Success, 10*(2), 1–11. https://doi.org/10.5204/ssj.v10i2.1299

Stucklen, E. G. (2019). Understanding and ensuring quality: Designing assessments and evaluations for online learning. In J. Vivolo (Ed.), *Managing online learning: The life-cycle of successful programs* (pp. 191–215). Routledge.

Summers, J. J., Waigandt, A., & Whittaker, T. A. (2005). A comparison of student achievement and satisfaction in an online versus a traditional face-to-face statistics class. *Innovative Higher Education, 29*(3), 233–250. https://doi.org/10.1007/s10755-005-1938-x

Sun, T., Martin, F., & Kim, S. Y. (2023). Establishing a student evaluation of online teaching and learning framework through analysis of existing instruments. *Online Learning, 27*, 356–382.

Surry, D. W., & Ensminger, D. (2001). What's wrong with media comparison studies? *Educational Technology, 41*(4), 32–35.

Tratnik, A., Urh, M., & Jereb, E. (2019). Student satisfaction with an online and a face-to-face Business English course in a higher education context. *Innovations in Education and Teaching International, 56*(1), 36–45. https://doi.org/10.1080/14703297.2017.1374875

Uttl, B., White, C. A., & Gonzalez, D. W. (2017). Meta-analysis of faculty's teaching effectiveness: Student evaluation of teaching ratings and student learning are not related. *Studies in Educational Evaluation, 54*, 22–42.

Whiteley, S. (2016). Creating a coherent performance indicator framework for the higher education student lifecycle in Australia. In R. M. O. Pritchard, A. Pausits, & J. Williams (Eds.), *Positioning higher education institutions* (pp. 143–160). Brill.

Winstone, N. E., Ajjawi, R., Dirkx, K., & Boud, D. (2022). Measuring what matters: The positioning of students in feedback processes within national student satisfaction surveys. *Studies in Higher Education, 47*(7), 1524–1536. https://doi.org/10.1080/03075079.2021.1916909

Youmans, R. J., & Jee, B. D. (2007). Fudging the numbers: Distributing chocolate influences student evaluations of an undergraduate course. *Teaching of Psychology, 34*(4), 245–247. https://doi.org/10.1080/00986280701700318

14 Being an online educator

Reflections on iterative design of a transdisciplinary humanities course

Julie McIntyre

Introduction

At the turn of the 21st century, Foster (2001) predicted that a "confluence" of changes – in employee skillsets, institutional resourcing, and grading – "occasioned by the infusion of technology requires an adaptability unlike any higher education has experienced in its history" (p. 116). This future of electronic technology in higher education has arrived. Sampson et al. (2020) encompass the contemporary impact on educators of e-teaching and e-learning like so:

> The delivery of higher education in online environments is far from being a mere transposition of the [pre-online] classroom practices to virtual settings. It demands the restructure of curricula, the evolution of teaching methodologies and the preparation of the students to the particular requirements of online learning. As more technology is created and modified to serve pedagogical purposes, and more higher education institutions embrace them to complement their classroom teaching methodologies, more doubts are created as to the best technologies and strategies.
>
> (p. vii)

For educators accustomed to the solitary intellectual labour of drafting traditional lectures, presentation slides, and tutorial notes for in-person classes, adapting to the design, development, and delivery of asynchronous online courses can be a challenging, multi-faceted learning process. This chapter shares reflections on how to successfully make this adaptation.

In my first foray from only teaching in physical university classrooms to also teaching online, I began to progress in the directions identified by Sampson et al. (2020). That is, the discovery of new teaching methodologies, expectations about guiding students to work successfully with digitally enabled learning, and decisions about which types of software to use. Despite the availability of excellent collaborative professional staff at my university, research-based scholarship on teaching and learning (SoTL) as a guide, and a

DOI: 10.4324/9781003505785-18

natural enthusiasm for change and digital technologies, I encountered doubts about how to proceed.

Online teaching is not only typically more technology-rich than face-to-face teaching; there are temporal variations. Online learning may occur either synchronously or asynchronously. Synchronous online classes are time-tabled, and students may view a lecture on a video-conferencing platform as it is delivered and/or attend a tutorial-style class in real time. Asynchronous online learning, however, takes place 'on demand' and is comprised of pre-produced content – usually a mixture of text, video, and activities like discussion boards. This heterogeneity can open new possibilities but can equally overwhelm the educator (Scherer et al., 2021).

The course that I am discussing in this chapter, centred on transdisciplinary research methods, was not a legacy course in its degree program (the Bachelor of Arts) but entirely new. No humanities precedents existed at my institution, and to the best of my knowledge elsewhere, from which to draw the substantive inspiration for my course or the other two new compulsory interdisciplinary humanities 'core' courses in the undergraduate program. It had not been tested with students in a face-to-face environment to inform an adjustment to online teaching. Often when a university educator designs, delivers, and develops a face-to-face course, the course they are working with has a disciplinary focus – in my experience, History – and has been tested and iteratively refined in lectures and tutorials, perhaps for many years (see, for example, Chapter 7). While by no means freshly minted as a university educator, learning to design and teach the course I am discussing here in a virtual setting felt 'greenfield' in content and format. This compounded my doubts and doubled the imperative to find solutions to these concerns.

By embracing self-reflection on the unexpected sense of disempowerment I encountered in learning to teach online, this chapter seeks to empower others. In research on technology-enhanced learning environments, Wang and Hannafin (2005) define iterative cycles as "analysis, design, implementation, and redesign" (p. 9) through successive versions of a course. The reflections in this chapter are based on my leadership of the creation and iterative design of the course BA (for Bachelor of Arts) Practice across six successive semester offerings, from 2019 to 2023. Overall, the contribution to the literature on online teaching is threefold. First, to demonstrate self-reflection on teaching practice as a source of professional knowledge. Second, to draw from this self-reflection to propose tools to address educator discomfort around transitioning from being a self-confident face-to-face educator to a self-confident online educator. Third, to expand understanding of the comparatively under-researched and under-discussed practice of designing transdiscipline learning in the humanities.

Methodology

This chapter first and foremost draws on Gibbs's (1988) reflective cycle of my teaching practice, in which I give my doubts and concerns as much attention as successes and achievements. Gibbs's Reflective Cycle involves a series of steps: describe what happened in a given situation, notice the feelings prompted, evaluate what went well and what went wrong in the situation, analyse the underlying causal and contextual factors, draw conclusions about prudent action, and make a plan for action. This chapter is the result of selected reflective evidence on the transformation I underwent as I became more experienced in online teaching and is aimed at offering advice on how to confidently make the shift from legacy to virtual educational settings.

This reflection-based methodological approach makes a break from scholarship on teaching and learning (SoTL) centred on quantitative or qualitative social scientific studies of online teaching. This witnessing of perceptions to achieve transformation in the classroom is widely applicable. In a critique of metrics-obsessed measuring of student learning outcomes and quantitative and qualitative data-based research practices in education, Biesta (2020) writes

> education 'works' as a result of the acts of reflexive agents [and this] implies that we need to think differently about its operation, not as a quasi-casual mechanical reality that happens behind the backs of those involved but rather as a (complex) social reality constituted by the conscious acts of reflexive agents.
>
> (p. 39)

Self-reflection is an authentic as well as "legitimate, rigorous, and necessary mode of writing" in SoTL (Cook-Sather et al., 2019, p. 15). The value of self-reflection in teaching practice is that it offers insights into the educator experience that cannot be adequately accessed with statistical data or ethnographic modes of outsider observation and anonymised surveys or interviews. Self-reflection as a research method surfaces the nuances of practitioner experience that are generally not accessible in quantitative and ethnographic social scientific studies yet are salient for other educators. Carey (2023) too emphasises that "higher education involves more than the mere acquisition of information and/or skill sets: it evokes (or could, and perhaps should evoke) the development of the human person as a whole" (p. 3), or ontological experience. Carey contends that educators benefit ontologically, or at the core of their being, from reflecting on their sense of being empowered or disempowered to belong in academia as well as through engaging in the epistemological practice of teaching and learning of knowledge and skills. Educator self-reflection reveals "the surprises, insights, questions, uncertainties, in-process musings, unproven hunches, and still forming hypotheses that animate SoTL work" (Cook-Sather et al., 2019, pp. 15–16). My reflections on unpacking, articulating, and unsnagging some interlinked ontological and logistical issues in online education may contribute to smoothing the workflow of others.

Background

In 2019, as I learned the difference between synchronous and asynchronous online delivery modes, I recall sitting at my desk, staring at the computer screen after watching a video presented by colleagues in the university's new department of media production about how academics could develop their own video content. During the closing credits of the instructional video, I felt a sense of rising panic about tensions between familiar, and in fact cherished, course design and delivery practices and the prospect of learning how to teach online. Prior to beginning to build an academic career in the early 2000s, I worked for 5 years as a broadcast journalist. I knew from creating, editing, and presenting audio content for radio and developing and presenting television news content that producing high-quality broadcast material required resources (time, team dynamics, equipment), and asynchronous online teaching would be a similar project in terms of involving different technologies and extensive planning. I anticipated an imperative to develop new institutional, pedagogical, and technical knowledge; I would need to think, decide, and act differently about the format of course materials while being conscious not to lose the usual energy I would bring to a live teaching session.

I also wondered how significantly online education would distance me from students as radio and television journalists are distanced from their audiences. Contact with students is a reason that I value being an academic. I obtain job satisfaction from being bodily and mindfully in the room with students in lecture theatres and tutorial classrooms. However, as Brenton (2009) asserts, "e-learning is not automated learning; it requires the teacher's presence as much as other types of teaching" (p. 91). Since first entering a university classroom in a teaching role in 2000, I gauged that students' questions during class signalled the need for further explanation and reflected later on how these moments could inform improvements. The difference between how students might interact with me and course materials in online synchronous and asynchronous modes was not clear in 2019.

Like many other teaching academics of my generation, prior to starting to teach online, I learned how to teach as an 'on-the-job' apprenticeship in higher education classrooms through being a traditional undergraduate student and from undergraduate tutoring as a postgraduate student, with mentorship from established academics. My academic discipline is History. Until 2014, when I obtained two graduate certificates in higher education, my certified specialisation was within my scholarly discipline, not pedagogy. I learned by osmosis, and trial and error, how to design, develop, deliver and evaluate curriculum content. My ontology as an academic arises in part from growing up and being schooled as a settler-colonial-descendant in a regional coastal area of Australia without ready access to a university. As a high-achieving secondary student aiming to attend university after high school graduation, my only choice was to enrol in distance education that was delivered by coursework mailouts, intermittent telephone conferenced tutorials and intensive residential schools. I embraced this distance learning mode during full-time employment in the media. Life circumstances meant that I became an on-campus student during early parenthood. On-campus completion of my undergraduate degree set me on a path to being a teaching and research historian. I am not a first-in-family academic; however, I began my university education in what is now termed an equity cohort: people living in remote locations, disadvantaged by their distance from a university. Underlying the doubts and concerns reflected upon in this chapter awareness of the accessibility benefits of online learning for equity cohorts as a factor in crystallising my sense of resolving the tensions between what I valued as traditional forms of course design, delivery and assessment and what I anticipated might be problems in online teaching and learning. This sets the scene for discussing the course that led to my transformation from legacy teaching to being comfortable in the virtual classroom.

The course

In 2017, the (then) School of Humanities and Social Science at the University of Newcastle began developing a suite of Bachelor of Arts (BA) compulsory core courses to be delivered face-to-face and in the new 'BA Online,' which would run parallel to the on-campus degree. The BA encompasses 21 disciplines or study areas that can be taken as a major or minor, from English to History to Global Indigenous Studies.

The core suite of compulsory courses BA Futures, BA Practice, and BA Project sought to build a degree cohort of students who, though they may be studying different majors and minors, shared a cohesive identity as humanities students. Another aim was to enhance graduates' employability. Australia's higher education sector focus on work-integrated learning was instigated in 2015 through collaborations between the national government that contributes to funding the university sector, business and industry, and universities. BA Practice, as the second-year compulsory course in the core stream, was originally envisaged as a research methods course that offered students intermediate-level insights into knowledge production in their majors and minors as the basis of transdiscipline workforce skills in finding information and knowledge.

Initial challenges designing online transdisciplinary learning

Initially, I, as the course coordinator, and anthropologist Hedda Haugen Askland and linguist Bill Palmer, as co-lecturers and co-designers, staffed BA Practice. The first semester intake in 2019 was 201 students. The original course proposal prioritised on-campus learning and was to entail weekly lectures and interactive workshops but was unexpectedly expanded to include a synchronous online offer. The original list of topics to consider covering in the course contained 15 topics, ranging from setting the scene (e.g. 'what is a methodology?') to focusing on specific research methods (e.g., policy analysis).[1] It was influenced by social scientific practices in teaching research methods to undergraduates, with some humanities inclusions, and with the aim of providing sufficient coverage of the majors and minors in the BA. I did not participate in the original design of course content and could not revise it in the initial iteration for administrative reasons. My role in addition to course coordination of the face-to-face course was to develop the online course on the Blackboard learning management system (LMS). I had support in the form of pedagogical advice and technical intervention from a learning designer. University policy stipulated that lectures for compulsory face-to-face courses be recorded and available on Blackboard for students who could not attend class. I edited these recordings of 50-min lectures from the face-to-face delivery into five chapters or 'chunks,' at appropriate content points, for the online students to work through. This seemed more feasible than making videos when my colleagues and I were developing our lecture content on a week-by-week basis.

Due mainly to habits of practice from face-to-face teaching, none of us on the teaching team had course content prepared before semester. This is a markedly different situation than the fore-planning presently invested at the institutional level in online teaching with digital learning support teams. As the lead educator on creating online content during the semester, I had an average of half-a-day per week to work on this task. Along with 'chunked' lecture recordings on Blackboard, online students accessed the same readings as face-to-face students and were provided with a directed reading list and an approximation of the face-to-face workshop activities. A learning designer advised me to visit the online version of BA Practice at least once a day to facilitate the comments and other discussion board queries, advice aligned with guidance on nurturing educator-student and student-to-student interaction online (Gherghel et al., 2023; Salmon, 2011).

Significant challenges arose during that inaugural semester about the week-by-week introduction of a social science model of undergraduate methods training to the humanities. As an interdisciplinary scholar, I have some grounding in social science methods, but not in how to teach them to undergraduates. Therefore I learned quickly, in an attempt to cohere the course for students. The social sciences structure their research around methods, in the mode of natural scientific hypothetical-deductive experimentation. In the Social Sciences, methods are named and taught during undergraduate education. In the Arts and Humanities, there is not traditionally a focus on methods and methodologies as the framework for learning and investigating. Arts and humanities are more accurately a form of reasoned argumentation with evidence, from which interpretation arises contingently, or – in disciplines such as English – the art of criticism, or knowledgeable evaluation of the value of literature as an artform.

At the conclusion of the inaugural semester, grade distribution in BA Practice was normal in both modes of delivery. But comparative overall Quality

Learning Experience (QLE) student feedback on overall satisfaction, while lower than the university average for the face-to-face course, was markedly lower than the university average for the online course. Although students responded positively to components of both the face-to-face and online offerings, overall there was confusion about the coherency of the curriculum. As I feared, distance from students in the online course version also proved to be a problem. I did not yet have tools or time as an online educator to be an effective interlocutor online.

Designing an asynchronous course

For the next iteration of the course scheduled for Semester 1, 2020, the online platform for asynchronous content delivery was no longer Blackboard but FutureLearn.[2] To prepare for this shift, I worked throughout the latter part of 2019 with a learning designer. This process was in tandem with teaching the face-to-face iteration in that semester. At the time I perceived the benefits of FutureLearn to be its visual appeal with clean interface and bold choice of thematic colours. FutureLearn's approach to designing learning using discreet 'steps' that directed students to complete them in sequential order offered a staged process for presenting course materials. Inspired by Laurillard's (2012) Conversational Framework, each step could present a different kind of content or activity, for example, videos, text, and quizzes. Comment fields at the end of most steps, in contrast to being located under a different tab on Blackboard, provided a clearer and contextualised pathway for students to engage with learning content. Changes to the course structure included 'modularising' content (allowing theming of related methods in ways that made more sense to students), greater instructional detail and transparency about learning in the course, quizzes for students to self-check knowledge, more places for students to ask questions, and welcome videos introducing the weekly focus. As discussed by Boyd and Singer (2011), "students learn best when they can see a purpose to their knowledge" (p. 56). Weighed against the benefits of this platform and the learning design it provoked, however, was the greater time necessary to present the more sophisticated learning materials compared with legacy styles of teaching preparation.

The sequencing, activity design, and modern presentation of materials on FutureLearn demanded significant 'lead time' for course development. The new technologies, and the heightened profile of the online BA degree in the university's portfolio, also meant more collaborators would be involved in the design and development. In contrast to the lecture recordings used in the first online iteration of BA Practice, I now needed to write scripts for videos produced with high production standards in mind. Extended development requirements seemed to mean that many aspects of the course would be developed and finalised weeks and months in advance of when students would receive them. The 'building' of the course on FutureLearn would be handled by learning designers. While learning designers could make edits during business hours, prioritising urgent issues, I could not directly edit the content if I had an idea on the spur of the moment in response to student learning or other stimuli. In synchronous teaching, inspiration is constrained only by the arrival of the deadline to teach the material; even then, changes can be made immediately, activities finished early, or the parameters of discussions changed in response to ad hoc and observational feedback. Deadlines for completing teaching content development are much earlier for quality asynchronous learning. Conversely, the online content was beta-tested with students to identify issues that might require revision. Overall, it was tricky to learn new patterns of time management for the development of online teaching.

I continued to consciously rethink my long-practiced habits of responding in a solitary fashion to making course revisions at my convenience to instead planning to create videos and other learning resources in collaboration with colleagues. I felt the importance of respecting the investment of time made by the teaching support staff who were unfailingly polite about this. Yet I wanted to push back against the restriction on future course revisions presented by the fact that learning materials with high production costs to the university, such as videos, would need to be re-used for a few years at least. To address this, learning design collaborators and I focused on making a concerted effort not to record videos or other digital 'assets' that would date. We also avoided recording information that would date the course. In this way, I felt I regained my sense of agency through planning ahead.

The collaborative action plan of iterative course design from 2019 onwards in response to formal and informal feedback, alongside concomitant institutional support for the transition to FutureLearn, resulted in student satisfaction doubling from the first version of the course. Overall, student satisfaction scores for BA Practice Online continue to hover around the university average, which is common for a large enrolment compulsory course such as this.[3] Still, the transdiscipline element of the course required attention. This is discussed later. Next, I outline strategies that I developed through learning to be an online educator.

Reflections on becoming a better online educator

Being a proactive collaborator

Proactively planning to adapt to the interconnected tasks in the process of creating, delivering, and revising online learning is essential for online educators. Parham (2013) sums up the discomforting sensation of multiple moving parts in operation: "Online classes are not entirely under the instructor's control. Instead [an academic] must rely on technical experts, editors, instructional designers, and others. It's enough to make one feel like a cog in a wheel as if they are working on an assembly line" (p. 21). She continues that "if there are enough support networks in place, an instructor may feel collaboration is a benefit and that building networks across campus is a positive process" (p. 21). Collaborating with stakeholders is an ongoing activity. As Fawns (2022) suggests, technology and pedagogy "must be understood as integrated within a greater, emergent entanglement that has no clear beginning or end" (p. 723). I contend that an online teaching academic ought to aim to be as proactive as possible and take a leading role with stakeholders in this emergent process. One way to do this is by mapping time and the role of each collaborator on the project.

To retain my agency as a teaching academic in an online environment I make time each year to discover changes to these technologies as developers are continually updating them. I map the relationship of the online tools to each other using a tool I am comfortable with as a historian: tables in Word documents. I proactively seek advice from digital learning support colleagues on how to best to mix emerging technologies to enable effective communication with students. I seek advice on accessing learning metrics within the online learning platforms, which is a widely adopted means of monitoring student engagement and adapting teaching in response (Sclater et al., 2016). Finally, I map my relationship and develop shared understandings of contexts and technologies with the colleagues who advise on or develop these online tools as time-based, as discussed later.

Team building with digital learning experts and media producers

Closely related to the earlier discussion, I recommend respecting different skillsets required to make teaching designs a reality, and being prepared to translate your needs into the terms that each expert colleague requires, as this builds trust. Teaching academics show leadership by being willing interlocutors in these processes. In practice, this may be as simple as learning the terminology that non-teaching colleagues use and sharing the terminology that you use. In higher education, 'microcultures' inform teaching and learning practices. Microcultures are "culturally constructed structures that include norms, traditions, recurrent practices, tacit assumptions, and so on" (Roxå & Mårtensson, 2015, p. 194). In other words, a 'hidden curriculum' can exist between those who support teaching and learning and those who teach students in disciplines (and interdisciplinarily). The effort that teaching academics make to learn what it is that digital teaching and learning support staff 'do' builds their capacity to in turn teach support staff what they, the academics, need from professional staff colleagues. Enabling mutually suitable communication across boundaries entails moving beyond help-seeking behaviour and fostering more frequent interactions between educators and professional staff. This might involve informal conversations and informal learning or more formal activities, such as developing shared communities of practice (Roxå & Mårtensson, 2015). Further, academics can contribute to unpacking the hidden curriculum and enabling collective action by seeking to understand the parallel timelines and competing pressures of expert colleagues, setting realistic deadlines, and meeting them.

Writing as if for publication

Online teaching academics are effectively participating in the publication of learning materials. Online course design, development, and delivery are similar to the drafting, writing, copy editing, proofing, and publication of a book, book section, or journal article. Conversely, notes for lecture oration and plans for tutorial discussions in synchronous delivery, whether in-person or online, are draft documents, not publications. This is an unrecognised distinction between contemporary online teaching and the lectures and tutorials that evolved prior to online learning. And the quality of the writing impacts student learning, with one study finding well-defined instructions correlates with engagement with investigation-based tasks on FutureLearn (John et al., 2024).

I found it useful to communicate with learning designers by creating individual table-based documents or spreadsheets for each step of an online learning week. I use a table-based document for online courses with three columns. The first column is the weekly step or page number. The second column is the type of online learning content, for example, a video or a 'drag and drop' exercise. Learning designers welcome the clarity of this working document and the interoperability of using variations in version filenames to streamline communication. I indicate changes in successive versions of the course templates with the old copy editor's tools of strike-through for removal of any textual copy or instructions and indicate new textual copy or instructions in different coloured types. Successive iterations of the completed templates are copyedited in the revision process during the semester for digital learning technicians to see clearly where changes are to be made, or content is to remain. This system of tables, 'old-school' copy editing and clear document filenames in turn provides a record of the course for successive semester iterations that I can keep on file. I do not have to return to an online platform to revise course content until I have reviewed the content in my files. This too allows for off-screen review and editing of content. Writing as if for publication promotes coherence across the whole of the course, aligning the multiple moving parts of the process.

Transdiscipline learning in the humanities

The principles of educating for transdisciplinary skills have been explored in information science (Christozov et al., 2019) but are less established humanities. Yet BA Practice possessed the characteristics of a transdisciplinary course where these features are defined, by information scientists, as focusing on "training competences and developing skills rather than transferring knowledge in the form of memorizing facts, [adopting a] problem-solving attitude and agility, building capability for lifelong learning and self-actualization, flexibility and adaptability" (Christozov et al., 2019, p. 22).

To more effectively balance the transdisciplinary qualities of BA Practice, I collaborated in 2021 with a learning designer to further redesign and develop the course, especially in the online mode. We aimed to improve the cogency of the content to enable students to grasp diverse ways of making knowledge. Innovations included using a greater array of guest lecturers from arts and humanities disciplines discussing research theories and techniques to engage students with their interests. This change is also aligned with the principle that educator presence is essential to high-quality online learning, as Brenton (2009) makes clear: "where effective e-learning takes place, it does so with the guidance and presence of a successful and thoughtful practitioner" (p. 97). We received highly positive peer feedback on the course, focused on my weekly introductory video explanations as a throughline for learning about research methods, the relevance of a methods-based skills approach to knowledge formation, and assessment. This indicated that iterative revisions to BA Practice had removed speed bumps in the process of designing and developing an effective learning experience.

Alongside being more transparent about the purpose of the course, we also offered rewarding and participatory opportunities to engage in the course. These included encouraging self-discovery of concepts, learning-level-appropriate readings and more compelling workshop activities such as interactive peer-based tasks and exercises that focused on 'real world' application. The framing for these activities was encouraging students to use the content of the course to develop a 'toolkit' for asking questions and finding answers. One of the main design components here was a discussion-based online assessment titled 'Workshop Notes.' As Heil and Ifenthaler (2023) conclude in their systematic review of online assessment in higher education, "[o]nline assessments impact not only students' learning outcomes but also influence motivation, self-regulation, engagement, or reflection" (p. 203). Although introduced in an earlier version of the course, the revised task was informed by observations of learning analytics on FutureLearn and student feedback, including embedding it more discreetly within the content to counter the issue of a minority 'skipping' ahead of the content to access the task. The iterative online assessment in BA Practice was also designed to embed trandiscipline knowledge and skills.

Students were directed weekly to engage with two set readings and then respond to a prompt related to the learning objective for that week. In their response, students were asked to write 150 words and respond to at least two of their peers' posts. The task was worth 20% of the overall grade, and students were graded on a selection of the posts. Although grading posts was time-consuming, it was also rewarding to see the growth in the community in the course, the sharing and evolution of ideas, and the building of knowledge beyond a student's major or minor. As a task that makes use of discussion boards, the assessment embraces the principle that "e-learning elements and activities will need to be integrated into the way the course is assessed" (Brenton, 2009, p. 91).

Returning to Christozov et al. (2019), they identify that transdiscipline programs require three features. These are, first, the development of adaptable competences and skills rather than knowledge learned rote. Second, respect for other methods of tackling problems. And third, the ability to think across disciplinary boundaries by knowing enough about them to move beyond limited frameworks and perceptions. BA Practice now embodies these features as generalist humanities research skills. The course description reads:

> In an age of online information overload, how can we think for ourselves about what is worth knowing or even true? Disciplines in the Bachelor of Arts emerged to create knowledge by seeking to understand, or think critically about, people's choices and experiences in the past and present, with an eye to the future. This means that we have useful shared principles for evaluating the quality of information. These humanities principles can be learned by focusing on evidence and what it means to be evidence-based and logical in writing and speaking. This course builds on HASS1000 by developing skills to discern when knowledge claims can be accepted as true, ethical and inclusive. Students completing this course will gain a toolkit for asking critical questions, and designing projects to provide quality answers.
> (University of Newcastle, n.d., "Course description" section)

Topics include, but are not limited to, evidence and scientific methods in the Humanities; Indigenous challenges to Western research methods; ethics, diversity, and inclusion in research; and aspects of research such as methods-based principles of project design.

Since 2020, BA Practice Online has consistently scored more highly in overall student satisfaction than BA Practice face-to-face. Arguably this is at least in part because in the online course students can more readily 'choose their own adventure' disciplinarily; an approach that aligns with good practice in flexible learning (Advance HE, 2024). This flexibility provides a strong anchor point from which to explore other evidence-gathering modes in the humanities than their own disciplines, and to perceive more clearly what it means to collaborate across the broad terrain of the humanities and social sciences.

Conclusion: a pathway in transformative change

Two decades ago, education researchers recognised that shifts in teaching and learning practices enabled by Internet technologies would have immense effects on our sector. Now that online teaching and learning are here to stay, this chapter has set out in concrete terms what it means for individual teaching academics to make the logistical and ontological transition from face-to-face pedagogies to asynchronous online course design, development and delivery. In 2019 I perceived the need for a new map and compass to make this change but being in the introductory stages of my experience, and the university's provision of digital learning design, did not know at first how or where to find these directional aids. Through drawing upon my existing academic and non-academic skills that were translatable to the online teaching environment, responding iteratively to student and staff feedback, and collaborating with colleagues, improvements have been achieved to the student experience of an online course. Throughout this chapter I have used the metaphor of multiple moving parts to describe the process of learning how to design and teach online asynchronously, especially with respect to teaching transdisciplinary content. In retrospect, as colleagues and I demystified and defined those discrete moving parts and iteratively moved forward, it felt like constructing a pathway where none yet existed. Each step of the way, we collaborated to fashion the 'paving stones' on which to find a firm footing through revisions for improvement in content and format. This path may be useful to others.

Notes

1 Course documents contained in commercial-in-confidence email correspondence to the author, 23 February 2018. This list of topics is no longer applied in BA Practice.
2 Blackboard was still used for assessment submission, grading, and announcements, but most teaching and learning occurred through FutureLearn.
3 Annual enrolment figures from 2019 to 2024 averaged 170 students.

References

Advance HE. (2024). *Framework for flexible learning*. https://www.advance-he.ac.uk/knowledge-hub/framework-flexible-learning
Biesta, G. (2020). *Educational research: An unorthodox introduction*. Bloomsbury.
Boyd, D., & Singer, F. (2011). The meaning and evolution of teaching excellence: A 'radical' case study from Radford University, Virginia. In I. Hay (Ed.), *Inspiring academics* (pp. 53–60). McGraw-Hill Education.
Brenton, S. (2009). E-learning: An introduction. In H. Fry, S. Ketteridge, & S. Marshall (Eds.), *Handbook for teaching and learning in higher education: Enhancing academic practice* (3rd ed., pp. 85–98). Taylor & Francis.
Carey, M. (2023). The faculty journey as ontological inquiry. *Turning Toward Being: The Journal of Ontological Inquiry in Education*, 1(1). https://rdw.rowan.edu/joie/vol1/iss1/6.
Christozov, D., Rasheva-Yordanova, K., & Toleva-Stoimenova, S. (2019). Challenges in designing curriculum for trans-disciplinary education: On cases of designing concentration on informing science and master program on data science. *Informing Science: The International Journal of an Emerging Transdiscipline*, 22, 19–30. https://doi.org/10.28945/4300.
Cook-Sather, A., Abbot, S., & Felten, P. (2019). Legitimating reflective writing in SoTL: 'Dysfunctional illusions of rigor' revisited. *Teaching & Learning Inquiry*, 7(2), 28–50. https://doi.org/10.20343/teachlearninqu.7.2.3
Fawns, T. (2022). An entangled pedagogy: Looking beyond the pedagogy – technology dichotomy. *Postdigital Science and Education*, 4, 711–728. https://doi.org/10.1007/s42438-022-00302-7
Foster, L. (2001). Technology: Transforming the landscape of higher education. *The Review of Higher Education*, 25(1), 115–124. https://dx.doi.org/10.1353/rhe.2001.0018.

Gherghel, C., Shoko, Y., & Kita, Y. (2023). Interaction during online classes fosters engagement with learning and self-directed study both in the first and second years of the COVID-19 pandemic. *Computers & Education, 200*. https://doi.org/10.1016/j.compedu.2023.104795

Gibbs, G. (1988). *Learning by doing: A guide to teaching and learning methods*. Further Education Unit, Oxford Polytechnic.

Heil, J., & Ifenthaler, D. (2023). Online assessment in higher education: A systematic review. *Online Learning, 27*(1), 187–218. https://doi.org/10.24059/olj.v27i1.3398

John, H., Kerr, J., & Andrieux, G. (2024). Beyond boundaries: The role of learning types in shaping MOOC learner engagement and progression. *Journal of Interactive Media in Education, 2024*(1), 1–19. https://doi.org/10.5334/jime.890

Laurillard, D. (2012). *Teaching as a design science: Building pedagogical patterns for learning and technology*. Routledge.

Parham, V. (2013). Learn something new everyday: One History professor's journey through online education. *Interface: The Journal of Education, Community, and Values, 12*, 19–24.

Roxå, T., & Mårtensson, K. (2015). Microcultures and informal learning: A heuristic guiding analysis of conditions for informal learning in local higher education workplaces. *International Journal for Academic Development, 20*(2), 193–205. https://doi.org/10.1080/1360144X.2015.1029929

Salmon, G. (2011). *E-moderating: The key to teaching and learning online* (3rd ed.). Routledge.

Sampson, D. G., Ifenthaler, D., & Isaias, P. (2020). Preface. In D. G. Sampson, D. Ifenthaler, & P. Isaias (Eds.), *Online teaching and learning in higher education* (pp. v–viii). Springer. https://doi.org/10.1007/978-3-030-48190-2

Scherer, R. Howard, S. K., Tondeur, J., & Siddiq, F. (2021, May). Profiling teachers' readiness for online teaching and learning in higher education: Who's ready? *Computers in Human Behavior, 118*. https://doi.org/10.1016/j.chb.2020.106675

Sclater, N., Peasgood, A., & Mullan, J. (2016). Learning analytics in higher education: A review of UK and international practice. *Jisc*. https://analytics.jiscinvolve.org/wp/2016/04/19/learning-analytics-in-higher-education-a-review-of-uk-and-international-practice/

University of Newcastle. (n.d.). *HASS2000 – BA practice*. Retrieved February 17, from https://handbook.newcastle.edu.au/course/2025/HASS2000

Wang, F., & Hannafin, M. J. (2005). Design-based research and technology-enhanced learning environments. *Educational Technology Research and Development, 53*(4), 5–23. https://doi.org/10.1007/bf02504682

15 Australian underworlds
Online teaching as a pathway to building scholarly networks

Nancy Cushing, Alana Piper and Vicky Nagy

Introduction

Amongst the institutions of higher learning, the connection between research and teaching is one of the key elements that has made universities distinctive. In Australia, as in many other countries, it is a regulatory requirement that universities demonstrate "scholarly activities and outcomes that inform teaching, learning, and professional practice and make a contribution to the advancement and dissemination of knowledge" (Department of Education, 2021). Different forms that the teaching-research nexus may take have been profiled: transferring knowledge to students about the results of research; engaging students in critical discussions of current research and research processes; modelling the research process for students; helping students conduct their own research through assignment work; and providing authentic research experiences by involving students in ongoing scholarly projects (Visser-Wijnveen et al., 2010). In the purest form of this teaching-research nexus, university lecturers are active researchers in the areas in which they teach. This positions them to convey to students the latest developments in their field, including their own unique contributions, in what has been called research-led teaching. Students benefit by gaining first-hand insights into how scholarship occurs and how fields advance and may be inspired to pursue research careers themselves (Kelley, 2018).

In the messy real world of the contemporary university, this matching of teaching and research has rarely been perfect. Leading researchers are sometimes 'rewarded' by being relieved of teaching, and those left with heavy teaching loads struggle to find time for research. Maintaining the connection between teaching and research has become especially challenging for the rising proportions of academics in teaching-focused or teaching-only roles, whether fractional, short term, or continuing (Probert & Sachs, 2015).[1] Teaching-focused academics are increasingly encouraged or required to maintain research activity through producing scholarship on teaching and learning, but such outputs are often less valued than traditional research in workload calculations and other measures (Godbold et al., 2023). Trends to offering reduced curricula of general core courses rather than an array of specialist subjects mean that even as doctorates become a minimum standard for entry to the profession, these well-qualified researchers are less likely to teach directly in their own research area. While still a requirement, the teaching-research nexus seems to be at breaking point.

This need not be the case. A nexus, of course, operates in both directions. Just as research enriches teaching, so teaching can inspire, facilitate, and create space for research in both the scholarship of teaching and learning and in a disciplinary (or interdisciplinary) field. This chapter explores a suite of research activities that grew out of the familiar predicament of taking on teaching outside of one's research field, using the University of Newcastle's intermediate-level History course, Australian Underworlds: A History of Crime in Australia, as a case study. That it was the *online* offer of this course which facilitated research activity was not coincidental. There is a strong ethos within the digital humanities towards collaboration and sharing. This is designed into projects. Data and means of manipulating it are often made freely available online for others to use, but the sharing goes much further. In many cases, the data management systems are also on offer enabling researchers to add to the core project with their own material. Where large amounts of transcription or data entry are needed, volunteers – also known as citizen scientists or citizen researchers – are invited to be part of projects not only to complete routine tasks but to share their own ideas on the subject matter in online chat groups or live meetings (Piper, 2020a). Developing an online course meant not only being able to draw upon existing digital humanities projects to inform lectures, provide demonstrations and furnish exercises for students, but being able to draw them into this digital world as participants. Instead of being an impediment to research activity, the teaching of Australian Underworlds online opened opportunities to expand research networks, establish new research collaborations, publish in a new field, and enable students to become researchers in their own right.

Background

Australian Underworlds was developed by Associate Professor Nancy Cushing in 2017 in response to a call for courses to complement the core curriculum of a Criminology major then being established within the Bachelor of Social Sciences. Cushing's areas of research expertise lay in Australia's social, cultural, and environmental history, but the history of crime had been of interest to her, leading to one publication (Cushing, 1996) and the incorporation of crime topics into her first-year Australian history survey course and upper-level courses on Australian popular culture and heritage. Recognising that while she was well-prepared to teach the context of the crimes, she lacked expertise with regard to how crime itself was being theorised by historians and current debates in the field, and so Cushing sought advice and support from scholars of crime.

It was in this process of course design that the opportunities for research collaboration began to emerge. Initially, Cushing looked to institutional colleagues in English Literature, Creative Writing, and Criminology who studied crime from their own disciplinary perspectives. They generously assisted by recording short videos for use in the course, recommending sources, and making introductions to their contacts. They directed Cushing to the Prosecution Project led by Professor Mark Finnane at Griffith University. Launched in 2013 with support from an Australian Research Council Laureate Fellowship Grant, the Prosecution Project's major public-facing output was an online database of Australian prosecutions. The database brings together records of the Supreme Courts in each colony (later state) from as early as 1788 and as late as 1961, supplemented by material from penal records, police gazettes, and other legal proceedings (Finnane & Piper, 2016). By 2020, Finnane and the project team of research fellows, postgraduate students, and associates, had used this valuable source to inform over 80 scholarly articles and book chapters (Prosecution Project, n.d.).

The Prosecution Project is a particularly productive example of the use Australian crime researchers have made of the copious records created by criminal justice systems since settler colonisation, and how this creates a valuable resource for use in the classroom. Australian historians of crime were early and enthusiastic adopters of the types of digital methodologies that would help them to analyse these data. As technology advanced from punch cards in the 1960s, through personal computers in the 1980s, to digitisation and big data in the 2000s, historians applied these new tools to answering questions about convicts in particular (Robson, 1963; Robson, 1965; Nicholas, 1988; Bradley et al., 2010). Demonstrating the culture of cooperation and collaboration in this field, the Founders and Survivors (2018) database of convicts transported to Tasmania along with another 49 datasets has been combined in the Digital Panopticon to document the lives of 90,000 individuals sentenced at London's Central Criminal Court, the Old Bailey, who were transported to Australia (Howard & McLaughlin, n.d.). The result is fresh new insights into the Australian convict system and those who passed through it, and into the later history of crime in Australia, infused as it was by fears of a 'convict stain.' These projects and those on the crimes committed outside of the transportation system are particularly helpful for online teaching as they bring digitised versions of original records and digital methodologies to students' screens, enabling them to pursue their own enquiries.

The Prosecution Project was part of the digital humanities sharing mindset and Finnane responded warmly to the request for assistance. This came in the form of feedback on the proposed course structure, suggested readings, and a guest lecture via Zoom from research fellow Alana Piper, a specialist in gender and crime history. The support so willingly provided enabled the design of an engaging and educational course that was accepted as a complement to the Criminology major and attracted strong numbers when offered on two of the university's campuses and in a basic online form, recorded by

Cushing at her desk. Piper remained involved, visiting in-person to record several short videos about the Prosecution Project and her own research for use in the course.

Having been successfully launched, Australian Underworlds benefitted from another association in 2020, when it was made part of the University of Newcastle's innovative BA Online. Delivered through the United Kingdom-based FutureLearn platform, the upgrading of the online offering was well-timed as students pivoted to study from home in response to COVID-19 restrictions. Following FutureLearn's template, Cushing worked with the University's Learning Design and Teaching Innovation team to break the course material down into a series of weekly steps consisting of short lectures, written text, and videos and learning activities, all accompanied by questions for discussion. Demonstrating the value of pooling a range of skill sets in course development, historian and learning designer Michael Kilmister and videographer Adam Khamis advised, inspired, and cajoled Cushing into bringing about a transformation of the course.

The response from students was immediate and positive. Enrolments rose and while some students did come from the now free-standing Criminology degree, the majority of the more than 600 students who have completed Australian Underworlds since its inception were enrolled in other programs, from the Bachelor of Arts to undergraduate degrees in Teacher Education, Business, Communications, Psychology, Law, and Construction Management. Their numbers provide evidence of the broad appeal of crime as a subject, History as a discipline, and the appetite for online study. The presence of such a diverse group of students has been enriching as students bring insights gained from other areas of study, such as Criminological theories on the causation of crime and insights into the role of the media from Communications studies, into the course discussions. The course has been rated highly in formal student feedback, and informally, some have said that it was the best and most interesting course they had ever taken. In addition to the University of Newcastle students, close to another 2,000 people living mainly in the United Kingdom, Canada, the United States, and Europe have taken the first 3 weeks of the course as a free massive open online course or massive open online course (MOOC) (Casing the Joint: Introducing Histories of Crime) and 600 through the edX platform. This confirmation of the appeal, quality and impact of the course was highly rewarding for Cushing as an educator, but Australian Underworlds also held another set of opportunities, centred on research.

Pathways to research

Cushing was only too happy to agree when Piper, having taken up a post-doctoral fellowship at the University of Technology Sydney, invited her to join a project with criminologist Vicky Nagy of the University of Tasmania. Collaboration is a vital tool for teaching-related research not only for the usual reasons of combining areas of expertise, access to resources, and sharpening insights through discussion but because of the social contract formed amongst research partners (Marquis et al., 2015). When one flags, others can step up, and a sense of responsibility to the collaborators can help with maintaining focus or making research a priority when it might otherwise be outranked by other demands. In this case, Piper and Nagy were interested in exploring how citizen social science – having students make a contribution to the work of a research project external to the course – could be embedded in undergraduate teaching and what its effects on student learning would be. The subject matter being dealt with was crime, an area of specialisation for both of these researchers, but the research would contribute to the scholarship of teaching and learning. That is, it would enquire into student learning in a way designed to advance the practices of teaching in higher education (Simmons et al., 2021). Having been involved with Australian Underworlds, Piper saw the opportunity to compare outcomes for History students with those amongst Nagy's Criminology students.

Their approach was not unusual as this type of interdisciplinary collaboration is characteristic of the digital humanities. The field is premised on bringing together those with expertise in the humanities and social sciences with scholars possessing complementary capacities in digital technologies, often with the involvement of museums, libraries, and archives holding the collections that sit at the heart of projects. As Láng and Megyesi (2024) note, in digital humanities research, "different skills and sets of expertise are joined, and common goals and research techniques are negotiated" requiring new vocabularies, practices and methods (p. 2). While Cushing had experience of collaborating across disciplines, the idea of forming a team for digital humanities research associated with teaching was novel, and very welcome.

The focus on citizen social science was also in keeping with digital humanities practices. Citizen social science, a variation on the better-known citizen science, is the practice of engaging those from outside of academia to participate in social science research projects as co-producers of knowledge rather than as those experimented on (Campos et al., 2021; Terras, 2015). While citizen science draws people into projects related to analysing and categorising large datasets from the physical environment, citizen social science focuses on matters related to people and their records. Research on citizen science suggests that men and women volunteer in relatively equal numbers, that participants skew to older age groups, and that they become involved for reasons of altruism, to express their personal values, to develop knowledge and as a form of recreation (Agnello et al., 2022). Similar motivations have led volunteers to take on tasks in the digital humanities projects discussed earlier, completing tasks that were beyond the capacity of limited numbers of paid researchers. In particular, the time-consuming transcribing of hand-written records to enable their integration into digital databases has often been done by citizen social scientists. When engaged in by students, this type of activity can also be considered as a form of work-integrated learning that moves out of the classroom into the wider world (Jacoby et al., 2024).

In her University of Technology Sydney Chancellors Postdoctoral Research Fellowship project, Criminal Characters, Piper analysed the large-scale data on the life histories and offending patterns of Australian criminals between the 1850s and 1940s held on paper prison records in the Public Records Office of Victoria. Transcription was a necessary first step. Piper linked her own project website with the Zooniverse platform, which claims to be the "world's largest and most popular platform for people-powered research," to invite volunteers to transcribe the records (Zooniverse, n.d.). Introductory material emphasised that the work would have a lasting benefit, not only for Piper's own research but also by creating a resource to be made available to the general public by the Public Records Office. Piper included help buttons, tutorials and other assistive features to guide participants, as well as a chat room where they could share their thoughts about what they were transcribing with her and other volunteers.

As they transcribed, volunteers came to know intimate details about the lives of offenders. Not only were their offences, sentences, and trial courts listed, but so were their year and place of birth, occupation, level of literacy, religion, marital status, aliases, and distinguishing marks, including those caused by physical conditions or disabilities. For some, there was information about their families, such as the removal of their children into state care, and on where the person went from prison: a charity home, asylum, or a pauper's grave. Many transcribers were moved to share their responses to what they learned from the records in the "Criminal Characters Talk" chat group set up for that purpose. The enthusiasm of the volunteers encouraged Piper to add prison records from NSW to the project. Nagy approached the Archives Office of Tasmania for their digital prison records and soon these too were added to Piper's "Criminal Characters" Zooniverse (https://www.zooniverse.org/) project. At the completion of the transcription phase, more than 15,000 volunteers had digitised the records of just over 100,000 offenders.

Having observed the responses of transcribers to the lives they had encountered in the prison records (Piper, 2020b), Piper and Nagy were keen to explore how such an exercise would affect student learning. This origin of the project addressed the frequent question of how those without access to even in-house funding schemes are to conduct research. By forming a team in which partners brought different expertise, access to research subjects, and infrastructure, Piper's funded research could be leveraged to underpin an unfunded project about student learning and citizen social science in higher education. Similarly, the generation of the research data was designed to occur as part of teaching activities rather than in addition to them, minimising the time needed to be found for this phase of the research. The data was generated in the form of an assessment task that required students to transcribe three historical prison records within the Criminal Characters interface, research the offenders and their crimes in other primary and secondary sources, and write a structured reflection about what they had learned. The responses would be analysed to assess the impact of active engagement with prison records on learning through both research-led (outlining a research problem and its theoretical context for students) and research-based (setting students on an authentic research investigation) activities (Healey & Jenkins, 2009).

There are certain key points at which scholars need to be cautious when combining teaching and research, and this was one of them. Agreeing to involve one's own students is a significant decision. While from the perspective of research, interventions must have some novelty to make them worth trialling, they must not be disruptive to student learning and indeed students should stand to gain practical benefits in exchange for their involvement (Bonney et al., 2016). In this case, the new assessment task had to relate to the established course learning outcomes. The stated outcomes undertook that students who successfully completed the course would have knowledge of key themes and concepts around the history of crime in Australia; be able to work with primary and secondary sources, including those that have been digitised; evaluate information, ideas, and arguments about the history of crime; express an ethical stance towards the history of crime; and demonstrate communication and information literacy skills. The transcription assessment task was an excellent fit for these learning outcomes and could readily be put in the place of an existing task focused on the close reading of primary sources and digital output.[2] Benefits to the students would be the opportunity to contribute to two research projects: Piper's Criminal Characters and the study of the impact of undertaking a citizen social science project on student learning.

The necessity to gain human ethics approval from both institutions was an opportunity to secure an external affirmation of the merit of the research in comparison with any potential harm to students. The collaboration had benefits in this process, as with both universities adhering to the National Statement on Ethical Conduct in Human Research, material prepared for one ethics application could be repurposed for the other. We agreed that to remove any concern students might have that not participating in the project could affect their marks, no work would proceed until final grades had been issued. Further, all information about the project including consent forms was distributed by people associated with the course but not part of the research team.

University of Tasmania students responded well to the call for participants with 42 completing their consent forms, while fewer than 10 University of Newcastle students agreed to participate. It is unclear why there was such a discrepancy in student participation between the two institutions. Amongst those who consented to have their work included in our study, we found that students had valued the opportunity to become citizen social scientists. Many were encountering historical records for the first time and the active, directed reading required for transcription meant that the words and images left a greater impression on them than the cursory reading many course materials receive. Learning about the offenders as people – their immigration status, eye colour, scars – created empathy and a desire to know more about them that spurred the citizen social scientists on as they sought additional information about these men and women in digitised newspapers. Criminology students in particular had an enhanced sense of the importance of historical context as they reflected on how people in similar positions in the present were treated in the contemporary criminal justice system. Although most were much younger than the typical citizen social scientist, once introduced to the possibility of contributing their labour to advance a research project, most students quickly found that they also enjoyed the opportunity for altruistic activity, expressing personal values, and developing knowledge. Many reported that they had engaged much more deeply with this assessment task than with any other one in their degree. Some were moved to transcribe more than the three required records and to discuss what they had discovered with family and friends.

Bringing students into research projects gives them a greater awareness of how knowledge is created and advanced and a sense of themselves as contributors to these processes rather than completing assignments as exercises with no application other than demonstrating capacity and generating a grade. This is in keeping with recent research findings on the value of authentic assessment, including digitally mediated authentic assessments, for building student agency and providing a space for them to actively learn and deploy their new knowledge (Nieminen et al., 2024). In keeping with the benefits claimed for involving students in research-based teaching that could lead to the generation of new knowledge (Kelley, 2018), we found that they were more engaged in learning and more motivated to complete and extend their studies. Both History and Criminology students learned that deep engagement with primary sources could yield new insights to be tested through critical thinking and synthesis with existing knowledge.

Recognition and publishing

The project was recognised by the Australian and New Zealand Society of Criminology by being selected for the 2021 Award for Excellence and Innovation in Teaching. We used the cash prize, with additional support from the University of Tasmania, to fund a hybrid symposium on "Citizen Social Science in the Classroom" in Hobart in July 2022. Running over two days, the symposium attracted university scholars and representatives of the GLAM (Galleries, Libraries, Archives, and Museums) sector. Presentations focused on how social scientists can collaborate with cultural institutions to enrich their classroom teaching and learning experiences while also advancing their own research, and how cultural institutions can meet their own aims of making collections more accessible through such collaborations. Building mutually beneficial relationships in this manner can open the way for future joint research projects and other benefits, including the hosting of work experience students by GLAM sector partners.

The next step in the collaborative research project was to write up and publish our findings. This was led by Nagy who identified two outlets focused on the scholarship of teaching and learning in criminology: the *Journal of Criminal Justice Education* and an edited collection on public criminology and education. Writing was shared, with sections drafted by one co-author reviewed and added to by the others. In due course after submission, both the article and chapter were accepted and appeared respectively in 2023 (Nagy et al., 2023) and 2024 (Nagy et al., 2024). Reporting on this innovative interdisciplinary and inter-institutional project made a valuable addition to the scholarship of teaching and learning, which we hope will provide a model for others considering embedding citizen social science in their teaching. For those in teaching-focused positions, publications like these are particularly important ways of demonstrating their active scholarship in the field of andragogy when seeking their next position or promotion (Probert & Sachs, 2015).

Drawing upon the network

In May 2021, while the citizen social science project was underway, Cushing received an invitation from a commissioning editor with Routledge's Humanities and Media Arts section to propose a textbook based on Australian Underworlds. In keeping with the aims of the publisher, she designed a book that could serve as a set or supplementary text for Australian history of crime or criminology courses but would also appeal to the wider reading public. As in the development of the course, she was again mindful of the need to include, rather than simply drawing upon, current work in the field of crime history. A structure was developed in which for each of the 12 topics treated, readers would be presented with a primary source and a short essay by a subject expert in addition to Cushing's longer chapter.

With early input from Piper and Nagy, Cushing drew up a wish list of contributors undertaking research in relevant areas. When approached, each person agreed to provide a piece that would enrich or indeed challenge the perspective on crime presented in the related chapter. Many were from the network already established around the course. These included Nagy and Piper, as well as Rachel Franks of the NSW State Library, and Cushing's colleague Catharine Coleborne, a specialist on the history of vagrancy. Others were field leaders with whom Cushing had had some earlier contact, such as Hamish Maxwell Stewart, while some were entirely new acquaintances. Very importantly for the book, these included Tyson Yunkaporta of the Apalech clan of Far North Queensland and Palawa man Michael Bryden, who were able to discuss Aboriginal Law from an insider position. The essays enabled topics to be added that addressed questions raised by past students of the course, including vagrancy and the policing of homosexuality, treated by Yorick Smaal. Space was made for emerging scholars and for those whose work intersected with crime history rather than being focused upon it. Amongst them was Michael Kilmister, a learning designer with a doctorate in History. Kilmister is one of a rising number of what Celia Whitechurch terms "blended professionals" working as a specialist providing teaching support while also continuing his own research and publishing (Probert & Sachs, 2015, p. 66). Kilmister's essay guided students through the process of using online databases for their own crime research. The contributors met a short deadline, and several were able to attend the launch of the book at the Australian Historical Association conference in Melbourne in July 2023 (Musgrove, 2023).

The *A History of Crime in Australia* book project was an opportunity for Cushing to extend her own forays into the writing of crime history and her network within and beyond this field. Although making a causal link is difficult, since its publication, she has experienced greater success in her own field of environmental history. This trajectory serves at least as a partial response to the concern some teaching-focused academics might have about the wisdom of directing scarce research time into sometimes under-recognised teaching-related research rather than their own disciplinary research (Simmons et al., 2021). Building one's profile, track record, and network through engagement in the scholarship of teaching and learning can have benefits for research activity as a whole.

Conclusion

One response to the challenge of keeping the teaching-research nexus vital in the contemporary university is to use one's teaching to generate research opportunities. As the case of Australian Underworlds online has shown, networks established in the development and teaching of a course, even outside of a familiar research area, can lead to opportunities for collaborative research with all of the benefits it brings. In this case study, a project investigating the use of citizen social science in teaching not only provided research outcomes for the academics involved but also generated opportunities for their students to gain experience in the conduct of a research project for themselves. Students helped to make the information in the court records available for the Criminal Characters Project and for other users of the libraries' collections and also learned for themselves how the immersion in documents required for accurate transcription can lead to new levels of understanding. By shifting the usual hierarchy and allowing teaching to guide research, academics can turn what has been perceived as obstacles into pathways to the creation of new knowledge.

Notes

1 In Australia, academics in a teaching stream rose from 755 in 2005 to 3212 in 2015. In the United States, in 2016, 73% of instructional positions were not tenure track and little or no support for research (Simmons et al., 2021).

2 The timeline assessment task requires students to identify a little-known crime using the Trove digitised newspaper database and create a timeline of events using Knight Lab's Timeline JS software (https://timeline.knightlab.com/), followed by a brief discussion of the crime in its historical context informed by scholarly secondary sources.

References

Agnello, G., Vercammen, A., & Knight, A. T. (2022). Understanding citizen scientists' willingness to invest in, and advocate for, conservation. *Biological Conservation*, *265*, 109422. https://doi.org/10.1016/j.biocon.2021.109422

Bonney, R., Phillips, T. B., Ballard, H. L., & Enck, J. W. (2016). Can citizen science enhance public understanding of science? *Public Understanding of Science*, *25*(1), 2–16. https://doi.org/10.1177/0963662515607406

Bradley, J., Kippen, R., Maxwell-Stewart, H., McCalman, J., & Silcot, S. (2010). The founders and survivors project. *The History of the Family*, *15*(4), 467–477. https://doi.org/10.1016/j.hisfam.2010.08.002

Campos, R., Monteiro, J., & Carvalho, C. (2021). Engaged citizen social science or the public participation in social science research. *Journal of Science Communication*, *20*(A06). https://doi.org/10.22323/2.20060206

Cushing, N. (1996). Woman as murderer: The defence of Louisa Collins. *Journal of Interdisciplinary Gender Studies*, *1*(2), 146–157. http://www.newcastle.edu.au/school/hss/research/publications/jigs/volume-1-2-sept-1996.html.

Department of Education, Australian Government. (2021). *Higher education standards framework (Threshold Standards)*. https://www.legislation.gov.au/F2021L00488/latest/text

Finnane, M., & Piper, A. (2016). The prosecution project: Understanding the changing criminal trial through digital tools. *Law and History Review*, *34*(4), 873–891. https://doi.org/10.1017/S0738248016000316

Founders and Survivors. (2018, July 12). About the project. *Founders and Survivors*. https://www.foundersandsurvivors.org/project.html

Godbold, N., Matthews, K. E. E., & Gannaway, D. (2023). Theorising new possibilities for scholarship of teaching and learning and teaching-focused academics. *Higher Education Research & Development*, *43*(1), 92–103. https://doi-org/10.1080/07294360.2023.2218809

Healey, M., & Jenkins, A. (2009). Developing undergraduate research and enquiry. *The Higher Education Academy*. http://www.heacademy.ac.uk/assets/York/documents/resources/publications/DevelopingUndergraduate_Final.pdf

Howard, S., & McLaughlin, J. (n.d.). About the project. *The Digital Panopticon*. https://www.digitalpanopticon.org/About_The_Project

Jacoby, D., Savage, S., & Coady, Y. (2024). Remote possibilities: Where there is a WIL, is there a way? AI education for remote learners in a new era of work-integrated-learning. *Proceedings of the AAAI Symposium Series*, *3*(1), 478–485. https://doi.org/10.1609/aaaiss.v3i1.31261

Kelley, P. H. (2018). *Incorporating research into undergraduate paleontology courses: Or a tale of 23,276 mulinia*. Cambridge University Press.

Láng, B., & Megyesi, B. (2024). An STS analysis of a digital humanities collaboration: Trading zones, boundary objects, and interactional expertise in the DECRYPT project. *Humanities & Social Sciences Communications*, *11*(1), Article 618. https://doi.org/10.1057/s41599-024-03135-w

Marquis, E., Healey, M., & Vine, M. (2015). Fostering collaborative teaching and learning scholarship through an international writing group initiative. *Higher Education Research & Development*, *35*(3), 531–544. https://doi.org/10.1080/07294360.2015.1107886

Musgrove, N. (2023). Review of the book *A History of Crime in Australia: Australian underworlds*, by N. Cushing. *History, Magazine of the Royal Australian Historical Society*, 161, 17.

Nagy, V., Cushing, N., & Piper, A. (2023). Public criminology in the Australian higher education classroom: Bringing criminology and history together through citizen social science. In D. Jones, M. Jones, K. Strudwick, & A. Charles (Eds.), *Public criminology* (pp. 169–194). Springer International Publishing AG. https://doi.org/10.1007/978-3-031-42167-9_8

Nagy, V., Piper, A., & Cushing, N. (2024). Citizen social science in the classroom: Criminology students' perceptions of prisoner records. *Journal of Criminal Justice Education*, 35(1), 218–234. https://doi.org/10.1080/10511253.2023.2179089

Nicholas, S. (Ed.). (1988). *Convict workers: Reinterpreting Australia's past*. Cambridge University Press.

Nieminen, J. H., Haataja, E., & Cobb, P. J. (2024). From active learners to knowledge contributors: Authentic assessment as a catalyst for students' epistemic agency. *Teaching in Higher Education*, 30(4), 970–990. https://doi.org/10.1080/13562517.2024.2332252

Piper, A. (2020a). Crowdsourcing: Citizen history and criminal characters. In P. Ashton, T. Evans, & P. Hamilton (Eds.), *Making histories* (pp. 199–210). Walter de Gruyter. https://doi.org/10.1515/9783110636352-017

Piper, A. (2020b). Digital crowdsourcing and public understandings of the past: Citizen historians meet criminal characters. *History Australia*, 17(3), 525–541. https://doi.org/10.1080/14490854.2020.1796500

Probert, B., & Sachs, J. (2015). The rise of teaching focused academics in universities. *International Journal of Chinese Education*, 4(1), 48–67. https://doi.org/10.1163/22125868-12340044

Prosecution Project. (n.d.). *Publications*. https://prosecutionproject.griffith.edu.au/publications/

Robson, L. L. (1963). The origin of the women convicts sent to Australia, 1787–1852. *Historical studies, Australia and New Zealand*, 11(41), 43–53. https://doi.org/10.1080/10314616308595262

Robson, L. L. (1965). *The convict settlers of Australia: An enquiry into the origin and character of the convicts transported to New South Wales and Van Diemen's Land, 1787–1852*. Melbourne University Press.

Simmons, N., Eady, M., Scharff, L., & Gregory, D. (2021). SoTL in the margins: Teaching-focused role case studies. *Teaching and Learning Inquiry*, 9(1), 61–78. https://doi.org/10.20343/teachlearninqu.9.1.6

Terras, M. (2015). Crowdsourcing in the digital humanities. In S. Schreibman, R. G. Siemens, & J. Unsworth (Eds.), *A new companion to digital humanities* (pp. 420–438). Wiley. https://doi.org/10.1002/9781118680605.ch29

Visser-Wijnveen, G. J., Van Driel, J. H., Van der Rijst, R. M., Verloop, N., & Visser, A. (2010). The ideal research-teaching nexus in the eyes of academics: Building profiles. *Higher Education Research and Development*, 29(2), 195–210. https://doi.org/10.1080/07294360903532016

Zooniverse. (n.d.). https://www.zooniverse.org/

16 Conclusion

Reflecting on the BA Online project

Catharine Coleborne and Clare Lloyd

Introduction: successes and challenges

The opening chapter of this book described the reinvention of the Bachelor of Arts degree at the University of Newcastle, a project that commenced in 2016. Looking back, we achieved much of the original intention of this project through the BA Online and our partnership with FutureLearn. The project expanded the degree's special 'Newcastle' and local identity by showcasing Aboriginal languages and ways of knowing, and the intercultural capability learning opportunity offered at UON. It foregrounded the degree's physical location through sharing the University of Newcastle's Indigenous knowledge and expertise. It created spaces for global learners in the open courses, with domestic students mingling with international learners. The project created a common thread or 'spine' in the degree by introducing core courses while also shifting the dial in terms of the administration and culture of the degree. The three core courses made it more possible to map student learning outcomes, forge a common student cohort, and enable a shared, interdisciplinary learning experience.

Readers will note that the separate sections of this book encompass the creation of the degree, case studies in online teaching and assessment, challenges and opportunities that arose during the project, and the impact and evaluation of the BA Online project. This reflective Conclusion reminds readers how the different drivers for degree redesign amplified by the BA Online – accessibility, innovation, and pedagogical renewal – ultimately made a series of positive impacts on academic staff and students over time. We also touch here on the way this BA degree reinvention provided specific opportunities for educators to work and collaborate with in-house designed and built online education by engaging with institutional learning designers.

Accessibility: improving market share, enrolments and flexibility

We know purposeful, quality online learning can increase opportunities for equity and "equity like" (Clarke et al., 2024, p. 6) students, such as students

DOI: 10.4324/9781003505785-20

attending university from backgrounds of relative disadvantage. This is explained Stone (2017), who explains online learning

> has a critical place in widening access and participation in education for a diverse range of students, many of whom are from backgrounds which have been historically underrepresented at university. Students from low socioeconomic backgrounds (low SES), students with disability, regional and remote students, Indigenous students, and students who are first in their families to enter university, are represented particularly strongly in online undergraduate programs.
>
> (p. 5)

During 2018, the focus of institutional thinking about degree renewal shifted to the development of excellent online offerings for students in the BA. Market insight research told us that we were losing students from our own catchment to online BA providers in the sector, both in NSW and nationally. There was a real argument for the BA to be offered fully online both in terms of revenue and accessibility. After the launch of the BA degree with four online majors, the growth in the Online enrolment was steady from 2019 to 2020. The offering not only allowed students to be fully online, but it also opened up more flexible study options for our face-to-face students, giving them the opportunity to mix their study modes and also manage their timetables and learning schedules. Our on-campus students now had more options for studying courses either face-to-face or online, which meant many students were also given greater flexibility along with new learning experiences via the different platforms for learning. For the first time, our undergraduate students experienced interactions and conversations with other global learners in the initial 3 weeks of their courses through short, 3-week open courses (MOOCs). Giving the UON students greater diversity of interactions through the open courses meant our learners could be in a virtual environment with global learners.

Innovation

Being the first at UON to partner with and use the learning experience platform (LXP) FutureLearn meant having to think about how to design and construct UON courses for this specific LXP. We also needed to consider and design ways to engage students in meaningful ways in this learning environment. The experience of working with FutureLearn was overall enormously positive and afforded an opportunity for academic staff to work across position and role boundaries with learning designers and new media content as they redesigned and designed courses for online delivery. The open courses generated public awareness of the BA at Newcastle, with the undergraduate degree acknowledged as a world first for FutureLearn. The online BA project was the first at the university to experience a learning 'taster' in a model where global learners were able to enjoy the first 3 weeks of a university course for free, as noted here earlier. This allowed learners to get a sense of the course content and quality to see if it was right for them. As Coleborne (2018) commented at the time of the degree's launch,

> What is exciting about this degree is that we are opening up our BA degree to new learners who are curious about the world and who are keen to create ideas. The degree will be flexible: students can tailor their study to their interests and career goals, also accommodating life's other commitments. We aim to showcase the exciting experience of being in an online classroom, with the added dimension of having students from varied perspectives and places participate.
>
> (para. 4)

Then came the COVID-19 lockdowns. Despite the greater impact on higher education, these too brought opportunity. The BA Online was not 'just in time' emergency education online (Ruegg, 2023) or adapted for the COVID-19 moment in higher education; it was purposefully designed before the pandemic started with the online learner in mind. This meant the project's innovations had something to offer the whole institution at this point in time, especially through a culture shift for educators in teaching and learning, design, and delivery.

In May 2020, Catharine, Clare, Michael Kilmister, and Annika Herb presented 'Moving Courses Online' to UON (Coleborne et al., 2020). Participants at that session learned more about the value of the BA Online as a way of thinking about purposeful online design and delivery.

The ways the BA project supported staff beyond the core project was evidenced in educators' experiences of online teaching during the second half of 2020. When the University made adjustments to delivery modes for on-campus students in large cohorts due to social distancing requirements in Semester Two, 2020, the institution surveyed teaching staff for comments about the adaptations to their teaching. Staff were asked, "What adjustments have you made in S2 as you manage student concerns about COVID-19? These might include additional online tutorials using Zoom or Collaborate; written exercises." Staff reported variously on their teaching experience was more positive due to having already worked on their courses in the BA Online project:

> I am teaching an online only course via FutureLearn. I have built references to COVID into the course materials and comments, but [do] not have to make any adjustments to teaching methods/delivery.
>
> All of my classes were already online, asynchronous offerings, so not much has changed!
>
> As we already have a full online version of the course . . . running in parallel, there's been very little we've had to do. We may need to open

an online tutorial if the numbers of students unable to attend continue to climb, but at this stage it's still too few.[1]

By contrast, staff feedback from educators who were not working with the FutureLearn LXP and who were teaching in other degrees, offered different concerns: "Obstacles include lack of time and creativity to adapting lectures or tutorials into online versions." Other feedback included points about the strains of online teaching more generally: "I think sedentary teaching (sitting at the screen) as opposed to being able to move when teaching has an impact on energy and quality."

Pedagogical renewal in the humanities

The BA Online was an important project to help with pedagogical challenges in the humanities and social sciences. It pulled staff in to work together, creating culture change and new forms of dialogue. The project was a new way of working for the teaching staff. They were part of a large project mapping the online degree, looking for consistency across the program while also giving each discipline space to pedagogically shine. Pedagogical uplift and renewal occurred for the disciplines as the project allowed staff to focus on their specific disciplinary needs. This made way for educators to create new ways of working. Students and their experiences with the online courses were the main priority, with a new emerging institutional focus on student retention. The staff developed a series of guides for staff teaching online around retention and student success alongside the degree changes. One of our former sessional staff, Annika Herb, now working in a learning and academic development role and a co-editor of this book, won the whole of University of Newcastle Staff Excellence award for her work with the BA Online and student retention. These were important outcomes because they pointed to the increased professionalism of the educators involved in the project with closer attention to student outcomes. A national Deans of Arts and Social Sciences session on online pedagogies around the country revealed similar strategies of design for online, also demonstrating that the project at UON was leading conceptual innovation in terms of pedagogy and renewal.

In the same 2020 survey of staff feedback about adaptations to their teaching, educators involved in the BA Online also used this opportunity to share their positive experiences. In response to the question, "Do you have any other constructive and helpful comments you are willing to share with colleagues?" one staff member responded,

> The FutureLearn model of varied steps in presenting course materials and activities is a good one. People should book into a FL course to experience this, and think about how they might incorporate elements of it into their teaching. I did this last year before the full conversion to

FL and found the students to be more engaged and likely to complete the week tasks.²

Feedback from educators in the project was often very positive, with comments indicating the "embedded professional development in learning design had enhanced their 'pedagogical skills in designing authentic formative assessment for online learning and creating interactive research-based collaborative learning activities'" (Herb, Kilmister, Lloyd, forthcoming).

Conclusion: final notes on the benefits and drawbacks of online education

The different chapters in this book make a strong collective case for the benefits of online education. Not only learners but also educators and universities as education providers can gain a range of positive outcomes from investing in online learning in partnership with innovative LXPs. The benefits include providing a greater number of students with access to education, as well as providing alternative models of educational design and delivery in the context of the institution.

Our collective work to create the BA Online with FutureLearn has been nationally recognised with invitations to speak at events focused on BA redesign projects including at the Australasian Council of Deans of Arts and Social Sciences events. As discussed in the first chapter of this book, the BA reinvention involved business and employer research; focus groups with students, families, and prospective students; and created new opportunities for academic and professional staff collaboration, creative, and productive work that was honoured by Faculty Staff Excellence Awards in 2018 and 2019. An early indication of the value of this degree reinvention was highlighted in an article on curriculum change in *Campus Review* (see Coleborne, 2017).

However, the authors of the chapters in this book also point to the problems they encountered in the process of designing and delivering online courses; among them, student engagement, online safety and the need for content moderation for diverse audiences; the stresses and strains for educators as they navigated the workloads and new approaches to teaching in complex environments; and the experiences of students who were not always adequately prepared for the online learning context: perhaps expecting different forms of interaction or who needed other forms of peer engagement, especially following the COVID-19 interruptions to face-to-face learning and the on-campus experience. Student feedback continued to be positive but also left room for improvement; direct surveys of FutureLearn students tended to be more positive than formal UON student surveys in the early years of the degree delivery.

In conclusion, our specific goals for the project have been largely met: we designed, created, and transformed a proportion of the BA to an online mode in eight key majors in the BA degree, allowing the BA to be promoted as multi-modal – online, blended, and face-to-face. Developing online courses for the BA degree new core courses, we innovated our pedagogy across the whole School, and in line with the New Education Framework, also developing educator skills in digital literacy in teaching.

A few opportunities remain unrealised. We are yet to extend our WIL capability into the online learning spaces through portfolio outcomes (although this process has begun). We would still like to invite relevant GLAM industry partners into the online teaching space, and we are yet to make significant progress in developing courses and components of courses as electives for different programs. However, given all online teaching and learning needs to be regularly reviewed and renewed, we look forward to seeing the next iteration of what the BA Online takes as we move the complex mission of humanities education forward into the future, especially in an era of constant change, digital innovation, and challenges to the value proposition of higher education created by generative artificial intelligence.

Notes

1 Internal document, School of Humanities and Social Sciences, 'Adaptations to Teaching S2', 30/09/2020.
2 Internal document, School of Humanities and Social Sciences, 'Adaptations to Teaching S2', 30/09/2020.

References

Clarke, S. L., Frawley, J. K., Kalman, E., Denham, R., Miller, B., Martin, R., Bridgeman, A. J., O'Shea, S., & Liu, D. Y. T. (2024). *Green guide: Enhancing the learning experiences of students from equity backgrounds*. The University of Sydney. https://doi.org/10.25910/cdd2-ef89.

Coleborne, C. (2017, September 13). UON revamps arts faculty to produce more employable grads. *Campus Review*. https://www.campusreview.com.au/2017/09/uon-revamps-arts-faculty-to-produce-more-employable-grads/

Coleborne, C. (2018, September 28). New FutureLearn partnership to deliver Bachelor of Arts online. *UON Newsroom*. https://www.newcastle.edu.au/newsroom/current-staff/new-futurelearn-partnership-to-deliver-bachelor-of-arts-online

Coleborne, C., Lloyd, C., Kilmister, M., & Herb, A. (2020). *Moving courses online* [Paper presentation]. The Educator Network, University of Newcastle, Australia. https://www.newcastle.edu.au/current-staff/teaching-and-research/academic-career-development/building-your-teaching-skills/professional-development/learning-lunchbox

Ruegg, R. (2023). "It's a pain, but it's not like the end of the world": Students' experiences of emergency remote teaching. *Australasian Journal of Educational Technology, 39*(2), 33–46. https://doi.org/10.14742/ajet.8147

Stone, C. (2017). *Opportunity through online learning: Improving student access, participation and success in higher education*. National Centre for Student Equity in Higher Education. https://www.acses.edu.au/app/uploads/2022/06/CathyStone_EQUITY-FELLOWSHIP-FINAL-REPORT-1.pdf

Afterword

Michael Kilmister, Clare Lloyd and Annika Herb

This book is the story of a 4-year project with ambitious objectives, tight deadlines, and dozens of personnel from different disciplines and various expertise working together in new ways. There was no institutional 'roadmap' for the design and development of a program for online delivery on a third-party platform. Also missing was guidance for integrating 'open' course into the structure of an undergraduate degree; in other words, designing learning that was appropriate for the public and enrolled degree students. These unknowns led to agility in project management and development, and a vibrant culture of collaboration. The intensity and collaborative nature of the work – a learning designer, a learning media producer, and a course convenor collaborating over a long-term period – led to fruitful knowledge exchange, mutual professional development, and creative solutions to novel problems. We hope this book tells the story of the countless creative entanglements between people and technology; entanglements that resulted in a successful project, but which still included hard-learned lessons. We have tried to capture these lessons in this book.

This is also a story of us: co-editors with manifold connections and deep respect for our colleagues and contributors. The three of us are Humanities graduates and educators. We came to the BA Online project at various times and worked in various capacities. Just as many embraced the BA Online as a development opportunity, they have also engaged by contributing to this book. They have opened their classrooms, their practice, and their lived experience as practitioners to you as the reader. There is a vulnerability in this act that educators can appreciate. We appreciate all the time and expertise that has shaped this book.

Our aim was to provide practical wisdom and recommendations via accessible texts grounded in evidence. While the experiences are responsive to and situated in a particular academic discipline, they are also adaptable to different contexts. Above all, we hope the key takeaway is the value of collaboration, human connection, and support to design and deliver online learning – an approach that transcends discipline, location, and institution.

Index

academic development 106, 169–170, 174, 184; role of peer review 195
academic skills: embedding support 8, 32, 37–38, 104; critical thinking 18, 23, 47, 50–51, 82, 83–84; using learning video to support 64–65, 89
access and participation 82, 90
accessibility 14, 147, 175, 181, 225–226; *see also* UDL
action research 169–170
Anthropology: teaching online 134; skills 136–138; virtual fieldwork 134–138
Arena Blended Connected (ABC) 6–8, 184
Ariotti, K., viii, 10, 97–109
artificial intelligence (AI) *see* generative AI
Askland, H. A., viii, 10, 134–149, 203
assessment 8, 100, 135–136, 160–161, 181–182, 209, 218–219, 223n2; authentic 8, 140, 220; feedback 38, 161; for learning 147
asynchronous learning *see* online learning

Bachelor of Arts degree: in Australia 3–4, 13–16, 25n2, 169, 193, 203, 225
Barnett, R. 29–30
Barton, K. and McCully, A. 110, 111, 113
Beirne, R. viii, 10, 78–93
belonging *see* community
Bennett, J. viii, 10, 97–109
Biggs, J. *see* constructive alignment
Blackboard *see* learning management system
blended learning 40, 103, 147, 153
Boud, D. 18, 82, 170, 184

Canvas *see* learning management system
captioning 59, 175
CAST *see* UDL
ChatGPT *see* generative AI
citizen social science 217–219; social laboratories 104
Coleborne, C. viii, 9, 11, 13–27, 221, 225–230
collaboration: between students online 52, 54, 55; between staff 162, 172–173
community, sense of 105, 145–148, 191
compulsory course *see* core course
constructive alignment 6, 8, 93, 100, 154, 219
constructivist pedagogy 20, 45, 52, 55; social constructivist 34, 46, 81
Conversational Framework 6, 34, 45–46, 51, 53, 81, 170; learning types 7–8, 102–103
Cook, J. viii, 9, 45–58
Cooper, J. viii, 10, 150–166
Cope, B. 30, 37
copyright 10, 72, 79, 81, 86, 90, 91, 175
core courses 15, 17–18, 20, 22, 34, 99, 136, 194, 200, 203, 213–214, 225; evaluation of 194
COVID-19 124, 146, 155, 169, 187; 'panicgogy' 28; readiness 29, 38, 74, 86–87, 97, 136, 176, 145–146, 216, 227
Criminology 14, 214–216, 220, 221
curiosity 80
curriculum design 115, 116, 219
Cushing, N. ix, 11, 98, 213–224

Davis, S. E. ix, 9, 59–77
digital humanities 214–215, 217

digital pornography 110, 113–116
digital technology 124, 128
discussion boards: assessment 84, 209; prompting of discussion 105; engagement within 49–51, 53, 84, 101; facilitating discussion 48–49, 105; moderation of 49–52, 105, 85, 204
distance education 46–47, 202–203

educational technology/tools 17, 19, 25, 28, 122–123, 132, 147, 159, 162, 174; Padlet 80, 89, 162–163; polling 103–104, 162
educator development *see* academic development
e-learning *see* online learning
Ellis, R. A. 30, 33
emergency remote teaching 25; *see also* COVID-19
employability 203, 217–218
engagement 79, 83, 103, 105, 116, 138–139, 147, 175, 183–184
equity, diversity, and inclusivity 16–17, 111, 116, 134–135, 135, 203, 225–226
ethnography 134–135; autoethnography 59–60
evaluation: Bachelor of Arts (BA) Online 91, 104–105, 170, 172, 193–195, 206, 216, 228–229; challenges and limitations 53–55, 177, 183–184, 187, 189–190, 192, 195, 229; comparing on-campus to online courses 190–192; metrics/'metrification' of 188, 207; research ethics 107n8, 219; response rates 194–195; satisfaction surveys 55, 177–178, 182, 188–189, 193–194; technology 192–193; value of 47, 55, 182, 187, 227–228
Evans, D. J. R., xi–xiii

face-to-face teaching: designing of 103–104; translating to online 97–98, 101–102, 125, 153, 175
first-in-family 16, 203
Ford, H. ix, 10, 78–93
Ford, J. ix, 10, 110–121
FutureLearn 20, 37, 46, 48, 55, 80–81, 85, 205, 209, 216; partnership 29–31, 35, 39–40, 225–226; pedagogy of 8, 19–22, 32, 34, 36–37, 112, 118, 154; staff views 228–229; structure 170–172; undergraduate degrees on 5–6

gamification 137–138, 147
Garrison, D. 46–53
Garside, T. ix, 10, 134–149
generative AI 74, 128–131, 195
Gherghel, C. 81–84, 204
GLAM (Galleries, Libraries, Archives and Museums) 220, 230
Goodyear, P. 30, 33, 39
guest lectures 64, 99, 103

Herb, A. i, 3–12, 169–186, 228
higher education: Australia 4, 13, 34, 97, 99, 187–188, 203, 213; United Kingdom 4, 31; United States 4
History: Australian 36–38, 98–99, 105, 214; challenges of teaching 97, 111, 214; European 60; Socratic discussions 104
Huett, J. B. 55, 63
humanities and social sciences: challenges 3–4; interdisciplinarity 208–210; pedagogy 18–19, 228; teaching research methods 135, 204; *see also* Bachelor of Arts; digital humanities
humour *see* pedagogy

Indigenous Knowledge 6, 22, 34–35, 37, 225
instructional design *see* online learning design
instructional designer *see* learning designer
instructor presence *see* presence
interdisciplinarity 78, 90, 203–204, 208–210, 221

Job-Ready Graduates 14

Kalantzis, M. 30, 37
Kessler, K. 79, 82, 84, 87
Khamis, A., ix, 9, 59–77
Kildea, G. and Leach, J. 135, 136–147
Kilmister, M. i, 3–12, 97–109, 134–149, 169–186, 216, 222, 227
King, M. ix, 9, 28–42

large class teaching 99, 227
Laurillard, D. *see* Conversational Framework

Lawrence, C. ix, 10, 134–166
Leach, J. *see* Kildea, G.
Learning Design and Teaching Innovation (LDTI) unit 16, 33, 40n1, 85, 154, 172, 216; *see also* University of Newcastle
learning design *see* online learning design
learning designer: academics working with 39, 100, 106, 140, 154, 175, 216, 226; building modules on FutureLearn 205–208; role of 23, 100
learning experience platform (LXP) *see* FutureLearn
learning management system (LMS) 18, 59, 80–81, 85, 91, 154, 204
learning media *see* learning video
learning types *see* Conversational Framework
learning video *160, 175;* planning 63–64, 67–68, 70–71, 206; production 62–63, 65–66, 69–74, 155, 158; editing 72, 89; length 84, 103, 204; pedagogy of 61–62, 84, 103; smartphone filming 63, 69, 157–158, 163; value of 59, 103, 162
Lloyd, C. i, 3–12, 23, 169–186, 225–230
Luckhardt, C. 62, 63, 64, 67

Massive Open Online Course (MOOC) 4, 30, 32–33, 35, 216, 226; and communities of inquiry 46–52; platforms 45; student discussions 84–85; *see also* FutureLearn
McIntyre, J. x, 11, 199–212
mediated violence 111, 114, 115, 116, 118–119
Mereles, A. x, 10, 134–149
Moore, M. G. 46, 47, 52
Musgrave, D. x, 10, 122–133

Nagy, V. x, 11, 213–224
networks (scholarly) 214–215, 220–223

O'Shea, S. 104, 225
online learning design 154–155, 169; blend of media 79–80, 83, 89, 102; in-house vs. outsourced design 33, 39–40, 63 (*see also* Learning Design and Teaching Innovation unit); modularisation 89, 101–103, 112, 205, 156, 170–171; revising 85, 208, 211; storyboarding 8, 102; translating from/to face-to-face 39, 79, 83, 101, 103–104, 150, 151, 154, 200, 202, 206, 227; *see also* Conversational Framework
online learning: asynchronous 50–51, 81–83, 90, 115, 123, 125, 204, 208; challenges 85, 151, 204–205, 228; emotions 37, 148, 152, 156, 178, 199; environments 38, 199; evaluating (*see* evaluation); flexibility 115, 118–119; interaction 47, 54, 55, 84, 151, 163; physical anonymity of 115, 116, 118, 190; staff enthusiasm for 32, 81, 103; supporting students 8, 82, 138–139, 177; synchronous 22, 34, 82, 183–184, 206
Online Program Managers (OPMs) 29; *see also* online program management (OPM)
open courses *see* MOOC

pedagogy/pedagogical 18, 170, 228; approach 6, 79, 86, 111; comedy as pedagogical tool 131, 151, 152, 155, 156, 157, 160, 162; online 19–23, 228; poetry 123, 124, 126–127, 132; team-based problem-solving 152; tools 124
peer learning 18, 20, 38, 50, 82, 84
Perović, N. *see* Arena Blended Connected
Piper, A. x, 11, 213–224
presence: cognitive presence 47, 52; educator/teacher presence 8, 22, 34, 37, 47, 49, 62, 103, 155, 161, 162, 170, 175, 176, 202, 204, 209; social presence 47, 49, 52
professional development *see* academic development

QILT 25n1, 188
quizzes 38, 48, 80, 104–105, 160–161, 205

reflection 38, 200–201
research and enquiry 89, 213–214, 218, 220, 222
retention 13–14, 18, 22, 24, 37, 47, 55, 103, 172, 183, 228
Roberts-Pedersen, E. x, 11, 187–198

Salmon, G. 155, 204
Scaffolding 118, 137, 192

Screen and Cultural Studies 78–81; audiovisual texts 79, 87; digital culture 110; disciplinary pedagogy 86–88; film viewings 87–89
Senior, K. x, 10, 134–149
sexting 111, 115, 117
Sharp, J.* H. 55, 63
Sijpkes, P. x, 11, 187–198
social learning 8, 20, 21, 22, 31, 33, 36, 37, 39–40, 45, 81, 82, 155
Stone, C. 17, 193, 226
student evaluation of teaching *see* evaluation
students 28; identity 136, 191; partnership 100–101, 105; underrepresented 99–100, 193, 203
sustainability 39; sustainable learning design 101, 106, 141, 147, 148n5, 164

Taylor, M. J. viii, 9, 45–58
teacher education 99–100, 105
teacher presence *see* presence
teaching research nexus *see* research and enquiry
team teaching *see* guest lectures

third-space professional 172; blended professional 222
transdisciplinary *see* interdisciplinarity
trigger warnings 113–114

UDL (Universal Design for Learning) 165, 172, 174, 181, 185n2
University of Newcastle (UON) xi–xiii, 3, 6, 16, 21, 33, 79, 98, 193, 225, 228; bush campus 34–35, 39–40; course production infrastructure 29–31, 63, 73

video conferencing software 28, 52, 82, 146, 227
video *see* learning video
videographer *see* learning video
virtual learning environment *see* learning management system
Vygotsky, L. 46

work-integrated learning *see* employability

Young, C. *see* Arena Blended Connected

Zoom *see* video conferencing software

For Product Safety Concerns and Information please contact our EU representative GPSR@taylorandfrancis.com
Taylor & Francis Verlag GmbH, Kaufingerstraße 24, 80331 München, Germany

www.ingramcontent.com/pod-product-compliance
Lightning Source LLC
Chambersburg PA
CBHW070308230426
43664CB00015B/2682